Mumblings
Pango

Rob Grimes

(The Collected Chimping Dandy)

Volume 1

the penguin's head

www.thepenguinshead.com

ISBN: 1493560212
ISBN-13: 978-1493560219

DEDICATIONS

To Linda, Dorla and Malachi - who told me that I should stop mucking about and actually write something.

(Even though Malachi denies ever saying this).

To Ben, Neil, and Nathan – Who have been a real inspiration.

To Bennett – My one regret is that this book isn't exactly 114.6 CM wide

To SMick - who played an active part in many of the stories.

To my Brother Pete and my Father Fred – Who allowed me to share their stories and slander their good names.

To Pete McGarel – Who hopefully knows why I am thanking him.

But mostly to you – For not using this book to level a wonky table or swat a fly or anything.

CONTENTS

	Foreword	8
1	I'm A Bigot, You're A Bigot, We're All Bigots...	9
2	Recipe: The 'Yeah, Should Be Fine' Chilli	11
3	Recipe: The Concussion Chilli With Rottweiler Sauce	12
4	So Long, Farewell, Auf Wiedersehen, Adieu	15
5	Your Name's Not Down, But Your Girlfriend Can Come In	17
6	What A Maroon!	20
7	This Is The Blog You're Looking For.	22
8	Excelsior!	25
9	Deconstruction Complete	28
10	The Catholic Church Does Not Make Mistakes	31
11	A/S/L?	34
12	Pandas, The Eastern Scourge	36
13	But, If'n I Wasn't Me.	38
14	Something For The Weekend?	40
15	If I Should Die, Think Only This Of Me	44
16	What A Long, Strange, Trip It's Been	46
17	That's Not Exactly What I Meant, But...	48
18	T-Wit - Who?	50
19	Whistle, And She'll Come To You My Girl	52
20	Tell Merrill To Swing Away	56

21	But I Feel Fine!	58
22	Dzit Dit Gaii	61
23	As The Superhero Said To The Stripper	64
24	Bandits At 2 O'clock! What Do I Do Until Then?	68
25	Take Me To Your Lederhosen	72
26	That Wasn't The Year That Was	76
27	Low Resolution	80
28	The Collected Barnaby Wilde	83
29	Boobs, Melons And Jumper-Lumps	95
30	Second Contact Closing Fast, Bearing 076!	99
31	Thermodynamics, It's The Law!	102
32	An Eye For An Eye.	104
33	Have You Tried Turning It Off, Then Leaving It?	107
34	But Will It Fly Smick?	111
35	And Then, I Shot Myself	115
36	Opinionated Isn't Even A Word	118
37	It Was Like The Somme!	121
38	And David Attenborough Was No-Where To Be Seen	124
39	We Don' Need No Steenking Dipthongs	128
40	Then I Posed, And He Took My Picture	140
41	Are You Experienced?	147
42	Piracy On The High Winds (The Edward Teach Stories)	151
43	You Do Know How A Button Works Don't You?	187

44	Title *Redacted* For Security Reasons	193
45	Danny In The Woods	195
46	Waiting For God-Oh!	201
47	The Barney Stinson Of The Animal World	205
48	A Bucket For Monsieur	207
49	All That And Brown Sauce?	210
50	It Was A Bright, Cold Day In April, And The Clocks Were Striking…	214
51	Just Call Me 'Sinestro'.	218
52	Maybe They Explained It Badly?	222
53	Leviticus 19:28	225
54	'Leg Godt' As They Say In Denmark	228
55	Ah'm With Ye Jacky-Boy	231
56	Then Smick Said That 'Chap' Was A Bad Word	233
57	A Discussion Of Pornography, Do Not Read	239
58	You'll Die, And It Will Hurt All The Time You're Dying	243
59	To Sleep Perchance?	247
60	Why You Little!...	250
61	So Here I Am Once More...	252
62	Well, That's Not Right, Surely	255
63	If Only Lock & Co Made Tinfoil Hats	258
64	When The Map Was Pink	262
65	Take Two And Call Me In The Morning...	265
66	A Space Helmet For A Cow?	270

67 I See A Tall, Dark Stranger 273

68 La-Piss Laloozy Is How It's Pronounced 277

69 Any Way The Wind Blows 280

70 No, No, No, No, No, No, Yes! 283

71 Steve The Hedge 286

72 They Came Out Of The Sun, All Dakka!-Dakka!-Dakka! 289

73 He Said Baby, Baby, Baby, Who? 293

74 I Need Your Clothes, Your Boots And Your Motorcycle 298

75 If I Hadn't Seen It I Wouldn't Have Believed It 302

FOREWORD

A long time ago, but in this galaxy, not one far, far away, sat an opinionated man in a comfy swivel chair. He was at a bit of a loose end, as he worked nights in a thankless job that didn't really tax him too much. He had done as much spinning around with his feet in the air and sneaking up behind his workmates and pressing that lever that makes their chair drop suddenly as he could really stand. He needed something to occupy his mind until the sun came back up and his internment was over.

He decided to force his somewhat skewed opinion on other people by commenting on their Facebook statuses. Then when he tired of that, because he was fickle, he started to post long, bloated, meandering statuses himself.

Eventually he started The Chimping Dandy Blog. (Which you can read for yourself at thechimpingdandy.blogspot.com if you are brave and kind, the sort of person who can stroke a Unicorn and not get horribly gored or trampled.)

That's where I come in, for I am He and He is Me and we are all together, as I believe a certain Liverpudlian Walrus may well have said once.

Our mascot is Seedy the Pangolin, who gets blamed for all the really bad stuff that we write, you can see her picture on the back cover.

We are The Chimping Dandy, what you hold in your hand are the songs of our people.

We hope you enjoy them, if you do, there may be cake. (For us… Send us cake, we really like it, any kind will do, but chocolate for preference.)

You can also follow The Chimping Dandy on Facebook –

www.facebook.com/TheChimpingDandy

or on Twitter

@Chimping_Dandy

1 - I'M A BIGOT, YOU'RE A BIGOT, WE'RE ALL BIGOTS...

My first real post was a little number about bigotry, but you probably got that from the title, because you're clever and sexy.

-oOo-

OK Friends, (I think I know most of you well enough to call you friends now) I'd like to talk a little bit about bigotry.

Not the piddly little types of bigotry that you can easily sweep under the carpet, like racial bigotry – I mean, when it comes down to it, does it really matter what colo(u)r the President of the World is? Do we have to cry 'it's only because all the minorities voted for him'? – If that's the case, it should make the 2024 Presidential Election interesting as I believe that's the one where, according to recent figures, Americans of white, Anglo-Saxon descent become the minority in what they still insist on calling 'their own country'.

Nor do I refer to bigotry about sexual orientation. I mean some of my dearest friends have nommed more Axminster than I could ever possibly hope to buy knocked off Chinese DVDs of, it doesn't make their opinion any less valid than those who enjoy their sausage with a side order of hot fish yoghurt does it?

Religious bigotry? Nope, not talking about that either. Despite not being what anyone in possession of all of their marbles would describe as a Christian, I go to Church every Sunday, and whilst I freely admit that there are people there who I would not trust to look after a straightened out paperclip, This has nothing to do with their religious beliefs, it's just that they're as mad as badgers!

No, I'm talking about that most insidious of bigotries… Musical bigotry! (there, I said it!) I know that I'm not an expert; I don't have a GCSE in 'Musical Appreciation' and I don't sing or play an instrument with any degree of skill or finesse but, as the Pope said when Michelangelo presented him with the painting of the Penultimate Supper (You know, the one with the kangaroo and the jellies and the three Christs) 'Look, I'm the bloody Pope, I may not know much about art, but I know what I like!'... Obviously I'm not the Pope, I've never worn a brown shirt, but you get the idea.

Can you think of a time when you've looked down on someone because they like Dubstep, or made assumptions about the intelligence of people who like any kind of music where the 'artist' has to mention their own name repeatedly in the body of the song so they don't forget who they're listening to? – I know I have, and I thought that that made me a bad person, a bigot of the highest order. But then I looked at my own musical tastes and realised that I was a victim too.

In the past people had laughed at me for quite liking Duran Duran and Adam & the Ants and this was bad enough until I said something during a discussion about popular music that has subsequently caused me to be treated like a leper. I remember it was a Thursday, and quite sunny, and we were all sat in Starbucks drinking Venti iced X 2 H O WC CRFL's when I uttered the fateful words 'You know, some of the stuff by Maroon 5 and Nickleback isn't that bad'

There are some things you can never take back... All the people at the table instantly took out their Non-generic smartphones and unfriended me from Facebook and I was given real Paddington hard stares from over the tops of their hipster glasses until I felt so uncomfortable that I had to put on my hemp flip-flops, get back on my leopard-print Schwinn Stingray and cycle all the way home.

I have never spoken to any of them again.

Remember kids, bigotry is bad, especially when it's directed at me.

2 - RECIPE: THE 'YEAH, SHOULD BE FINE' CHILLI.

This is the first story featuring my good friend 'Scots Mick', we've known each other for something approaching twenty-five years and have had many fine adventures – Here's the first.

-oOo-

So, with everyone giving it the 'Ohh, I'm cooking the Hairy Biker's Barbeque' or 'I've just made the Hairy Bikers Jam Roly-Poly' - I've decided to share some recipes that me and my old mate Scots Mick used to throw together, In that we've both an interest in motorcycles and we're both (to a greater or lesser extent) hairy.

- Hang around outside a function room that's holding a badly attended party.
- After the few guests leave and the organisers troop out with the food, muttering about what a waste it all is, ask them 'Are you going to throw that away?'
- Look at them like Puss in Boots from Shrek
- Realise that that doesn't really work when you're not a cartoon
- Get them to empty everything off the plates and platters into a bin liner.
- Go home and pour the contents of the bin liner into a cauldron
- Pour in a couple of cans of chopped tomatoes
- Add a bottle of chilli sauce.
- Put on a slow heat and stir, occasionally saying things like 'Is that cauliflower?' and 'Should we have taken the bread off the egg mayonnaise sandwiches first?'
- Go to pub
- Leave pub, remembering that you don't need to go to the Greek as you have hot food at home
- Divide the chilli up between all willing participants, setting aside anything you can't actually recognise
- Eat, incredibly gingerly
- Wish you'd gone to the Greek

3 - RECIPE: THE CONCUSSION CHILLI WITH ROTTWEILER SAUCE.

This is the second of the two recipes; you'll notice that it's also a chilli as at this particular stage in my life, chilli was my signature dish. Well, I say signature dish, it was also my title dish, my body of the letter dish and my address dish. We all ate a lot of chilli back in the day.

I once sent this recipe to Dave Myers, half of the famous 'Hairy Bikers'. But he didn't reply. I was disheartened, but not entirely surprised.

-oOo-

Regular readers will remember that I promised to slowly release recipes from the 'Real' hairy bikers - i.e. Myself and Mike Farrish.

Today it's the turn of - 'The Concussion Chilli with Rottweiler sauce'

One thing to bear in mind is that although the ingredients and method are (with one fairly major exception) things you will find in the average kitchen, the complete dish takes a total of six months to complete - It can be prepared in advance.

You will need for the chilli: The standard ingredients to make a completely normal chilli - meat, tomato (fresh or tinned), onions, chocolate, herbs and spices, but specifically, and I can't stress this enough, no baby carrots.

You will need for the sauce: one 100lb+ good natured Rottweiler and a high-pressure water supply.

- Take a large pot and make a chilli as per any one of a thousand recipes as can be easily found on the Internet.
- Get slightly drunk and taste the chilli - decide it is nowhere near spicy enough and put in four more whole chillis.
- Get slightly more drunk and taste the chilli - decide it is nowhere near spicy enough and put in four more whole chillis.
- Get really quite drunk and taste the chilli - decide it is nowhere near spicy enough and put in four more whole chillis.

- Drink all the beer that is available and decide that you may as well put in all the chillis that you can find in the house.
- Wake up and lift the lid off the chilli pot.
- Stop crying and look around at everyone else in the room with an expression of disbelief and mild panic on your face - as if to say 'I don't know anyone stupid enough to try that'.
- Remember that you do, in fact, know someone - And call your very good, but incredibly gullible, friend (ours was called Steve, but feel free to substitute your own as you see fit).
- Make sure that there is a clear path between the chilli pot and the nearest toilet (this is VERY important).
- Give 'Steve' a fork and ask what he thinks the chilli needs.
- Be completely surprised when he says 'Why have you put baby carrots in it?'
- Turn to each other and mouth the words 'Baby Carrots?', then turn around just in time to see a fork with half a dozen whole chillis on it be swallowed whole.
- Congratulate yourself on clearing such a nice path to the toilet.

Now, for the sauce:

Wait six months (Yes, six)

- Have a party at your house on a Saturday night that gets completely out of hand and culminates with everyone becoming unconscious on the sofas, floor, hammock, garden or sideboard (It is important that the Rottweiler is invited, but 'Steve' is not)
- Approximately 10:00 on the Sunday morning, arrange for 'Steve' to burst into the house and yell 'Helloooo' at the top of his voice, in payback for having long-term colonic shock due to the Baby Carrot incident.
- The Rottweiler should now launch himself at the interloper and stick a good 8" of doggy tongue down his throat - In a completely friendly, non-threatening way.

- 'Steve' will recoil from this and grab the first thing that comes to hand to wipe his mouth - You should make sure that this is the blanket that the dog sleeps on, for added gaminess, if you are a connoisseur of such things, it will help if the dog is slightly incontinent.
- Explain to 'Steve' what he has just done, he will make his way at a brisk pace to the kitchen, stumbling over slumbering bodies along the way, whilst trying to hold in his breakfast.

  [Interlude] - I should probably explain that the house I was living in at the time had quite high water pressure, to the point where if you held a glass under the cold tap and turned it on full, it would blow the bottom out of the glass - [/Interlude]

- 'Steve' will now hold his head under the cold tap and turn it on full.
- Marvel at what a strange sound the human head makes as it bounces off the rim of a stainless steel sink.
- You now have three choices as to how you wish to finish off the sauce:

  1 - Call an ambulance
  2 - Continue to laugh until you feel quite sick
  3 - Let the dog lick him awake

  (We chose a mix of 2 & 3 - but obviously you should let your conscience be your guide)

4 - SO LONG, FAREWELL, AUF WIEDERSEHEN, ADIEU.

This one here is a goodbye letter. Remember that terrible job that I talked about in the Foreword? Well, this is what I sent out to my closest workmates when I left. They still talk about me there you know, I'm a legend probably, or something.

-oOo-

So, that was my last shift for the unstoppable global technological supergiant that is [My previous employer].

It was quiet, but then you'd expect that I guess, with the first part of the Helpdesk transfer to India now being completed.

Firstly I'd like to say that on the whole, the past sixteen months or so (apart from anything involving actual work or being able to pay my bills of course) has been, at worst bearable and at best, uproariously funny.

The people I've worked with have been a mixed bag, mostly mad as badgers (But in a good way) a couple certifiably psychotic, and still fewer with their heads so far up their respective poop-chutes that it's a wonder they don't jump to another dimension every time they break wind.

OK, so this is the part where, traditionally, I should rail against all the injustices that I believe have been visited upon me without fear of retribution…

Well, here's the turn-up for the books – I'm not going to. It's pointless, we all know about the history of ill considered, knee jerk reactionary, short-sighted, parochial decisions that have been made on a more and more regular basis over the past six months or so. We've all received the same morale-sapping, draconian, divisive emails. And if any of us had cared enough for it really to have been a 'showstopper' as our colleagues over the pond might say, then we would have stood up and tried to do something about it or at least voted with our feet.

Instead, let's remember some of the good times:

The night the drunken old guy got in and urinated down the stairs before the Police arrived.

The ghost of the cute little girl upstairs (Now I'm not sure that anyone who hasn't worked the nightshift has ever experienced her) but you can often hear her running around up there in the early hours of the morning – And it's quite an experience the first time you get woken up by her giggling or tugging on your shoe if you've fallen asleep on the sofas in reception during your break. (And as of last night we have two new believers).

The vending machines with the undocumented gamble feature – I don't mean the gamble you take that there's actually anything in the vending machine when you come on shift and the shops are closed (Same applying to tea, coffee and/or milk) – But the gamble when you put your money in and it either eats it then sits there looking at you with that 'Come at me Bro' expression on its readout, or the crisps (because it's invariably crisps) get stuck against the glass and you spend your next 60p using another bag of crisps (bag price 49p) from the row above to try and knock them down.

So, time to sign off because I'm starting to bore myself, and I've got a lot longer attention span than most of you.

I'd just like to take this time to thank [My Manager] for doing the best job he could be expected to do with the tools he was allowed to use (and finally agreeing to put me out of everyone's misery) and [The Customer Services Manager] for reminding me on several occasions of the importance of not indiscriminately murdering your workmates with a blunt instrument.

I'm not going to send everyone an individual 'I liked you because..' message, because I'd probably forget someone, and there's the whole thinking of nice things to say about everyone issue, which most of you by now, will know that I'm not particularly good at.

Good luck to the Helpdesk team and Luke, I hope you make a go of your new positions within the group (P.S. Luke, my Dad – Who spent a lot of time in Germany after the War - advises using this formal, traditional German greeting every time you meet someone new "können Sie mir helfen? Ich habe meine Hoden in der Küche Schublade gefangen")

It's time for me to go now, but let me leave you with my one and only regret…

I only ever got to see one of you completely naked (and if that single, completely true statement, doesn't put the rumour mill into overdrive, I don't know what will)

5 - YOUR NAME'S NOT DOWN, BUT YOUR GIRLFRIEND CAN COME IN.

I've done a good few jobs over the last thirty years, some good, some bad, most of them odd. This is the first one that I talked about online. It's all about the time that I spent as a Door Supervisor or 'Bouncer' as we used to be called in the 'Good Old Days'

-oOo-

This may surprise a few of you - But I am actually a fully-fledged, licensed and notarised 'Door Supervisor' (What we all used to call a Bouncer).

In the dim and distant past, probably about twenty years ago, as I'd done some freelance bailiff work, I would occasionally get accosted by the bouncers of local biker bars and clubs (Whom I'd known previously, I mean these guys didn't just spy my rippling biceps and go - 'He looks like he'd fill a doorway') and asked if I'd like to 'watch the door' whilst they stepped away from their posts for a bio break or to *cough* check some young lady's ID *cough*.

This slowly evolved into me becoming one of those people that everyone hates - 'The guy who gets into places for free'. You'd rock up at the door of your venue of choice, the bouncer would ask 'Working?', I'd reply, 'Can do, if you're busy' and then there'd be some fist-bumping or that fist-handshake thing and I'd go and get a bottle of Dog and sit down for the rest of the night. The only proviso was that if things did kick off, you were seen to be in the front row, handing out righteous judgement with whatever blunt instrument came most readily to hand.

This very seldom happened if I'm honest as, contrary to popular opinion, biker bars (in the UK certainly) tend to be self-policing, and also, bikers in general are a pretty good natured bunch - Visit one, you'll love it, but it's probably best not to wear a tie unless you like people pointing at you and laughing. (This does not apply if you're female and dressed as a schoolgirl, feel free to wear a tie then, although in fairness, you'll probably still get pointed at - Although it's unlikely to be with a finger.)

However, it all tailed off as things got more and more regulated, you started to need certification, you had to have a 'Little Blue Badge' issued by the local authorities, then the SIA (Security Industry Authority) got involved and it all went to hell in a handcart... Bouncers became Doormen, then Door Supervisors, the bats and socks full of pennies got replaced by politeness and psychology and it became 'safe'... OK, let's qualify that bit, I mean it became safer for the punter. You were significantly less likely to wake up in a ditch, looking at a selection of your own bodily fluids, wondering why you could see the back of your own head. It was no safer for the guy in the monkey suit saying 'I'm sorry sir, not tonight, try again next week' as the local authorities had not seen fit to regulate the behaviour of drunks to the same extent, it was still quite acceptable for them to lash out with glasses and broken WKD bottles and whatever else they carried about their persons.

I thought myself to be well out of, for want of a better word, you could describe as 'A mug's game' and settled down to a life of comfort, videogames and beer. That is of course until my wife commented that I should probably 'Do something in my spare time', it seems that sitting, drinking beer and playing games aren't 'something' as far as the current Mrs Dandy is concerned. I took this to heart, and within a couple of months I was offered a place on a Door Supervisor training course - Spooky!

Our instructor was a little Scots fella, who had been invalided out from 3 Para after (IIRC) smashing both of his legs (or arms) to pieces after a faulty parachute deployment - And he was, without doubt, the most double-hard b*st*rd that I have ever had the honour to meet. He would merrily go through the official SIA Door Supervisors Training Handbook with us, then slam it shut and say 'Tammorae, I'll tich ya poufters whae ya rally need tae knae'

And he did... We learned what bits to poke, where to chop or twist, how fast, how hard and how long for - In fairness, he did preface every demonstration with 'An ya shoul' ne'er do thas, but ye'll nee' to knae how to defen agin it' - It was the first time I ever saw anyone use the 'sleeper hold' to its natural conclusion and also the first time I saw a guy who was probably only 5'5" subdue a guy around a foot taller, one handed.

(It should be noted that the big fellah wasn't just tall, he was probably about 300lbs and has once been sacked for knocking someone out with a live chicken - He works for the BBC now I think, or at least he did the last time I met him)

And he also HATED first aid training, don't get me wrong, he still taught it, and taught it well, but his opinion was that it made you soft and you'd worry about hurting someone if you thought you might have to fix them again afterwards. To this end, he organised a bit of 'role play' the day after the first aid training. He set the classroom up to mimic a darkened nightclub layout and slumped one of our number in the corner, then he let us in, one at a time and told us that it was the end of the night and the rest of the club was clear, 'Whad'ye dae?' Of course, we were all still in 'Helpful First Aider' mode, we checked for breathing and consciousness and stuff and went to help, whereupon the guy opened his eyes, brought an empty syringe from behind his back, and stabbed us in the neck, 'Yer deid, if ya lucky, it wae jus drogs, if ya wea onlucky it wea infected blod, if ya wae rilly onlucky it whuz jus' full o' air !' he cried, with more than a little glee - The only guy who passed this test was the one who he'd put in the sleeper hold - Maybe it focuses the mind?

I've used it a couple of times since, even done security for bands and suchlike. All in all, a pretty great experience, people who are interested in self-defence should definitely look into it - I've taught a lot of what I learned to my daughter, and will be doing the same when my son's a little older - So that's something for the next generation of bullies to look forward to.

6 - WHAT A MAROON!

In this chapter I have a quick pop at fashionable people, it's not just because I'm not particularly fashionable (Although I'm not) or old (Although I am) or bald (guilty) but because I think 99% of them are gits.

-oOo-

I saw a joke, well - not really a joke as such, I'm sure there's a proper word for it, but it went something like 'What's the most difficult thing about being a Gay, Vegan, tattooed, Wiccan, single parent to an adopted Somali child, who runs marathons regularly and rides a Harley? Trying to figure out which one to shoe-horn into the conversation first when you meet someone new."

Whilst I realise that there are people who might find that offensive, especially if they tick more than one box, it does highlight the recent trend for 'just being bloody Gods-Damned interesting'

Now, let's get the feather smoothing out of the way first, Don't get me wrong, there are people who are born gay, there are people who don't eat animal products or wholeheartedly believe in The Summerland because of deeply held moral beliefs, people who have tattoos to document meaningful events in their life or to show affiliation to specific groups etc. But there are an increasing number of people who do it just so that they can say that they do it.

Or, as I like to call them, Gits.

The kind of people who, if you stripped away the overpriced clothes, and their amusingly ironic accessories, they'd be a medium sized steaming pile of not very much at all. Slavish followers of whatever the style magazines (Because they're too 'now' to watch TV of course) say is 'Bang on trend' this month. People who try so hard to be interesting that the day-to-day populace would rather pluck out their eyes with rusty pickle-forks and throw them to the ravens than have to look at them.

What these hyper-informed, too cool for school, infra-fabulous people should realise is that your average human being is an amazing piece of kit, as the Prince of Denmark once said to Rozencrantz: "What a piece of work is a man, how noble in reason, how infinite in faculties, in form and moving how express and admirable, in action how like an angel, in apprehension how like a god! The beauty of the world, the paragon of animals." (Although I have seen the word Paragon replaced with Paramour - And that's a whole different website) - If they just relaxed a bit, took a day off from being an aspirational lighthouse, they could celebrate their individuality by being an individual, be the best person in the world at being themselves. They'll find they have a much smoother ride.

Unless of course, they're aspiring to be Batman... Then they should definitely try to be the best Batman they can be...

7 - THIS IS THE BLOG YOU'RE LOOKING FOR.

I like Star Wars, the films, the books, the action figures, the soap-on-a-ropes etc. But I found the explosion of hate that echoed around the Internet when George Lucas sold the film rights to the next four hundred or so Star Wars films to Disney a bit, well, rabid. So I abused my position as a Celebrity Blogger and tried to calm the people. I was about as effective as a scouser in a tracksuit, with a microphone perm wandering around flapping his arms and saying 'Caaaalm dowwwwn, Caaaalm dowwwwn!'

-oOo-

In hono(u)r of my first real follower (Anakin.1138, the Chimping Empire is glad that you have found us, and hopes that you will be a powerful ally in our assault on the Rebel Blogosphere) I have decided to tackle a thorny issue - One that has divided the most astute minds of our, and no doubt many other generations to come.

Will anyone actually die because Lucasfilm is now a part of Disney?

Simple Answer: No - The End. (Shortest... Chapter... ever..!)

Ah, right, you want more? Fair enough.

Let me explain my basic standpoint on the current six films, I liked them all. Not every part of every one, I mean, they could probably have cut episodes I-III down to two films by cutting out all of the Shaak riding and the no dialog, soft focus 'Oh how deeply in love we are' bits, then bulked it back up to three films again with more Pew-Pew Dakka-dakka-dakka "Ah! Jedi scum, you've only gone and cut my other arm off". And Jar-Jar? Meesa Likea kick yousa in da Poodoo... But other than that, on the whole, pretty good.

Did I like the special editions I hear you ask? - Again, some good bits, some bad bits - Mos Eisley was a lot more impressive, Han treading on a slimmed-down Jabba's tail - not so much.

And, of course... HAN SHOT FIRST! - That-Is-All

Did George Lucas ride roughshod over our collective childhoods with his spikey death boots of death? No, not really - As I understand it, the accepted reasoning says that there were things he wanted to do in the original trilogy that the technology wasn't up to - so when the technology was available, he added the extra bits and got some of it a bit wrong. And it's not just me that thinks this, actual real people think the same thing, take the popular blogger Bob Suicide for instance - She's very passionate about it

(If you don't know who Bob Suicide is, she's a Suicide Girl, I suggest you don't Google her unless you are over 18 and not at work)

All in all, taken as a franchise, they're good, old fashioned, Saturday Morning fun films - I mean even the wipes and fades that are used between scenes evoke that feeling, completely intentionally I might add.

So, I hope we can all accept that they're a source of entertainment and not a religion or a way of life (Even though I freely admit that put Jedi on my Census document).

Put yourself in Uncle George's (Spikey Death) Boots (of Death) - You make a trilogy of films that take the world, quite literally, by storm - They're globally applauded as the best thing since hot and cold running sliced bread. You make a potload of cash, you ride the wave for ten or so years and start re-mastering the originals - They're not so applauded, it's the kind of applause you get when a magician pulls a rabbit out of his previously empty hat, but it's dead - Still pretty impressive, but there are a lot of people who would have preferred not to see it. Then a few years after that, you go back to the beginning of the story and go a bit SFX-mental with fully digital actors and suchlike. You try to sell the story to a new generation of kids who expect everything to float, glow, be Wi-Fi / HiFi / HD / 3D / 5.1 Surround and Smell-o-vision. The kids love it, but the Fanboys hate it, and when I say hate, I mean squeeze your pet Pangolin through a mangle then wear it as a codpiece style hate. This time the rabbit's not just dead, the magician's left holding a pair of cute little bunny ears that look a bit green around the edges and smell like a zombie's jockstrap. So you realize that the kids are the future and produce an animated series, targeting the kids directly.

Then you re-imagine the cartoon series in full CGI - Then you realise that you may well have 'Jumped the Shark'.

So, whaddya do? Who could resurrect this franchise that's spiralling down towards Coruscant without a fireship in sight? Who knows more about selling stuff to kids than anyone in the known Universe? Who didn't kill the Marvel franchise when they bought it? Who's already been successfully marketing Star Wars toys for at least the past 10 years?

I reckon that it was his only real choice. Of course if Episode VII is completely dingo's kidneys (fetid or otherwise) then I shall replace this chapter with one that's just a picture of George Lucas being crucified - in 3D. And then deny that this version ever existed, you can think of it as "This IS the Blog you're looking for - The Special Edition"

8 - EXCELSIOR!

This chapter was an epiphany, it was where The Chimping Dandy stopped just being a name that I called myself, or indeed a long, long way to run. It became my Supervillain alter ego. The Pangolin-centric construction of a twisted mind, and when things started to get a bit more 'fun'.

Actually, this is two stories screwed together, because the second one didn't make sense without the first. This is my first agglomeration of many. You have been warned.

-oOo-

A few weeks ago, I was walking to school to collect the BoyChild from his daily servitude and I chanced to pass by a young mother with a toddler. Now this little chap must have been about 4 years old, all shiny cheeks and tousled hair -

(Actually, for the punchline to make sense, you'll need to know what I was wearing... It was windy and sunny, but not particularly warm and those who know me well will be aware of my fascination with full-length coats - So I had on a long, lightweight leather 'duster' with my leather cut-off over the top, black jeans, my New-Rocks and shades).

As I passed by, the wind caught my coat and made the tails flap in an alarming but seemingly heroic fashion.

He turned to his mother, and in a hushed, serious tone said - "Mummy... That man's a Superhero"

Well, made me chuckle anyways.

As has already been mentioned, I am a Superhero... At least to small children who don't know any better. And as Stan Lee once said (or FDR, or Jesus, depending on who you believe) "With great power comes great responsibility" This is of course totally true, and now I am greatly empowered by the Internet, I will try to become responsible for at least some of your entertainment.

Isn't it strange that (arguably) the two 'coolest' Superheroes - Batman & Iron Man, have no superpowers whatsoever, no unassisted flight, no transmogrification, telepathy or ability to smell things from a profoundly long distance. What they do have is cash and plenty of it - Want to fly, see in the dark or have weaponry extruded from your own orifices? Well, cold hard cash is your friend - According to Forbes, approximately $10,000,000,000 will see you be able to set yourself up as either of the cool crusaders.

If I'm honest, I don't have that kind of money... So, what do you do if you can't buy Superhero-dom, you're not from another dimension/planet and you don't fancy being bitten by anything (radioactive or otherwise).

Well obviously, you make it up... But then that opens another can of deep fried, crispy, Winston Hobbes'. What superpowers do you arbitrarily give yourself? You can discount the whole flying thing straight away, I mean, you can't pretend to fly...

Well, I mean you can, but usually only the once, and onlookers would probably describe it more as falling, especially to the reporter from the local paper, just before they said 'He was a nice man, he kept himself to himself'. You could probably, just about, give yourself super(ish)-strength - Given enough time, discipline and motivation I suppose... Which are, of course, the three main reasons that I'll never have that. (See also: Mad acrobatic / Ninja skills, swordplay, accuracy whilst throwing stuff or even being able to play 'Smoke on the Water on the Electric Guitar)

So, we need to think outside of the box, really get the grey-matter jiggling about - Go to the esoteric end of the scale - I have thought about, and rapidly discounted:

- Being able to make things taste slightly different
- Lengthening the shelf life of cut flowers
- Instantly doubling the number of bubbles in a standard bottle of carbonated drink

But only because of their lack of crime fighting applications and the fact that they are a bit pants. Then I found it, the perfect pretend super-power...

Wait for it...

I can stop time! - for as long as I like!... You don't believe me?

OK, I'll do it now. 3... 2... 1... *Bamff* Ha! you didn't notice did you? That's because I actually stopped time, you were frozen in an actual bubble... of time! My only problem is, I stopped too which is a bit of an issue where using it for anything even remotely heroic is concerned - I'm working on it, honest.

Just think though, if you could actually do that, with a thought, or pressing a button on an old watch you found in an antique shop that had magically disappeared when you tried to take it back because it never told the right time. With a *click* or *Bamff* or *Boop* everyone around you freezes and you are free to do whatever you like... Think of the possibilities... Erm... Ah... Now try to think of possibilities that don't involve changing rooms, stealing money or anything involving the words sneaking, inappropriate or without being caught.

Oh my Gods... I'm a SuperVillain

9 - DECONSTRUCTION COMPLETE.

I have several passions, there's motorcycles, computer games, science fiction and writing for a start (Good Gods, I'm a geek!) Then there are things that I can't really write down here without some embarrassment on other people's parts or the Police being called.

My one guilty pleasure is Charity Shops. As made famous by that Macklemore chap in his recent (in 2013 at least) rap hit 'Thrift Store'. I love having a good old delve through dead peoples' junk.

Hang on… No… That didn't come out right.

-oOo-

I just love Charity Shops (Thrift Stores, for my legion of American readers) - They're a veritable Aladdin's cave of dead people's stuff and broken toys. My local 'shopping centre' has about seven and every time I go out to buy the ingredients for an Ocelot Stew, or Sweet and Sour Crispy Peacock I try to pop into as many as I can. I don't necessarily want to buy anything - It's kind of like a trip to the museum, but with added mothballs.

There is nothing you can't get (OK, there are a huge number of things that you can't get, just shuddup and go with it) and if you wait in the store long enough, you will see every single consumer item that has been sold in the past hundred years or so. I've seen everything from Hello Kitty Handbags to Victorian Violet Wands on those hallowed shelves (Before you ask, no, I didn't buy it, there was too much month left at the end of the money). We all need to support these places; they can't be allowed to die out.

Don't get me wrong, for me, it's nothing to do with the Charity, for all I care the money could go straight to Albanian gangsters who live only to wallpaper their houses with kittens' eyelids. It's the whole digging through the crap aspect of it that appeals to me, a bit like you guys must feel reading this Blog... Most of the time it's all odd shoes and canteens of cutlery with all the knives missing - But occasionally you'll find an original copy of Action Comics Number 1 - In A1 condition. OK, so someone's drawn a penis on the cover in sharpie, but still..

Anywho, I was in one a few months ago, digging through a tub of naked Action-Men (GI-Joes), odd Sticklebricks and Matchbox cars that had so few wheels between them that they'd only be completely at home in Back to the Future 2, when the very worthy lady behind the counter asked;

'Are you looking for anything in particular?'

Now, I froze, because I didn't want to say, 'No, I'm just pretending to be an archaeologist' - Which was the sad truth, so I replied with the first thing that came into my head, 'I don't suppose you have any Lego do you?'

She thought for a second, she actually did that thing where you tap your index finger on your lips and look up (which I know you're all doing now, so stop it!) then said,

'No, I don't think so, but if you give me your number, I'll give you a call if some comes in'

Ok, I mean she wasn't completely unattractive in a 'Person who works in a charity shop and probably has a part share in a rescued pony' kind of way, but I couldn't take the chance that she was hitting on me, after all, I'm a married man... So, in true tabloid style, I made my excuses and left.

A week or so later, I was walking past the same shop when I saw what I thought was a first edition StarScream in the window (It turns out it wasn't) - As I was deciding whether to in, the worthy lady's face appeared and mouthed 'OO-ee God, sumly Go!' (You're doing it again... stop it!). She beckoned me into the store like Morpheus asking Neo to show him Kung-Fu and said,

'It's just come in, you can have first look!' And then she did that excited stiff handclap thing.

It took me a good few seconds to figure out what the blinking-flip she was talking about, and I still didn't twig until she brought out a cardboard box with Lego in it.

'I'm afraid it's not all Lego, but feel free to sort out what you don't want.'

So, picture the scene, avid readers, I'm sat on the floor, in a busy-ish Charity shop, sorting out a box of mixed toys that was about 80% Lego, when she came up and said,

'Let me know when you've got that one sorted and I'll bring you the next one'

Now, I did that thing where you go all slittly-eyed and look from side to side (Again? Stop it!) and said, 'There's more?'

'Yeah, a couple of small ones'

So all in all there were three decent sized boxes of Lego and a box of assorted rubbish, which I kindly re-donated to them. Quite gingerly I asked, 'And how much would you like for all these?'

'Well, I'm sorry, but Lego's quite expensive to buy isn't it, I'm afraid I can't let it go for less than £20...'

I nearly pooped an actual kitten in my rush to get out my wallet.

'Tell, you what,' I said, 'It's all in a good cause isn't it? I'll give you £25.'

You know, I think she was genuinely touched, and I desperately tried not to blurt out 'But it's worth, like £200 Muhahahahaaha!' and twirl my moustache.

So, once I'd filled out the Gift-Aid certificate - It seemed the right thing to do. I picked up the three boxes of Lego and struggled out of the shop. Now, I didn't have the car with me because the shops are only about 10 minutes' walk from my house. So I had the two open boxes balanced on top of each other in front of me, and a box, with what I thought was a fairly close-fitting lid, gripped with the spare fingers of my right hand... You can guess what happened, by my usage of 'what I thought was', right?

The lid came off the box, and spewed about a kilo of Lego all over the pavement. Embarrassing enough you might think, but no, it chose to let go at a traffic island, on a three lane road, at rush hour, with halted traffic.I don't think Bono got anywhere near that amount of applause when he announced that he had single-handedly saved the entire African population from starvation - And to get the same amount of 'Woooo!'s I would have to have been wearing a severely short skirt and little else. My face actually felt like it was about to spontaneously combust.

Was it Karma? - Would it have happened if I'd offered what some people might say was a 'fair' price?

Yeah, it probably would... Because even though they say that Karma's a bitch, she's also got a bloody good sense of humour.

10 - THE CATHOLIC CHURCH DOES NOT MAKE MISTAKES.

I have a lot of friends that regularly go to Church, Hells! I go to Church myself, fairly regularly, but it's OK, I have a note from God to say that I can sit at the back and snigger.

Every one of them that have read this thought that it was great. The people who wouldn't say that it was great don't have the Internet, or the Devil's word tube as the probably call it.

Also, I sent this to Kevin Smith, I'd like to think he read it

-oOo-

OK, the title is a quote from Dogma, a great movie by Kevin Smith, it was said by the character Cardinal Glick, played by George Carlin, an even greater person who is sadly no longer with us.

If you've not seen Dogma, or heard of George Carlin, then go and do some research now - In fact, go and watch as many of Kevin Smith's films as you can - They're all great, sweary, but great. When you've gone that, Google George Carlin... I'll wait, it's worth it, believe me.

Done? Good weren't they? - You know the stocky chap in the long coat and the backwards baseball cap in the films? That was your actual Kevin Smith! - Hardly a Hitchcock style cameo - But if you're gonna make great films, then I say why not star in 'em too?

Anyway, enough frivolity, I'd like to talk to you about God (was that the sound of a hundred *back* buttons being pressed?). I don't necessarily mean your actual Judeo-Christian, Monotheistic, Capital G type god, it could be your multi armed, blue coloured one, or your elephant headed one, or any one of a thousand different deities that people have blamed stuff on for the past few thousand years.

As the more eagle-eyed of you will have spotted, I am a regular church-goer and I believe in a supreme being, I have Faith. What I don't got is Religion.

"But if that's true, why do you go to church?" I hear the four people who are still reading this say.

There are a number of reasons really, Mrs Dandy is a confirmed Anglican Religionite, and there are some nice, friendly and most of all odd people there, but mainly it's because I enjoy running the mixing desk (this is the 21st. Century people, it's not all massive organs and people going Ah-ah-aaaahhhhh in an angelic fashion now) it makes me feel like Rick Wakeman - It also gives me the chance to poke fun at the fundamentalists...

OK - That will have made some hackles rise, so let me explain what I mean by fundamentalists - I take the word to mean, someone who believes that the Bible (or any religious text pertaining to a particular belief system) is infallible, an historic record rather than a book of moral stories and hints and tips on how to live a better life.

This becomes so all-consuming to some people that they forget all about the 'Be Excellent to each Other' stuff (See, Bill & Ted, George Carlin again - Isn't it amazing how this stuff all fits together - I don't just throw this down on the page you know?) and concentrate on the 'Thou shalt not' and 'Righteous smiting of the unbeliever' stuff. In short, they get caught up in the Dogma (Oh my Gods it's like I've got a plan for this thing, right?) - The words of the text themselves rather than the meaning.

There're also people who just go to church because they want to be seen to be important, the kind of people who like to slip into everyday conversation 'So, I said to the Vicar....' They really ruffle my cassock - These are the people for whom I really hope there is an afterlife, 'cos they got a big old shock coming to them with the whole rapid downwards motion and the fire and the pitchforks and the 'Oh no it burns - freunlaven!'

On a different note, if you'll pardon the pun, there was a song sung a couple of weeks ago called 'Our God is greater' - Inoffensive little song, quite jolly and stuff. But it got me thinking, greater than what? Is it kind of a religious football chant? Should religion be so confrontational?

So what do I actually believe? Do you really care? Do I care if you care?

I believe that the state of the world we live in is not ALL down to chance - That there's a guiding influence. I'm not a creationist, I believe in evolution, but I have no problem with the idea that the evolutionary system has been pushed in a particular direction at different points in history.

I don't believe that there's necessarily a plan for everyone, or anyone for that matter. But I do believe that there's something greater than us that on occasion, helps out - I don't mean in the 'God bless Mummy & Daddy and please can I have a Pony' way. I mean in the 'Holy Crap my brakes aren't working, we're all gonna die!' way - Although they do say that everyone becomes a believer in situations like that.

It could all be luck, I don't profess to know - It could be Aliens, Gods, Goddesses, a giant bowl of spaghetti and meatballs reaching down with his Noodley Appendages.

But as far as I'm concerned, there's something there... After all, if there wasn't there'd be times when I was just sat in the car talking to myself - And that would mean that I was mad.

11 - A/S/L?

Here's a story about a milestone in the history of the Internet, when we moved from individually strumming the bits of data along a length of wet string to shooting them down a bendy glass pipe with a real, live Star Wars superlaser.

-oOo-

In the early 90's I had my heart torn out and handed to me on a plate - Luckily, I'm a big boy and I got over it fairly quickly, with the help of massive amounts of alcohol and free Compuserve CDs. Compuserve? What's Compuserve I hear you youngsters cry.

Well, remember before Hotmail? No?.. OK, do you remember AOL CDs on the front of Games magazines? Right, excellent, we finally have a frame of reference. AOL gave you an Email address and access to the Internet, before Sky & BT and everyone and his brother were including it in monthly packages - It was rubbish, and it used to frak your PC on a regular basis, but it was pretty much all there was.

Now, imagine that, but having to pay by the minute... using a dial-up connection at 28.8Kbps - There was also a monthly fee, but if you uninstalled the software and re-installed it from a different CD every month, you didn't have to pay (It just meant that you had a different email address every month).

Compuserve used to filter the Internet for you, not that there was a great deal of content back in the day, but it was mainly comprised of what they called 'Forums' - Which were just posh chatrooms really, divided into different subjects and interests. I say different, they were all pretty much full of teenagers (or people pretending to be teenagers) trying to get off with each other. and Usenet Newsgroups - Which were the forerunner, I guess, of places like Tumblr and Twitter.

It was through being a part of these forums that I was introduced to the mating call of the early 90's Internetter, "A/S/L?" which of course stood for Age / Sex / Location which in turn, was shorthand for Am I committing a federal or statutory crime by talking to you about your underwear / are you the complimentary gender that I am looking for / are you local enough for us to meet up or far enough away for your parents to not be able to kill me when it all goes horribly wrong.

And while we're here, I'd just like to state on record that, despite evidence to the contrary, I never pretended to be a precocious 14 year old girl from California called Mindy to go trolling for paedophiles... *cough* not once.

If I were to use a fishing analogy, the A/S/L is the 'bite' and then you'd have to 'play' the 'fish' until 'it' was 'tired' and could be 'landed' - The most effective, and certainly most popular method of playing with your fish would be (and I kid you not) to quote popular songs of the day to your intended paramour - I didn't recognise a lot of the lines that were being used, as they were American songs that hadn't 'broken' in the UK - But towards the end of my Compuserve years, the chorus of the Savage Garden song Truly Madly Deeply became the go-to track for reeling love-sick teens in hand over fist - It went a little like:

I want to stand with you on a mountain.
I want to bathe with you in the sea.
I want to lay like this forever.
Until the sky falls down on me.

Remember it now? I never saw this fail, not a single time, never used it myself of course... That would have been immoral, and not to say a little creepy, as I would have been fast approaching 30 at the time, and therefore, positively pre-historic in comparison to everyone else there.

No, I moved to the much more sanitary newsgroups. These were like a notice board where people could post images, of anything, although the subject matter did all tend to be much of a muchness (Certainly in the alt.binaries. groups) - With pictures of young, and not so young ladies, in various states of dishabille and / or contortion - that would load, onto your 640 x 480 256 colour screen, at the rate of approximately 1 line per second... Meaning that a full screen image could take up to ten minutes to load - Just enough time to make a nice cup of tea and get control of any unnatural urges that you might be having.

I think that this was a secret plan by Compuserve to try and get young boys out of their bedrooms and into the fresh air... What I think actually happened was that those young boys who were too shy to quote Savage Garden lyrics to cheerleaders halfway across the world spend all their time getting the grainy, false colo(u)red images of 'Debbie, 21, from South London' to download faster.

And thus was High-Speed Broadband created.

12 - PANDAS, THE EASTERN SCOURGE.

I've long been of the opinion that there's something just 'wrong' about Pandas. They don't bother to camouflage themselves, although saying that, I guess you don't really have to sneak up on bamboo do you? They've got big, sharp bear teeth and claws and stuff and eat brains. No, sorry, they don't eat brains do they?

I'm thinking of something else aren't I?

-oOo-

Pandas, by which I specifically mean the Giant Panda or Ailuropoda Melanoleuca for the taxonomically inclined amongst us. What are they all about?

I mean, seriously - What the flip is going on with them? - A decent sized Panda weighs about the same as a small Grizzly Bear (about 25st) they've got huge teeth and claws, big enough to tear you limb from limb in a heartbeat, Yet they seem to be the sweetest natured animals on the face of the Earth - I tried (for research purposes - Try typing Angry Panda into Google, it just feels weird) to find instances of angry pandas - And could pretty much only find evidence of one pretty grumpy one called Gu-Gu who bit three people who got into his enclosure, one of whom bit him back! - I'm guessing he was only upset because he was named after the first words the zookeeper's baby said.

There's a video on YouTube that comes up when you search, I wouldn't bother watching it, it's pretty much a Panda barking and waving his paws at a couple of other Pandas who got too close to his pile of bamboo. If that's what goes for an 'Angry Panda' nowadays, I think they need to change the title to 'Somewhat miffed Panda coughs politely and points out what is obviously his lunch'.

Then you've got the whole bamboo thing! Pandas have huge carnivore teeth, rippey, bitey, tearey teeth for eating goats and yetis and other things you'd find in the mountains... But no, they eat bamboo which has less nutrient qualities than celery and you need a completely different set of teeth to eat it successfully. They have to eat about a tenth of their bodyweight a day, in bamboo, to get anything out of it - Where's the sense in that?

Luckily they're not completely stupid they do supplement their diet in the wild with the occasional bit of carrion and... erm... grass and bees and stuff probably, but still, they should ideally be hiding in trees, pretending to be... erm... [Insert name of huge black and white thing you'd expect to find in a tree and wouldn't seem strange at all] by the side of secluded trails, dropping down on unsuspecting sherpas and eating their brains with a spoon. (Oh... Zombie Panda.. File that under 'Next Flash Fiction story ideas')

You know, in captivity, they feed them cupcakes? - Not all the time I grant you, but all the same, feeding the cutest animal in the world with the cutest food item in the world - It's amazing that anyone accidentally seeing this spectacle doesn't just explode by achieving critical cuteness. You can picture the scene -

[Chinese] 'And here ladies and gentlemen, you will see Mung Mung being fed blueberry muffins by my lovely assistant Doof Lee Chung' (Noises off: series of small, wet explosions from the direction of the crowd) 'No! it's happening again! put down the cupcakes Lee Chung... Put down the Aaargggghh!' [/Chinese] Fade to black

Oh yes, another thing that I didn't know before today... They've got thumbs (kinda) and if evolution goes their way, then it won't be long, in a geological sense, before they start to use them... I don't mean hitch-hiking their way out of the bamboo line and going for a trot down Peking High Street, I mean fashioning bamboo into swords and shields and inventing coconut powered lasers and suchlike.

And Kung-Fu Panda is a very real concern, you know how they let gorillas watch TV in the zoos to keep them entertained? What if they do the same with Pandas - They maybe already do... One day, Ping Chin Min the Panda wrangler decides that it's Bloop Bloop's birthday and he could do with a bit of cheering up, sticks on Disney's finest and before you know it, you've got 350lbs of black and white fury spinning around it's enclosure flinging cupcakes at people and playing Tenacious D guitar solos! Don't laugh guys, it's stuff like this that keeps me awake at night.

It wouldn't take much for an evil genius to make an unstoppable army of Pandas would it?

I for one, welcome our monochrome overlords with open arms. Now... Where's that cupcake recipe?

13 - BUT, IF'N I WASN'T ME.

We all have those feelings sometimes don't we? Where you wish you were better or stronger or faster, without all the pesky going back to 1974, changing your name to Steve Austin and getting a bit banged up in a spaceplane crash (Yes, I know it was technically a lifting body that crashed, but do you expect anyone who's daft enough to buy this book to know what a lifting body is? No? Me either.)

But I had a simpler wish, I wanted to be a TV hard-man, with a hairy chest and piercing eyes.

-oOo-

Even the most content of us must have sometimes thought 'I wish I had that' or 'I wish I could do that' mustn't we?

I know I have, jealousy is the engine of aspiration is it not? If we were completely happy with what we had, why would we ever try to better ourselves?

But have you ever thought 'I wish I was him (or Her - Delete as necessary).'? Meaning that you could actually sit inside their head like a phantom marmoset and experience what they experienced, get the adulation that was meant for them but you so richly deserve. Go to the right parties, get invited to the grand openings, have intimate knowledge of the right, if slightly underweight, supermodels?

No?

Really? It can't be just me surely... Bugger!

OK, I guess it's declaration time, I'll do that thing that they make you do at your first AA meeting (or so I've heard)...

My name's The Chimping Dandy, and when I was ten years old, I wanted to be Martin Shaw! You know, out of The Professionals With Lewis Collins and the butler dude from Upstairs Downstairs. I swear, if you looked up the word 'Man' in a dictionary, in 1978 there would be a picture of Martin Shaw, naked to the waist, with an RPG in one hand, a half-eaten side of beef in the other and a simpering blonde curled around his feet looking up at him adoringly.

There was nothing Shaw couldn't do, he could kick his way through doors, slide over the bonnets (hoods) of 3.0s Ford Capris, kick, punch, spit and everything else that the modern (70's) man needed to be able to do.

He was a Gerd (as in ErmaGerd!) and I may have modeled my image on him for longer than was strictly necessary. In fact, I remember a school art project where we were asked to draw a self-portrait over the holidays, and my art teacher said 'It's very good, but I didn't ask you to draw Martin Shaw' - I was also still wearing fake leather jackets and Loon Pants / Bell Bottoms well into the 80's - Which, with hindsight, could have been one of the things that crimped my chances with more fashion conscious girls, or girls in general for that matter, Although...

It wore off of course, as these things so often do... I mean it's not completely gone, I don't think you can ever truly forget the first person who you wanted to go all 'Single White Female' on. Occasionally, I catch an episode of Judge John Deed, look longingly at his full head of hair and a tear comes to my eye.

I've grown out of all that now of course; one puts away Childlike things doesn't one?

Although, thinking about it, I reckon wi' a bit o' practice, ah could get clurse t' motorcycle racer Guy Martin's accent... Aye, grew aht me sidebons, put on t' boil'rsuit - Aye, that's reet nice, When's next bert f' th' Isle o' Mann? - Smart as Y' lake.

14 - SOMETHING FOR THE WEEKEND?

Now, my day job (believe it or not, writing semi-funny stuff is not my day-job.) I work in IT… For a Hairdressers – A big hairdressers, who you probably won't have heard of, I mean I hadn't before I started working here. In fairness, I am bald though, so that could be the reason.

There will be a number of IT related stories in this book, some of them will even be funny.

-oOo-

Hands up, all those people who thought it was funny when your Ever-Lovin' Chimpster got a job at a Hairdressers? One, two, some, many - is that two people at the back or one person with both hands up? What? Oh, that's not your hand... You're very kind sir, but I'm not that way inclined.

OK, keep your hands up if you thought was even funnier when I found out that I had to work one day a year in an actual salon, with real people, who have actual hair?

And keep them up if you thought this was even funnier when you remembered I am, for all intents and purposes, bald?

Now, take a look around at all the people who still have their hands up, don't forget the one guy standing behind the pot-plant in the corner, pretending to be a... a... What the hell are you doing to that Sturgeon? Put it down! No, not there!, nobody's going to want that now are they, Where the hell did you get a wheelbarrow full of butterscotch Angel Delight? - Anyway, I digress, none of you are getting Christmas cards this year, you people who put your hands down at any point? Neither are you. It's nothing personal, I'm just not sending cards this year, I'm skint.

Back to the story - I called my local Salon to announce that I would be arriving first thing in the morning to 'Do my thang!' You could hear the faint smell of panic and tightening of sphincters all the way back here in the office. I put the phone down and made inappropriate jokes about my minimal amount of power over people who didn't know who I was. Then I heard a funny noise.

'What was that?'

'What?'

'That noise - The Beep-Beep noise?'

'You've had a text on your BlackBerry'

'Really? Weird'

'Never had a text before?'

'Not on my work phone, no.'

So feeling a little stupid, I read the text, it said: [Do you like Black or White coffee?] Now, you have to admit that this a strange first text for anyone to receive. I assumed that it was from the salon, and made a mental note to pick up some milk on my way in, nothing like being prepared. Then, again, Beep-Beep! Knowing now what this noise signified, I checked my phone, it said: [Do you like puppies?] - Never has my Flabber been more Ghasted! (c) Frankie Howerd 1973. At this point, my colleague over the other side of the office dissolved into fits of giggles, it turns out that he had remote controlled the salon's computer, and got it to send me the texts. Touche Monsieur, Touche!

So I arrived at the salon at the crack of 9:30(ish) to be told that the manager had rang in sick, and the poor stylist had no real idea what was going on.

'I'm here to help you guys out; I can do whatever you need me to'

'You're not here to spy on us and report back on all the things that we're doing wrong?'

Did I mention that I'm a terrible liar? 'No..?' I squealed, like a constipated gecko. I think there was a chance that she may have seen through my complex web of subterfuge and deceit.

'Would you like me to, erm, clean something?'

'OK, how about those shelves?'

'All those? But there must be all of about, oh, I don't know, eight of them or something'

If I'm honest, the next three hours flew past pretty quickly, and by the time I'd finished the first shelf I had gained the trust, and if I'm honest, grudging admiration of the entire staff, of one person... With my lightning powers of calculation, I figured that the other seven shelves would take me twenty-one hours to complete. I am not a born shelf cleanerer it seems. I decided that my further efforts should be concentrated in a purely managerial / audit capacity. I weighed up the options, balanced what I knew about the salon against what I needed to know, turned to the poor stylist that I had been torturing with my very presence and said'

'I'm going for lunch'

Lunch was a pretty grown up affair consisting of a litre of Chocolate milkshake and a slice of pizza, that took me exactly the one hour to consume *cough*

On my return to the salon, things were getting busy, real people were having real treatments done to them by qualified people who seemed to actually know what they were doing, I felt very much out of my depth.

'I'm going to pop down to the other salon, and see what I can do down there'

'Uh-huh,' said the stylist. In fairness, I could have said 'I'm going to take this tin of beans and see how long it takes me to make it boil by just staring disapprovingly at it.' And she would have cared exactly as much.

Down I went, into a similar situation again, Different salon, different stylist, same air of 'I know you're trying to help, but will you just get out of my way and let me do what I'm good at.'

Luckily, we had three salons in the town, so I went to the third. Here at least, I made an impact. Oh yes... Impact.

If you were to think of the four words guaranteed to chill the blood of the average person, what would they be?

You're going to die?
I'm afraid it's positive?
Yes it is loaded?
Why should I care?

I feel that I found four words that trumped all of these today... 'I'm from Head Office' - It struck fear into the very entrails of the assembled staff, brushes were dropped, jaws hit floors, customers chairs spun around uncontrollably making the Zoidberg 'Whoop-whoop-whoop' noise, all hell was, quite literally, let loose.

Do you remember the seagulls from Finding Nemo? - Instead of 'Mine!' the cry that went up from the assembled staff was 'You want the Manager!' So the manager was found, I explained who I was, we all had a great laugh as we hosed the urine out of the salon and I completed my audit, such as it was.

All in all, not a complete waste of a day.

(Please note, there is a significant amount of artistic license used in this dramatisation, everyone I met on that day was great and I would have no problem spending an entire day cleaning a shelf for them sometime in the future - Whether any of them feel the same way, well you'd have to ask them)

15 - IF I SHOULD DIE, THINK ONLY THIS OF ME.

We all get sick sometimes, it can be anything from a bit of a runny nose to actual parts of your body falling off whilst you're wandering around the supermarket. But all these ailments have one thing in common.

None of them are as debilitating as Manflu… In fact, I think I feel a tickle at the back of my neck just thinking about it.

If anyone ever asks you, it's big and black, it looks like it's been burned, put out with dragon urine, burned again, lovingly sanded and repainted a rather fetching Baby Blue, then burned, with burning dragon urine and put out with a meat tenderising mallet. It has skulls and spikes, batwings and buckles and other, assorted things that you might find in a particularly interesting Goth girl's 'special' underwear drawer.

What am I describing? My current location of course - Death's door... I have been laid low by that most virulent of mortal agues, Columbian non-returnable suppurating man-flu. I am officially dead, I am dictating today's Blog from beyond what you mere readers, would describe as 'The Grave' to a small medium (can you have a Small medium? are all mediums by their very nature, medium? - That would explain why they all wear such similar clothes) called Gracie who just happened to be wandering past Dandy Towers as I was in the final throes of putrefaction.

Every time I cough, my lungs actually swap places.

When'ere I sneeze, I have to reel my eyes back into my skull with a handle on the side of my head, mounted for just that purpose.

To describe the inside of my head as 'Wooly' would not do justice to the 1.8 million sheep, all called Francoise, who are currently in residence within my metacortex.

If I lie down, there is a very real chance that I will drown in my own filthy, undulating ichor.

If I stand up for more than a few seconds, I feel as if I am about to fall, poleaxed, like an AT-AT that has been tripped by a virus-laden tow cable.

My eyes relay the world to me as a series of disjointed, abstract flashes of colour and brightness that I can only make sense of by looking at them through closed eyelids.

You may mock, especially if you are of the female persuasion. But it is a serious illness to which more of the National Health Service's research budget should be diverted... Possibly away from things like 'Having a bit of a tummy ache' and 'Finding out why people sometimes cry uncontrollably when they're drunk'

I suggest that an entirely new branch of medicinal research should be instigated, purely to provide ways of dealing with the symptoms of this insidious virulence. There should be clinics full of nurses who would be trained to make sure that the infected was never without those really soft tissues that men are too manly to buy, but are really nice on your nose. They should have something approaching a Utility Belt that contains various curatives, both medicinal and otherwise, such as medicated sweets and hand-held games consoles.

(Hang on, just need a second to work out the Nurse's Uniform / Batsuit combo)

(Nope)

(Gonna need another couple of minutes)

Anywho, enough of my problems, I'm trying to soldier on, stiff upper lip and all that, mustn't grumble. Although now that I come to mention it, I am a little short of breath... Beads of sweat forming the outline of a hang-gliding lion on my forehead... Vision... Fading... Ears... Ringing...

Nurse!

16 - WHAT A LONG, STRANGE, TRIP IT'S BEEN.

As we've covered before, I quite like Star Wars, as I am a big kid. My favourite character, through all the films, books and toys is one Mr Boba Fett.

I was forced to write a short post about him by an unexpected gift.

Well, the gift didn't force me, the act of receiving the gift did, although thinking about it, there wasn't any actual force involved, not really… No force at all.

I'd go as far as to say that the force was quite weak with this one… (I'm sorry... really very sorry about that)

-oOo-

When I got home from work last night, there was a package waiting for me, it was some very good friends of mine who now reside in (or near at least) Boston MA. It was squidgy and soft. My first thought was that it was the possum gizzards that I'd asked them to look out for, but no.

It was a rather spiffing T-Shirt with the slogan Boba Fett For President.

I was immensely pleased with this item as Mr Fett is my favourite:

- Mandalorian
- Sarlacc survivor
- Star Wars character

(Thinking about it, if I'd changed the order of that list a little I could have saved me some typing - Hey, I don't pay by the character, stuff it!)

The thing is, I have no idea why he's my favourite - I mean, he wears an outfit cobbled together from a boilersuit, BMX pads and shoes that look as if they're made by Converse, he doesn't say very much in the way of pithy one-liners, every time he uses his jet-pack it always ends up with him having some wacky flight control problems and he doesn't seem to be able to shoot straight to save his life.

If you just take your view of Bubba Boba from the films then he's a bit of a loser, But then you think - The poor kid's earliest defining moment was prising his Dad's still warm head out of his helmet with a fish-slice, so I guess we should maybe cut him some slack.

I think it might be the idea of Boba Fett that I like rather than the reality (reality of a fictional character? - wheels within wheels dude!) The merchandising, the mythosaur skull logo - He's like an Intergalactic James Bond flying an orbital sander, the 'Bad' version of Han Solo.

I don't know, and it doesn't really matter. He's totally Badass.

What I do know is that I'm wearing the shirt to work on Friday, before my daughter steals it and I never see it again.

17 - THAT'S NOT EXACTLY WHAT I MEANT, BUT...

There are things that you shouldn't say aren't there? Especially in these days of unfettered political correctness. They tend to be personal opinions about people or situations. You may think that the new girl from accounting likes cake a little too much or that the guy you see at the bus stop doesn't really have the ears for that style of hat.

But it doesn't stop there though, often when you say things, they get misunderstood, people read a subtext into them, they try and guess what you mean, rather than what you've actually said.

And that, dear readers, is where the trouble starts.

'Change your material to fit your audience' they always say - Although they also say 'Cut your coat to suit your cloth' and 'Many a slip twixt cup and lip' and they may as well be Klingon for all the sense they make to me. One day, I shall hunt down these 'They' who say all these things and slap their nonsensical legs with a spikey deep-sea fish of some kind.

Anyway, material / audience... Right. There are some things you cannot say to some people - You can't say F**khead or W****r or S**t-eating Hobbit-faced slime-spewer who I would quite literally rather R*m-j*b a dead goat than talk to, to a small child who had just dropped their lollypop on the carpet.

You cannot say 'Race you!' and run off up a flight of stairs to someone suffering from a spinal injury and currently using a wheelchair (however temporarily) unless there is ample, high-speed, disabled access to the next floor up.

It is also frowned upon to call into question the cabling and electrical termination ability of our cousins from the Indian Subcontinent, unless you are a male member of the Royal family who can trace their recent parentage to the Hellenic areas.

However, the most fragile, the most pitfall strewn, the most likely vocal interaction to see you hung by the neck until you are dead is simply the one between an adult male and an adult female. There is not a single, solitary thing that one can say to the other that cannot be misconstrued as an attack on their masculinity/femininity/size/weight/length/sense of humo(u)r or general physiognomy.

Seemingly simple interrogatives such as 'Are you OK?' or 'Would you like me to do that?' are often misheard as 'What the hell's wrong with you this time, you petulant harridan' or 'For Jebus' sake will you stop fannying around with that and let someone significantly higher up the food-chain have a go'

You cannot comment that a member of the opposite sex is anything other than yoghurt-explodingly ugly unless you want your throw-away comment to be processed by your nearest and dearest's brain into the phrase 'Yes, they are a significantly more appealing sexual partner than you, and I would, should an opportunity present itself be up it (or on it) like a wombat on tepid custard'

I can virtually guarantee that everyone, male or female is nodding in agreement at this moment in time, apart from Mrs Dandy, who is thinking 'He's talking about me!' and hatching a plan to separate me from parts of my anatomy that, which though sadly no longer functional, I still have a certain masculine attachment to.

Why do we do this? Are we all so insecure? - You'll notice that I said WE there, I am just as likely to mishear 'And then Brian said...' as 'And whilst Brian was taking me roughly from behind, four other naked, priapic, men came in carrying a sign that said...' as anyone else, more so probably as my imagination is somewhat colourful compared to some.

Are we so eager to believe that our loved ones are evil that we constantly try to find the hidden meanings in what they say to us? Or is it that deep-down, we don't believe that we deserve to be loved?

Crap! we're all freaks - We should plan a yearly event, maybe one that lasts a whole month, where we take everything that anyone we supposedly trust says to us at face value. No second-guessing, no reading between the lines.

We could call it, erm... Oh bugger, I don't know, something like Truthtember (only less twee-sounding) and celebrate it with cards that say things like 'Your Sister's good looking' and 'I work with someone whose shoulders are wider than yours'

I think it would be good for us all in the long run.

18 - T-WIT - WHO?

We're a pet-loving family, the Dandies (no, not like that) And I can't actually remember the number of dogs, cats, fish or rodents we have had to buy food for over the past twenty years or so.

But I can remember that we've only ever had one owl, and this chapter is about him… or her… No, it was a him – I'm 94% sure.

-oOo-

Did you know, that it's physically impossible to move your hands wide enough apart to indicate how awesome owls are? Give it a go now - spread your hands apart as wide as you can... Is that it? No, sorry, owls are significantly more awesome than that. Probably at least twice as much.

They're like Birds of Prey V2.0 - I mean, your average Eagle, marvellous bird, don't get me wrong, can pick up a sheep and carry it back to the nest and feed it to its young, you don't get blackbirds doing that do you? But an owl, any old owl (with the possible exception of those tiny ones that live in holes in the ground) could do all that... Only silently - It could do it before the sheep / lizard / haddock had even woken up. One second the prey's having a lovely dream about grass or tapioca or something , the next it's torn up into chunks and being swallowed by something that looks a little bit like a transvestite zombie ET.

Weird thing that, owls are one of the few things in the animal kingdom that have ugly babies, I mean, I like owls... A lot, but you happen upon a nest of owlets when you're out for a stroll in the countryside and the whole 'Kill it with fire' instinct kicks in - They also smell incredibly bad and make a noise not unlike Satan with his Man-danglies caught in a revolving door.

We used to have a resident owl at Dandy Towers, there are photos of him on my Facebook page for my stalkers to take a look at. His name was Twist and he was frighteningly bi-polar. Incredible bird though, beautiful plumage. A European Barn Owl, who would sit, imperiously in the corner of the kitchen like a judgemental biscuit tin, watching you with his cold, dead, shark's eyes - right up until the point where he deemed you below his contempt and closed them. Ever been ignored by an owl? It does nothing for your self-esteem.

Owls are not the perfect indoor pet; they eject their waste from both ends with unpleasant speed, accuracy and regularity. They seem to void the bodily fluids of their food separate to everything else and that is not a sight, or smell that you quickly get used to. But if you persevere, they can become merely incredibly troublesome rather than a right-royal pain in the rear.

They're nice to take out for a walk though, they'll sit on your shoulder quite happily, or more likely on your head - And you'll get a lot of attention. In fact, I once got stopped by a couple of female Police Officers when I was out with the owl and one of the Rottweilers - Once all the coo-ing and the aww-ing had died down (It helped that the Rottie was particularly cute too) one of the uniforms turned to me and said,

'I bet you don't get mugged very often'

The owl took this as her cue to flap the short distance from my shoulder to my head, and relieve herself down the back of my neck. This did not do wonders for my already limited appeal to the opposite sex and they quickly continued on their patrol avec le grande vitesse.

If you Google the word 'Owls', pretty much every picture of a real owl that appears has an implied tag of 'Owl thinks: I will kick your ass'; and the ones that don't, look as if they suffer with some fairly severe mental retardation, this does nothing to assuage their general air of ass-kickery as they can now be filed under psychotic predators with inch long claws and no remorse.

They can do unnatural stuff too - Everyone and their rabbit knows about the whole head spinning 'round like Linda Blair watching speedway, but did you know that most of them can turn their heads upside-down too? Some of them can make one of their front toes point backwards to create inescapable double talons of tearing - Although they're not all conquering instruments of death of course, otherwise we'd all be speaking owlese and living in holes in trees.

They've been given a couple of disabilities just to keep them in their place - They have no peripheral vision and their ears aren't on straight.

Despite all this, I would have one again quicker than you can stir fry a possum, this time I might have something a little bigger, maybe a Great Grey or an Eagle (Owl) - Something I could fit a saddle on, or at least have a half-suit of armour made for.

I'd call him Trevor

19 - WHISTLE, AND SHE'LL COME TO YOU MY GIRL

Apart from the stuff we've already covered above, one of things 'things' that I like is the supernatural. I love a good horror film, in fact I quite like rubbish horror films. Werewolves and ghosts and suchlike are my meat and wine, or whatever that slightly anachronistic phrase is. Yvette Fielding from popular television show Most Haunted even follows me on Twitter!

It seems that I may have passed some of my feelings on to my Daughter, The MiniDandy, although as with most of today's young people, she's taken it just one step too far, and invited the supernatural into our house.

-oOo-

As Christmas has many associated traditions, I thought I'd reel some of them out in a 'Good Gods, what should I drone on about today' Kinda way.

The first one that I would like to have at is the Christmas Ghost Story. In the past, the BBC have done a cracking job of adapting the works of MR James (And others) into stories in the style of those told by the older generation, to the younger generation around open fire when the only lighting was provided by stuttering candles.

I present to you my own family Christmas Ghost story, a true account where names have not been changed, as no-one is truly innocent, are they?

It was the winter of 2002, we were a smaller family then - just the three of us. My Daughter was an accomplished talker and had quite a vivid imagination, despite only being three years old. She would often hold long conversations with her toys, posing them around a tea-service or arranging an impromptu picnic for them.

Her mode of conversation was very adult, she would ask Piglet a question and politely give him time to reply, nod sagely and move to the next stuffed animal or doll, to see what their opinion on the situation was. This was the rule, rather than the exception and was thought to be quite 'cute' or even precocious by any assembled onlookers.

One afternoon, when Mrs Dandy went upstairs to collect her after her regular nap, she heard our daughter laughing and having one of her conversations, the gaps where she would normally wait for her toys to reply were slightly, but noticeably, longer. It also sounded like the toys were asking the questions, and my Daughter was the one doing the answering.

When the chat seemed to have reached its natural conclusion, Mrs Dandy entered the room to see our daughter sat on the bed, alone. Alone in this case meaning no other toys, not the treasured Piglet or any of her other plushy inner circle.

"Who were you talking to Baby?"

"The Lady." she replied, in a completely disinterested tone.

"Which Lady?"

"Don't know, just the Lady, what's for Dinner?"

This was talked about for a couple of days as an odd occurrence, but nothing really came of it and the assumption was made that 'The Lady' was an imaginary friend, based on a half remembered character from a Disney Cartoon or a Narnia book.

A few weeks later, we decided to make a photo-wall in the dining room, with family pictures from the past fifty or so years. The project took some time, with photos being printed then framed and mounted on the wall. I walked into the dining room one day to see my daughter staring at the pictures.

"Who's that?" I asked, pointing at a picture of her

"Me!" she shouted, excitedly

"OK, who's that?" I pointed at a picture of my Brother

"Unca Pete! - Who's that?" She asked, turning the game around and pointing at a picture of Mrs Dandy.

“That's Mummy!"

"Who's that?"

"That's MY Mummy" I replied, preparing to tell some stories of my youth.

"No, silly Daddy, that's The Lady!"

"Which Lady, Baby?"

"The Lady," In a tone that implied that I was quite possibly the stupidest person on the entire planet, "That comes and talks to me in my bedroom!"

I should probably explain that my Mother had died of cancer some fifteen years previously.

After some small amount of coaxing, my daughter told me that 'The Lady' regularly visited her and would ask if everyone was alright and if she was happy. So far, so spooky, but that's not where the story ends.

As the identity of The Lady had now been established, a strange pall fell over the house; everyone seemed to be treading slightly lighter, a room you would normally walk through without turning on the light became a study in moving shadows and half-seen figures. Every creak of floorboards from the first floor was met with a strained silence to see if it evolved into footsteps.

As escalations go, the next 'stage' of the experience was strange, but for anyone who knew my mother, completely understandable.

My Daughter was (and still is) a reasonably sound sleeper, once she was asleep nothing short of a tactical nuclear strike would wake her up. Mrs Dandy often used 'Naptime' as a couple of hours that could be spent on housework that was otherwise difficult with a toddler in tow, such as dusting upstairs. One afternoon, she decided to try vacuuming, knowing that she wouldn't wake our daughter up.

I think she managed to use the vacuum for around fifteen seconds before it turned itself off, not at the vacuum, but at the switch on the socket. It took her some time to realise that that was what had happened as she assumed that something was loose, or the machine itself had overheated. The switch was turned back on and cleaning commenced for another few seconds until it was turned off again by the unseen hands.

My wife put down the vacuum, took a deep breath and turned to address the empty air:

"Look, Grandma Dandy, I'm not going to wake her up, everything is fine, we don't mind you visiting, but let me get on with my work"

The silence was deafening, which made the roar of the vacuum turning itself back on all the more of a shock.

After that The Lady's visits became less and less frequent, we think that she visited my Son a couple of times from things he's mentioned in conversation - But not to the extent that she did with my Daughter.

She did always say that she wanted a Grand-Daughter though.

And recently, some eleven years later, although we've moved house, my Daughter has started complaining that she can hear whispering, as if someone were talking very quietly behind her. The only word that she can actually make out is her own name.

She's not particularly worried, she described the smell that sometimes accompanies the whispering to me – It's Sandalwood by Yardley, one of my dead Mother's favourite scents.

20 - TELL MERRILL TO SWING AWAY.

So you've read that I like Sci-Fi and horror, now I'd like to tell you about a film that is neither particularly Sci-Fi (though it features aliens) and not particularly horrific (although it does feature some graphic finger chopping off action) but it still puts the wind right up me.

Has anyone got a film that affects them emotionally?

I don't mean 'I cried at the end of <Insert any film except Twilight>'

I mean from when you hear that it's on, through watching the opening titles and right up until the 'No animals were harmed in the making of this motion picture, soundtrack available on Geffen Records' message, your heart would pound and you would have feelings of excitement / fear / happiness / dread?

I would like to admit that have an unreasonable fear of the 2002 Mel Gibson vehicle - Signs, by M Night Shawaddywaddy. I don't mean I don't like to watch it, I watch it whenever it's on - It's just that I watch it from behind the sofa, with a pillow in front of my face and my fingers in my ears. And for a great portion of the film I'm actually looking at the fireplace, just underneath the TV rather than at the TV itself.

For those of you who haven't seen it, it's about a Reverend, played by Aussie Mel, who loses his wife in a particularly grizzly car accident, this proves to him that God doesn't exist and he loses his faith.

(Ah, yeah, I'm going to assume that as the film's ten years old, if you were going to see it you would have done so already - So, as my fictional friend Melody Pond might say, beware *SPOILERS*)

He lives with his son (Asthmatic), his daughter (Who can't finish a whole glass of water due to some OCD-like deviancy) and his brother (Mad, but good at Baseball) on a farm in Pennsylvania. Where they suddenly start finding crop circles. Queue alien invasion, flashbacks, tinfoil hats, Cameo by the Writer/Director (M Night Shebopaloola), fingers being cut off, messages from beyond the grave and the eventual realisation that having Asthma, OCD and being a bit mad, but good at baseball, might one day save your life, and that living with people like that can restore your faith.

Nothing there that's particularly scary, It's no Hostel, certainly. And I don't have these feelings about any of M Night Shamalamading-dong's other films, The Sixth Sense had some 'Made me jump' moments, I'll freely admit, and Mrs Dandy worked out the twist about ten minutes into the film, as she will gleefully tell anyone who will stand still long enough. Unbreakable was, erm... Well... a bit rubbish in fairness, even with SLJ being a major character. The Village was OK, and I didn't see the twist coming in that one either. Devil was fairly good in a 'stuck in an elevator' kinda way. And The Happening wasn't a bad flick, all considered, a decent premise and no feel-good ending - which is strange for a US made film.

Someone once suggested it was the Baby Monitor bit, where it was discovered that you could hear the aliens talking to each other with clicks and whistles using a baby monitor, but only if they were quite close. Or that it was the scene where they catch an alien on video from a kids' birthday party, and it just goes about its business, not caring that it had been spotted. I understand that quite a lot of people don't like that bit.

Maybe it was the way it was depicted realistically, the whole 'This could quite easily happen' vibe you get, or I get at least. I don't know.

All I do know is that it scares the willies out of me, but I really want to watch it now, I wonder if it's on?

21 - BUT I FEEL FINE!

On the 21st December 2012, the World ended.

Well, obviously it didn't, or you wouldn't be here sat on the toilet trying to remember whether you'd paused the TV before you left the lounge. But some people were convinced that it was going to, they were mad people, but people all the same… We shouldn't judge.

No-one seemed to know exactly how it was going to end, I suppose it wasn't really important when it comes down to it, it's pretty final, you're not going to sit through it and go 'Oh! Was that it? I was expecting more Tsunamis.'

So, I came up with some ideas of my own, and it turns out that ridiculous as they were, I was still closer than those people who actually thought it was going to happen.

Gods-Dammit! I should have kept the Nickleback 'If today was your last day' post until today shouldn't I?

Anywho, it seems that tomorrow is the end of the World, and if it means I don't have to travel the complete length of the M42 at 10mph again, I welcome it with open arms. I got to thinking, whilst I was sat in traffic, for two hours, this morning... What form will Armageddon take?

Hollywood has given us several different possibilities - Films with deeply original names like '2012' and 'Armageddon' have covered the natural disaster angle quite extensively - We've had ELE asteroid impacts, floods, ice-ages, solar prominences & alien invasions - All the big bang endings that can be depicted with massive special CGI effects and Dolby / THX surround sound.

I'm convinced that the end will come tomorrow with a whimper, rather than a bang. The end will be gradual - I mean it'll still be fairly quick, we've got to cram it into the 24 hours after all, but it won't be all 'Ah! what's that?' Bang! *Dead*.

Below I list some possibilities that I think have a very real chance of ending the world:

The magnetic North and South poles will swap places - This will render all GPS devices non-functional causing apocalyptic car-crashes all over the planet - The only people to survive will be iPhone 5 owners who suddenly find that AppleMaps is now correct - Unfortunately a significant proportion of these people have under developed genitals, and the remainder of the human race will slowly die out.

There will be a massive explosion of radiation from the sun which will grow ducks to the size of horses and shrink horses to the size of ducks. This will, at a stroke, wipe out global bread reserves as flocks of giant mallards descend on supermarkets and bakeries and also destroy 90% of the agrarian economies around the world as it suddenly takes 200 horses to pull a plough. It will also cause the almost instantaneous fouling of our inland fresh water supplies - I mean, ducks are pretty filthy animals to start with...

The Moon will turn out to be the egg of a giant, mutant, Star-Goat (As I have always secretly suspected) and planet earth will be grazed to the mantle whilst the uncontrollable tides boil the seas away into space.

The amount of IT/technological waste that companies have been stockpiling due to people not really understanding the WEEE regulations will achieve sentience, we will be subjugated and decimated by millions of suddenly self-aware DVD players that have gotten tired of having shiny discs inserted into them and want to know how we like it when they do it to us.

The hidden back-masking embedded in the REM track 'It's the End of the World as we know it' will kick in as it is played incessantly by radio stations around the world. This will turn us all into mindless zombies who... Oh.. I don't know... Shave our heads, look painfully thin and eat each other's brains, or something.

But you don't need me to tell you, after all, most of you are incredibly intelligent, or you wouldn't be reading this Blog, that the chances are we're all still going to be here on Saturday morning - I don't mean here, at my desk, in Coventry - I mean generally where all of you are now, within a few miles at least.

Unless of course, there was just some massive mix up in translation... Where some aged scientist sat in a dusty office somewhere thought the Mayan Calendar said, 'The chain will end by a huge Comet on 21/12/12' and it actually said 'Huge electrical chain Comet will cease trading on 21/12/12' - If you take into account Gregorian shift and leap years and stuff - They were bang-on.

Just as likely in fairness...

22 - DZIT DIT GAII.

Conspiracy theories are the Internet's middle name, and 99% of them are incredibly easy to poke holes in. Occasionally, you find something really, really odd, hidden in plain (or plane in this particular case) sight. You do a bit of a double-take, feverishly Google the facts, such as they are. And then start stocking up on old copies of 'The Catcher in the Rye' and tinned food.

Read on dear reader, and be amazed-zed-zed-ed-d

Imagine you're going on holiday, somewhere nice and warm, Barbados or Guatemala or somewhere like that - Somewhere you need to fly to though. You buy your tickets and pack your pants and your towel, because that's all you really need in places like that, right?

Your departure date comes around, the taxi arrives and you're whisked to the airport. Upon arrival, you are calmed by soothing music, the happy smiling faces of other travellers and the carefully thought out decoration of the terminal itself. Grandiose pictures and statuary with a global, geographical theme perhaps? Aircraft through the ages? Famous people with aviation backgrounds? All things that you're quite within your rights to expect...

Not if you fly out of Denver International you aren't - On initial arrival at the airport, you are confronted by a 30' high statue of a rearing horse with glowing red eyes, the locals have entered several petitions to have it taken down, siting that it is evil - In fact, the statue actually killed its own sculptor as it fell on him whilst it was being completed!

If you manage to make your way inside with your wits intact, passing by two gargoyles bursting out of suitcases, you come across the dedication plaque, or capstone from when the building was completed. Apart from the large, Masonic Square and Compasses in the middle, which is enough to set the conspiracy nuts off all on its own (Doesn't bother me, some of the nicest people I know are Masons) it houses a time-capsule to be opened in 2094 and it has a raised dais, with a vague resemblance to a keyboard that houses a repeat of the Masonic symbol and a braille translation of the inscription. There are them that say if you press the symbols in the correct order, the door to the secret underground bunker will open.. (Did you read that in a hushed pirate voice? - You should, it sounds much better)

There are inscriptions in the floor, including the chemical symbols for gold and silver on the side of a mine cart and the Navajo phrase 'Dzit Dit Gaii' which means 'The Mountain that is White' - The inscription 'Mt Blanca' is also repeated in various places around the terminal - A very important place in Knights Templar mythology.

But the strangest thing you'll see, in my opinion at least, are the murals - I'm not going to post them here, because they're all over the net, but I will describe a couple to you. Try to keep in mind that we're in a public space, at an international airport, in the mainland USA, not a despot's palace in an out of the way corner of what used to be the USSR or a terrorist based republic in the Middle East.

There's one that depicts a giant nazi-esque figure, wearing a gas-mask and great-coat, with a giant sword spearing the dove of peace. He's surrounded by a slew of grieving mothers holding dead babies, in the bottom corner is a poem, written by a 16 year old child who died in Auschwitz... Just what you want to see before you catch your flight to Eastern Europe. There's one where the main feature is a scene of a group mourning three people in open caskets, surrounded by extinct or nearly extinct animals whilst the rainforest burns in the background - A poignant image, certainly - But would you display it at an airport? Yet another shows the children of the world coming together, some of them carrying a selection of swords wrapped in the flags of warring states including the Palestinian & Israeli, Indian & Pakistani and British & Irish amongst several others, standing on a fallen statue of the unidentified gas-masked villain. Strangely, some parts of the murals have been recently painted over at the request of customers...

Weird, I think you'll agree - There are other odd things about the place, for instance, from the air it bears a close resemblance to a swastika. It was paid for mainly by a private investor, to the tune of some $5 Billion. It's alleged that five pentagonal structures were built, twelve stories high and then buried and used as foundations, rather than demolished as they were reportedly not to specification. It has triple-redundant water & power systems and a ventilation system that stretches for miles outside the airport environs. It seems to have a higher incidence of windscreen and fuselage cracks than any other airport, this has been speculated to be due to high (or possibly low) frequency pulses emanating from below the airport itself.

Of course there are more than likely perfectly reasonable explanations for all of the above, the main one being that it's posted on the Internet it's probably tosh. But do a bit of research for yourself, immerse yourself in the world of the tin-foil hat wearing brigade, see what you can find - It might keep you busy over Christmas.

23 - AS THE SUPERHERO SAID TO THE STRIPPER.

We've established the Chimping Dandy as a Super-villain, one who can stop time with a thought. But how was he created? Why did the world suddenly need him? And what has this got to do with Pangolins?

-oOo-

I must stop using the phrase Super-Hero, as we established a few weeks ago, my made-up superpower - The ability to stop time - can only be used for evil, at least, as far as I can think of things to do with it.

Technically, I'm a Super-Villain, and as my Daughter reminded me, Villains get the best clothes.

So the time is here, pull up a bat-winged chair, that one over there upholstered in the suspiciously beige leather with the faint tattoos on it should still be warm, top up your skull shaped goblet with 'Claret' and I'll tell you the story of the origin of The Chimping Dandy.

Our story begins in the small West-Midlands hamlet of Birmingham, in a bar - as all the best stories do, I mean, I've yet to be enthralled by a story that begins 'The best thing about where we were was that there was free beetroot'. There were a number of us, and we were approaching that stage of drunken-ness just before the 'Hold my beer and watch this' casualty-fest.

It was a stag night, so it wasn't going to end well, we had no illusions about that - In fact, one of the guests was the bride to be's ex-husband - And was, after a number of drinks 'Loaded for bear'. The sensible thing to have done at this point would have been to go somewhere and get a meal, so that we could sit down for a while, get our breath back, sober up slightly, and line our stomachs with unfeasibly spicy food. What we actually did was to find another bar, and have another drink. We repeated this downwards spiral a number of times up (and then back down) Broad Street.

Then someone uttered the magic question 'is it Naked Lady Time?' In fairness, this had always been a planned part of the evening, to the point where the groom to be, had been stitched up like a kipper by his fiancée in that she had pre-arranged for him to be man-handled (well, woman-handled) by a selection of young(ish) ladies on the stage, on a throne, with shaving cream.

After a final beer, we adjourned to either The Rocket Club, or Legs Eleven - I forget which, and for the purposes of this story, it matters not - Both of them are establishments where semi-pulchritudinous ladies will remove 95% of their clothes for a small monetary consideration. For those who have never been to one of these establishments (or those that have told their partners this at least) I will describe the scene. The main area was a large, darkened room, decorated in early 'Poundshop Transvestite Christmas'. There was a central stage area, populated by a single chair, complete with handcuffs. This in turn was surrounded by a selection of booths with banquette seating for ten or so people each.

There were three types of people in the room:

Punters - Men (almost exclusively) who had come to prove their superiority over women by remaining clothed whilst the women got naked.

Strippers - Girls who had come to prove their superiority over men, by charging them £10 to watch them get slowly undressed over a three minute period.

Security - Huge (and I can't state that enough) gentlemen, usually of Afro-Caribbean descent, who's aim in life was simply to enforce the rule that the punters and the strippers never got closer than 2" away from each other.

Like so many of my stories, some description of the clothing worn by the group may assist in your suspension of disbelief. The brief had been 'Smart to smart-casual' mainly to enable us to enter any of the myriad drinking establishments with a minimum of fuss. I had bought a new suit for the occasion, and it was silver - Now, I don't mean that it was shiny silk, at the time I was neither that rich, nor mental enough to believe a silk suit would survive the evening, no - it was made of finest rayon/polyester mix, jacquard printed to look like the sort of pattern you see under a leaky car on a rainy day. Yes, it was about 300% more vulgar than you're currently thinking that it was.

Anyway, the evening progressed much as you would expect, every few minutes a young lady would wander into our booth and say 'Dance?' Now, nine times out of ten, one of the other guys would say 'Yes' and gyrating would ensue. I am not saying that I didn't say yes myself because I was some kind of saint, or that I felt guilty to be looking at another naked lady whilst I had a wife waiting for me at home, it was purely because watching the guy next to me get a dance was free.

Now, this seemingly hadn't gone un-noticed by some members of staff and I was approached by what I can only assume, was one of the 'senior' girls - I'd seen a couple of the other girls talking to her and pointing at our group and she had seemed to have been offering advice to them.

"Hello," she said and sat down next to me.

"Hey!" I replied, in what I hoped was an off-hand, but inoffensive way.

"Don't we have anyone you like the look of?"

"Ah!, no, I see, Maybe later, I'm still making notes."

"Notes?"

I looked around furtively, hushed my voice and said, "Look, don't tell anyone, but we're doing research for a new show on Bravo" (For those unaware, Bravo was a channel that produced 'lads' programming - it's now mutated into Dave, which just shows Top Gear repeats)

"A new show? What's it about?"

"Well, we're going to visit various strip clubs around the country, but we're going to be filming an anchor segment from one place, like a base, every week, we're still trying to decide where to use"

"Oh, I did wonder." She replied, looking me up and down.

"What did you wonder?"

"Well, we don't get many people in here dressed like that - We figured that you were 'somebody', but none of the girls recognised you. Would you be filming the girls too?"

"Well, that would be up to the management, obviously, but I was wanting to include a couple in the title sequence, we'd have to see how it went. We'd have to audition obviously"

The young lady then stood up, and without monetary assistance, proceeded to audition, for two songs. She then sat down, waved at one of the security staff and mouthed the words 'On my break' to him. He nodded with the slow surety of a Norwegian glacier and continued scanning the room for distance infractions - A drink appeared on the table in front of her, and seeing my raised eyebrows she said;

"Don't worry, it's already paid for. You must have seen some stuff"

"Sorry?"

"Doing programmes like that, is it all the same kind of 'adult' shows?"

"Yeah, mainly... Swinging, Dogging, Chimping, that kind of thing."

"Chimping? I've never heard of that. Do I want to know?"

I leaned in close, keeping the regulation 2" distance of course, and explained it to her. The look of revulsion on her face started a change in me at the subatomic level, I could feel my time-bending abilities throbbing into life, I felt empowered, and I knew that things would never be the same again.

By proving to a jaded stripper, that there were still things in this world that could disgust even her, I had become...

The Chimping Dandy!

24 - BANDITS AT 2 O'CLOCK! WHAT DO I DO UNTIL THEN?

Do you remember I said that I'd done some strange and wonderful jobs?

Did you want to hear about the time I flew a Fighter/Bomber over Russia on a daring mission?

Me too, it sounds very exciting!

-oOo-

I remember it like it was yesterday (even though it was over twenty years ago). I'd launched from a small airbase on the eastern border of Finland, the one it shares with what is now Karelia - But was at the time, as far as we were concerned, just another part of the western USSR. I was flying low and slow, trying to minimise my radar signature, not easy in such a mountainous region.

The sanctioned mission was simply to destroy a train, transporting tanks and ammunition to fortify the small, but strategically important town of Onega, but, as ever, I had maxed my weapons loadout, as there were always brownie points available for hitting targets of opportunity. It took me almost an hour of flying over barren steppe to find the target, it was on an uncharted line just west of Pavlovskaya. I could just see SAM sites on the edge of the detection range of my passive radar, not close enough to bother me of course, but worth remembering all the same.

looping around to bring myself onto an intercept vector, I thumbed the weapons select switch until the AGM-65E(i) came on-line, my centre MFD showed an image of the train below and I checked the range. 20 Clicks, within range but only just, I waited for a few seconds until I'd closed to 15, rotated the stores bay open and then launched the first missile. No matter how many times you do it, the jolt of the munitions dropping away and the roar as the rocket engine engages is something you never get used to.

The small screen showed me the weapon's track as it sped towards the target at over 1,000 KpH. Seeing as I wasn't paying, I thought that I'd send in another one to keep it company. I launched the second Maverick, rotated the bay closed and turned south-east, realising that the air would soon be filled with MiGs looking for payback. The first missile chose that second to hit and I saw the plume of flame, the screen changed to show the track of the second missile, just as it detonated inside what must have been the ammunition storage car, this second explosion dwarfed the first and caused the almost instantaneous derailment of the entire train.

Looking down at the battlemap, I noticed that I'd received a message from an E-3 orbiting high overhead. It seems that my secondary target had been confirmed as a Typhoon class nuclear submarine due to be launching from the repair-base at Severodvinsk - I had to destroy it before it made it to the safety of the polar ice-cap. I set the waypoints and headed north towards the coast. As I cleared the foothills of the mountains and started across the vast swages of pine forest, I detected several mobile SAM sites blocking my way to the north, I should have known that it wouldn't be that easy.

I lost altitude again until I was skimming the treetops, knocking the powdered snow from their top branches with the vectored exhaust from the turbo-fans, I canted gently to the left and headed out over the White Sea. The missile launch alarm caught me completely by surprise, I hadn't seen a radar site come online anywhere close enough to detect me. I'll admit that I panicked, I'd become complacent after a ten completed mission streak returning a plane to base without a scratch had earned me a place in the base's Sierra Hotel... Big mistake!

The threat classification system identified the inbound as a Grail, with passive infrared guidance. That explained why I hadn't seen a SAM site come online, somewhere behind me was a Russian soldier who just happened to have a Grail-launcher with him, and no doubt a field radio. Things were going to get hotter from now on. A barrage of flares confused the rocket for long enough for me to try to get out of range, in case he had a similarly equipped friend. I knocked the throttle forward and ordered the terrain-following autopilot to hug the waves, coming around in a long, slow loop, I set course south-east again, intending to fly right down the throat of the sub-pens.

It only took a few minutes for my forward cameras to make out the base, there wasn't much to see, a collection of hardened concrete boxes descending into the water, huge steel pressure doors blocking their entrances. All except one, one door was wide open and in front of it floated the massive, 40,000 tonne bulk of the target. My radar showed SAM sites lighting up all around the docks like killer Christmas decorations and I realised that a low-altitude run might be the best way to take out the target, but it would leave me with around twenty four S-75s trying to tear chunks out of my rear end as soon as I ran for it.

I targeted the sub, and selected my single ASALM missile. As soon as I had a positive lock, I rotated the weapons bay open, pulled back on the stick and lobbed the munition into the air, over a tonne of ordinance leaving the plane changed the flight characteristics fairly sublimely and I had to fight to keep from turning turtle. As soon as I had hit vertical, I rolled the plane through 180 degrees and pulled back on the stick, pointing myself back at the base, but this time upside down. Performing (even if I say so myself) a perfect snap-roll, I targeted the four closest SAM sites and launched Mavericks, then let loose the two CSW's that I'd had the quartermaster load on a whim, I'd never used them before, not really trusting the new, so called 'Smart' weapons.

It must have taken only two or three seconds from the start of my attack to the start of my exit run, but it felt like years, everything slowed down almost to the point of stopping, I could see my MFDs refreshing themselves. And I was hammering the chaff and flare release buttons so quickly that I didn't notice the 'OUT' indicators until I was 5 Clicks south of the site.

Three SAM sites had managed to get off a shot before they'd been wiped out in the firestorm (I learned to trust Smart weapons after that) and I was out of countermeasures. There was nothing I could do but get as close to the deck as possible and hope that I could evade them until they either hit something solid or ran out of fuel. I started to jink but the missiles continued to close. This was it, there was no way out, they had three times my speed and they were seconds away from being in detonation range. I pulled hard left and realised they weren't following me... Of Course! How could I have forgotten that the S-75 was guided from the launch station, the same launch stations that were now burning piles of twisted metal?

My self-congratulation was cut short as two of the missiles detonated behind me, luckily their approach vector was too oblique to tear any major chunks out of the plane, but they caused some minor damage to my control surfaces and as my port engine swallowed some shrapnel, I lost thrust.

There was nothing left but to set a direct course back to base, I had virtually no weaponry left, no countermeasures, no hope of escaping using engine power or manoeuvrability. My only chance was to keep the plane in the air long enough to make it back over the border to Finland, it didn't matter what happened after that.

Unfortunately, a flight of MiGs had different ideas; I'd made it as far as Lake Onega, not so far from where I'd hit the train. The threat detector was solid red, the air was full of Aphids and Atolls and I made the conscious decision not to spend the rest of my days in a soviet prison. The end, when it came was in a riot of alarms and bright colours and if I'm honest, the pain was more from the realisation that I wouldn't be able to get credit for the disabling blow I had dealt.

I leaned back into my chair and stared at the screen, it said 'Retry Mission?' I pressed 'N' and turned off my old Commodore Amiga - I'd forgotten just how much I enjoyed playing F29 Retaliator.

25 - TAKE ME TO YOUR LEDERHOSEN

So I've told you about my girlie feelings for the film 'Signs'. The next chapter might go some way towards explaining them.

-oOo-

I'm feeling self-referential this morning, so I'm going back to a subject that's close to my gizzard.

Alien Abduction...

People who know me and/or have visited Dandy Towers will appreciate that the first floor library is mainly comprised of Science Fiction books, a smattering of Horror, many, many 'Fo' dummies' books and an English to Dutch phrasebook. I like a getaway from reality to be a getaway and how much further can you getaway than to the thirteenth bifurcated throne-room of Emperor Fun'dun'kmant'ine the Socially Inept who happens to command a fleet of ten thousand gravity-powered, cloakable, Star-Killerons and is father to the shrew-gratingly beautiful F'nurk'ma'chewb'utfutnut, whose attributes are both talked about in and visible from, low orbit.

I'm not biased, I like everything from the high space opera stuff as described above to the 'It was Earth all along' shock twist in the tail, OMG I'm so original, genres. I've been reading this sort of stuff for the best part of forty years and I've read pretty much all the basic stories and some of the not so basic ones, there can be some stuff you really have to think about, like;

Boy meets girl, girl turns out to be thousand year old alien and runs away. Girl meets other boy; boy dies bravely in intergalactic war, boy revived by enemy soldier. Spaceship turns out to be the killer; girl turns out to be the spaceship. Boy turns out to have imagined the whole thing; both boys are the same person. Girl is one of the boys' Grandmother, but not the other's.

You see, with my training and experience, I understand all that - I mean it helps that I wrote it, but still... You'd think I'd be immune to all the associated Sci-Fi tomfoolery. But the whole Alien Abduction stuff does tend to put the wind up me a bit - I can read about it, no problem - I've got many books full of accounts from people who claim they've been abducted, taken aboard your actual spaceship, by your actual aliens and either been viciously subjected to vicious experimentation or given a bit of a tour and had a lovely chat about the threat of impending thermonuclear war and dropped off with only an itchy sub-dermal implant to remember them by.

I think I might just be a bit gay about the idea of being anally probed - Hang on, that might not be right, not to mention slightly homophobic, I just mean that I'm really not a fan of the whole idea.

You know how in the horror films, you've got the soon to be victim, running through the forest in the middle of the night, being pursued by (If it's a decent director) a half-glimpsed monster, when she comes across a rickety woodshed, forces her way inside and slams the door. She immediately feels safe, even though we've previously seen it tear a train apart using only its nipples and eyebrows. Well, you don't get that respite from alien abduction, most abductees are asleep when they're 'taken'. You might get a bright light and a wooooo-wooooo-wooooo noise if'n you're lucky, but that's about your lot until you wake up in a white room full of the little grey dudes with the big black eyes giving it the old 'This might sting a bit' routine as they plunder your nether-regions with a nuclear powered eggwhisk.

And that's the other thing... If you'd asked a bunch of kids in the '60's to draw you an alien, you'd have got a mix of wild and wonderful pictures from two-headed parrots to octopus footed centipedes and everything in between. Do that now and the chances are you'll mostly get the picture that most of you just thought of (OK, apart from you people who misread 'AN' alien as 'THE' Alien) - You know, the little dudes with the pear shaped heads, massive black eyes and no visible genitals, known by one and all as Apple Store Employees... Erm... I mean Greys.

It's something I've been thinking about for a while, is this image being drummed into us? Are we being made ready for a big 'reveal' by a conglomeration of Western Governments? So that when the curtain is pulled aside and it turns out that we've had Zarp and Plurb from Zeta Reticulii coaching the direction of mankind's development since the Roswell crash we all just go 'Ah, right you are then'?

I read recently that according to a recent study even young babies recognise pictures of Greys as being a 'thing' rather than just an abstract shape. This brings up another two questions;

- Why are they able to do that?
- Why would anyone be doing that research?

I think we should all be desperately worried - Either that there's an alien invasion going on by stealth - Or I'm as mad as a donkey wearing lederhosen on a tightrope.

Either way, no-one's sticking anything up my butt, without at least buying me dinner first.

26 - THAT WASN'T THE YEAR THAT WAS.

So, picture the scene, it was New Year's Eve 2012 and I'd been reading the myriad 'Reviews of the year' that spring up all over the Internet at that time of year.

I thought to myself 'I should do that, but I should make it a bit edgy, a bit different.' So I decided to do a review of things that hadn't technically happened.

-oOo-

Well, I suppose - As it's the last day of 2012, I should do some sort of hoitsy-toitsy review of the year... High points, low points, mid points - What trended on Twitter, how many people found the Blog interesting, how much my personal Facebook index flopped around like a halibut in a Zumba class.

But I'm not going to, I have a memory like a sieve and the few things that I can remember actually happening, I can't remember when it happened or to who and with what.

I might make some stuff up I suppose - Hey, that might work - In fact, that's what I'm going to do! A month by month guide to things that didn't happen in the last year.

January.

An early news report from Khazakstan informed us that civilian contractors were transporting a Sperm Whale by air, using one of those huge Russian sky-hook style helicopters and an intricate system of thin straps and pullies - It turns out that the whole thing had been organised by an Italian company and the instructions had been translated from Italian to Khazakstani by the same Icelandic chap from the Dutch East Indies who writes out the instructions for Ikea. Within minutes of taking off, the poor cetacean suffered terminal garrotting and fell into six neat pieces. Luckily, local villagers were able to follow some supplementary instructions, and fashion the remains into three free-standing bookcases and a very avant-garde table-lamp.

February.

Shoppers in Sheffield, UK, were startled to find that due to an issue with autocorrect at a local advertising agency, a launch event for the Blu-ray release of the X-Men origin film 'Wolverine' had become a little more feral than expected. Where the original instruction had been 'Make sure the guy in the Wolverine suit gets to Meadowhall by 09:00' - It appeared on the Talent-Wrangler's iPhone as 'Make sure you release 900 live Wolverines in Meadowhall - Guy'. In the ensuing chaos, four people were bitten to death - two seriously, one by a policeman.

March.

March will be remembered, more than anything, for the temporary repealing of the laws of conservation of momentum by the US Senate. The reason that this was a temporary change was that not much research had been done beforehand and no-one realised that this would make any form of 'Coasting' impossible - This alienated one of the largest US demographics - i.e. The 15-35 year old, itinerant, disillusioned skateboarding company director - And Google threatened to launch a class-action suit due to lost productivity at its HQ, as no-one was able to use the swings and slides.

April.

Apple fanboys were shocked to learn that they had been taken in by a complex ruse perpetrated by Samsung. An email had been sent offering them the chance to take part in the new Beta Test of the printable iPhone 5. The 'dupes' queued for hours at their own home printers, after being told that the device would be launched at 00:00 on April 31st, a completely new day, that would only exist for the Apple glitterati - At 11:59 on the 30th, a print job was generated that printed out a picture of a house-brick with a smiley-face painted on it by a duck. The joke was on Samsung however, as this proved to have slightly greater functionality than the standard iPhone 5.

May.

Plans were unveiled by NASA to recreate the original Starship Enterprise in Earth orbit. The $60 Billion dollar project stalled however, as not enough people could be found who were willing to be boarded into the walls for the entire five-year mission and operate the sliding doors whilst making the 'Shhhht' noise.

June.

June played host to the hottest day ever recorded in the history of the known universe. It occurred when an office party prank at the Large Hadron Collider at CERN in Switzerland went horribly wrong. A group of scientists, bored with making drinks that changed colour indicating the arousal level of the drinker, decide to see what would happen if you accelerated a shish-tikka-donner mixed kebab (with extra salad) to lightspeed. The effect was devastating, but thankfully short-lived. As the chilli sauce reached 299,792,459 m/s its quantum state changed to anti-chilli and a small, but quite fragrant sun was instantly created - raising the local temperature for Western Europe to approximately 74.2 bajillion degrees.

July.

On the 8th. Due to an unusual weather pattern, 95% of the world's remaining 17,600 White Rhino performed The Timewarp - from Richard O'Brien's Rocky Horror show. The quake produced when they all initially 'Jumped to the left' caused massive flooding in Botswana and large cracks to appear on the peak of Kilimanjaro - It's not known why the remaining 5% didn't join in, but the prevailing research shows that they were probably Mama-Mia fans.

August.

August shall be remembered for the temporary cessation of all sporting activity on the UK mainland - Absolutely nothing competitive happened. TV programming that would normally have been sport related was replaced by re-runs of Come Dine With Me. Even conkers was outlawed. Anyone caught flouting this new ruling was taken to Sebastian Coe's underground hideout and birched ruthlessly until they'd learned their lesson.

September.

Danish inventor Myrtryk Von Hunboltzon premiered his world-beating new invention - The Cat-a-porter, a method of instantly transmitting cats from place to place globally. Initial trials proved effective as cats of all sizes, colours and personalities were transmitted around the world. Unfortunately, it all turned out to be a massive con, as the cat that was being 'transported' was in fact, being minced by hidden equipment and not transported at all. All Von Hunboltzon had actually invented was a device for spontaneously creating cats out of thin air.

October.

The world of Fortean Research gained another martyr in early October as Brigadier Hawksworth McTavish-Silverplib (Retd.) completed his two year stalk-fest of the Beast of Bodmin in spectacular fashion. The Brigadier, known to local Beastarians as 'Mad Dangler McTavish' due to his habit of hunting the beast with a Magic-tree car air freshener tied to his genatalia to mask his scent, was believed to have cornered the animal in a disused barn. His mangled remains were discovered in various places scattered around Cornwall. He is survived by an English Springer Spaniel called Leonard.

November.

Almost nothing of any note happened in November, the tides continued in their sploshey up-down motion, birds flew south, cheese matured and the complex system of checks and balances that we call life continued unabated. Right up until the point where every man, woman and child who lived through the 1980's was discovered to have been some kind of paedophile or assorted rapist, sheep worrier or sodomiser. Apart from Bruce Forsythe, he was outed as a vampire and ritually staked by Tess Daley on the set of 'Strictly Come Dancing'

December.

Hollywood news that peaked in December was centred around the revelation that Kristen Stewart, 'Star' of the Twilight films and Snow White and the Huntsman, did not actually exist. She was outed as a completely digital construct by her ex-partner Cedric Pattinson. When questioned by a representative of the Jo McCarthy Rights for Real Humans group, Pattinson admitted that he thought it strange that Stewart disappeared every time there was a power outage at their shared apartment in East Compton, LA. However he thought that this may have been due to her childhood spent in California. It was also discovered that it was during one of these power outages that her facial expression subroutine had been deleted.

Well, there you go, a month by month list of things that didn't happen in 2012 - I hope to continue making you guys shake your heads in mild disbelief in the new year.

27 - LOW RESOLUTION.

Following on from the last entry, where I gave a rundown of monthly events that didn't happen, I thought I'd share with you my list of New Year's Resolutions that didn't actually happen either as it turns out... Spooky!

It gives you a bit of insight into the things that make me tick, and it's not just that huge comedy key in my back.

-oOo-

So we're well into the New Year now, I mean, I'll still be writing down '12' at the end of the date for... Oh, I don't know... Maybe the next six months or so, but 2013 is definitely here to stay.

Now, I've never been one that subscribes to this idea of setting myself unattainable targets, or even attainable targets for that matter. But there are some things that I will try to do this year. Actually, 'try' might be putting it strongly - What I'll probably do is carry on as normal and then if I accidentally do any of these things, I'll feel all smug and self-important and tell you all about it.

1. Get more involved in Burlesque.

I've been nipping at the edges of burlesque for some years now, the words 'Flamboyant' and 'odd' are ones that you could quite happily use to describe me (amongst several others of course, but those are the two I'm highlighting now) and I think that that sums up my feelings on Burlesquerie. It's not all about the strippers, although I'd be lying if I didn't freely admit that that is a part of it. It's more about the whole feel of it, the anachronism, the ostrich feathers, the music. Although I think the main thing is that it's one of the few 'Glamour related' pastimes that is totally non-judgemental where body shape/size are concerned. Real sized people are welcomed with open arms, and a lot of the professional artistes can't be described as stick thin by any stretch of the imagination.

2. Shine at my chosen career

This one is probably the most unlikely in fairness. I've been doing what I do, jobwise, for about thirty years now. I'm pretty good at it, it (just) pays the bills and I tend to get a lot of repeat business, in that places I've worked at, or people I've worked with, tend to ask for me if they have things that need doing that I can do. Thing is, this has virtually nothing to do with the fact that I am any better at these things than anyone else - It's usually because I make people laugh, at the same time as doing a half-assed job. The ability to fit into an already established team with the minimum of discomfort has been a mainstay of my repertoire for a long time. But now I've moved from being a contractor to being a permie, I might just have to get good at what I do.

3. Draw more

2012 will be forever remembered as 'The year when I actually started actively selling my stuff Internationally' - I've always been a 'hobbyist' as far as my artwork is concerned, drawing mainly for pleasure and I'd considered myself firmly in the 1st. year art student school of drawing. I mean, I'd designed a couple of tattoos for friends and family that they seemed happy with, but I'm certainly no H.R. Giger. I need to practice more, copy some stuff by more talented people than myself - I might even post it, and give a shout to the people I am hopelessly plagiarising - If'n I remember that is. I might specialise in erotica, that always sells well, what with the Internet being populated almost exclusively by perverts.

4. Work on my Anger Management issue.

I hit my alarm clock with a 2lb lump hammer last night because it wouldn't let me change the alarm time - This did not enhance my general user experience, my wife is buying me a new one today... (And no, you don't need to know why I keep a lump hammer by the side of the bed)

5. Finish my bloody trike

I have a rather lovely Honda VF1100 trike in my garage - All blue with silver flames (See flamboyant, above) , it was the love of my life until I sent it away to have it professionally finished. The diligent and trustworthy professional I sent it to had a few problems and he ended up having it for a number of years (rather than the number of months that he originally quoted) and I kind of lost momentum. The damn thing's been sat there for over a year now with no real progress being made. It needs maybe a few hundred quid throwing at it and days (rather than weeks) of time. I seem to always find a reason for not looking at it, ranging from 'There's something else we need to spend the money on', through 'It's raining' to 'I've found some beer that I'd forgotten I had'. This really isn't good enough, I seem to be coming across as a bit of a procrastinator. In fact, I would be the King of procrastinators, but I can't be bothered - All bow down before your regent, Prince LazyAss the fifty-third - Bathe in my reflected protraction.

6. I will stop feeling guilty for doing things that I enjoy.

Actually, this one's probably never going to happen either. Maybe it's just my made up middle-class sensibilities, or maybe I'm just too gorram passive-aggressive - As the Offspring once sang, 'The more you suffer, the more it shows you really care (Right, yeah!)'. I tend to show this particular nonsensical defect by going without so that others don't have to... Makes no sense at all - I earn the vast proportion of the yearly family income, why should I feel guilty for buying myself the occasional PC Game or Ladyboy? No-one berates me for spending my own money, it's all self-contained - I think I'm probably not as well adjusted as I thought I was?

Anywho, enough of my bleating, I hope you've found something here to help you rationalise your own impending failure to keep to your arbitrary resolutions. After all, if a Super-Villain such as myself can't hit his own targets, what chance have you guys got?

(Feel free to use this as an excuse to your nearest and dearest)

28 - THE COLLECTED BARNABY WILDE

You may have picked up by now that I, on occasion, enjoy things of a motorcyhicular persuasion. I've ridden on two wheels and three wheels and have found that due to me having the balance and co-ordination of a new-born deer on a frozen tea tray suspended on a hammock over a... a... well, something that jigs about uncontrollably – Possibly Lee Evans, I'm sticking to three wheels for the time being. There follows a number of stories about the various times that the weather, machinery and my own ineptitude have conspired to try and kill me or loose me friends.

It features the word sphyncter quite a lot, usually prefaced by the word twitching.

-oOo-

I remember the very first time that I rode a trike, thinking back, it was probably a sign - I should have quit whilst I was ahead. It had a 1275GT Mini engine, with a gear linkage made from plasticine and cocktail sticks. When you changed gear, it involved a stirring motion, akin to the one you see in any cartoon where witches and cauldrons are mentioned - The gear you actually got at the end of this process was as random as you'd expect. I rode from the house of my very good friend Scots Mick (He of the Chilli recipes fame) to my own house, some four miles in total. Along the way I clipped the apex of every, single corner - In this instance, you should take 'clipped' to mean rammed into, mounted the pavement and then careened off the other side. In fact, a number of times, I clipped the apex of several perfectly straight roads, which didn't even have apexes.

I was being followed by Mick in his car, in case anything fell of the trike, including myself. We had planned to take the trike to a van hire company where one of 'the boys' worked, so that we could get one of the tires re-seated as it was leaking. Now, before I relay the punchline I have to explain that this particular trike was fitted with what we, in the trade, call 'Ape Hangers' - These are a particular type of handlebar, designed by the devil himself, to make any type of motorcycle that they're fitted to virtually uncontrollable. They do give you that Concussed American Starfish riding position that seems to be popular (or was in the 90's at least.) - Take a minute, Google them, see what you think.

So, we pulled into the car park and I changed down to 2nd gear and attempted to pull into a parking space. Of course, what actually happened was that I accidentally hit the 'Gamble' button on the gear selector and got 1st. This caused me to go skipping across the carpark with the front end in the air (thus rendering the steering inoperable) and punched the back quarter of a parked van with my left fist. Have you ever punched a van hard enough to leave a dent in it the shape of your fist? - It really hurts... Of course my assembled friends ran to my aid, checking that I hadn't done any irreparable damage to myself - Actually, no, what happened is that they stood, having to lean on each other because they were laughing so much. I think one of them actually wet himself - Especially when they showed me that the trike had skidded to a halt about 12" from a 6' drop.

On another occasion, I left work at 06:30 in the morning to discover it had snowed quite heavily during the night. The snow was deep enough that the rear axle was dragging in it, which played merry hell with the handling. I managed to wrestle the trike out of the industrial estate by bouncing gently off the pavement kerbs as I couldn't see exactly where the road finished and the pavement started. Once out onto the main road, things got a little bit easier as the virgin snow was replaced with black slush. I admit that I got cocky, fishing the back end out on purpose and spinning the rear wheels. Of course, as so often happens in these situations, I got bitten in the butt.

As I approached a busy traffic island and tried to brake, nothing happened - Well, nothing involving slowing down happened, a number of things involving going in the wrong direction took their place. In the 60' trip across the island, the trike spun through 540 degrees - A full one and a half turns, with me hanging onto the Apes for grim death. Luckily the other vehicles using the island at that time of the morning managed to avoid me completely. When the trike finally came to rest on the wrong side of the road I had to wait a good ten minutes before I carried on my journey - Not because I was shaking (though I was, like a Portuguese Man O'War with Parkinsons), but purely because the vacuum that had appeared between my clenched sphynchter and the seat meant that I couldn't move.

The next recounting involves a trike that didn't actually belong to me as such, it belonged to a young lady that I co-habited with for a while and was powered by an 850cc Reliant Robin motor. Don't laugh; it's a great engine when you strip all the fibreglass body from around it. It used to suffer every once in a while from the carbs freezing, but other than that it was bulletproof.

Anywho, we were on our way back from doing the weekly shop (one of the redeeming qualities of trikes is that they can usually carry more cargo than a bike) in the pouring down rain. You know that rain where you just have to look out of the window and you're soaking wet? Well it was heavier than that, heavy enough to frak with the electrics and cause misfires. So, it took a while to get home, sometimes on three cylinders, sometimes on two, but not very often on all four. I chanced to look down between my knees as we pulled onto the drive and noticed that a couple of the HT leads (The leads that go to the spark plugs) were 'tracking' - This means that they were making pretty blue sparks and dumping their precious electricity somewhere other than where they should - In this case they were swapping it between themselves and also with the cylinder head, very kind of them, but not exactly what you want in a perfect world.

N.B. The next two seconds of this story involve the complete disconnection of my hands from my brain.

I thought to myself, 'If I just separate those leads, I bet it'll run a whole lot better.' Now, the HT leads on a Robin carry about 30,000 volts (as opposed to the 240 volts in the sockets of your house) at an amperage, luckily, just below that required to stop your heart stone dead, so obviously I reached down and went to move the cables apart. The belt I got was sufficiently strong to lift me off the seat, throw me to the ground and cause me to lie in the rain, jumping around and laughing uncontrollably for a good few minutes.

The young lady who owned the vehicle in question, once worked at (and then owned I think) a trailer manufacturing business, their workshops were based in an old yard, about fifty yards long with about a 15 degree slope from the sheds, past the office, to the road. I used to help out there occasionally, wiring things up and making trailer covers etc. to earn a bit of beer money (Which was all reported to Her Majesty's Revenue & Customs of course). On this particular day, clocking off time came around and I decided to be efficient and move the trike from the yard next door and park it outside the office.

I won't go into all the dicking about with opening huge wooden gates and getting out onto the main road, then shutting and locking gates - But it took a good ten minutes to get the trike into the main yard. I then thought that I'd turn her around so that she was facing the right way for a quick getaway. The yard was shaped like a backwards 'P', with a wider area at the top where you could just about turn a car around, so I rode up the slope, slowly turned around and started to head back down.

I had to stop halfway, as a customer had pulled into the yard and left his car outside the office, exactly where I was going to park. So I did what you would normally do on a bike, I knocked it into neutral, held it on the front brake, and put both my feet down (Remember that last bit, it's important) assuming that he wouldn't be very long, as it was closing time.

I was right, less than a minute later, he came out of the office, saw me, gave that embarrassed grin and wave so beloved of people who've realised they parked like an idiot, and reversed out of the yard. I put the trike in gear, released the front brake and lifted my feet about an inch off the ground. They floated backwards slightly, as they sometimes do before you get 'em back on the footpegs. Unfortunately, my left foot hit the rear, left hand wheel and got dragged under - there was a loud and interesting crunchy-snappy noise.

So, if you'd just like to take a deep breath and let me describe the scene. I'm sat, almost upright on the trike, with my left foot, upside down, under the wheel - I was wearing para-boots (which probably stopped me having to have a shiny new foot fitted) and shouting for help. Luckily, there were no other bikers in the immediate area, so no-one was too busy laughing to respond. Long story short, the trike was moved off my foot and I was helped off and laid on the ground, my foot kind of 'sprung' back into place - which hurt probably about as much as when it had first snapped and caused one of the assembled workers to comment 'For a big bloke, 'e screams like a girl dun’t 'e?'

One small X-Ray later the doctor confirmed that I hadn't actually broken my ankle, what had happened was that it had completely dislocated, but one of my tendons had refused to snap and had pulled a 'plug' of bone out of the top of my foot. Once the ankle bones had been re-located, they had to 'manipulate' that plug back in before they could put it in a cast.

And yes, that bloody hurt too - But this time they gave me something to bite on, so I couldn't scream like a girl.

I used to work in Nuneaton, at the head office of large childrens' clothing store. Every morning I would ride through all the little villages between Derby and there, past Twycross Zoo, past Bosworth Battlefield, past all the little birdies cheeping happily in the trees. It was great, a wonderful ride - You should try it.

Just as I entered Nuneaton, I'd pull up at a garage just before the town centre and take off my helmet and replace it with a pair of wraparound shades. What with being a rufty-tufty biker and needing to look cooler than a polar bear's podules and everything.

Anyone who knows Nuneaton and has come in from the A5 side will know that there's a twiddly-bit where you need to turn left in the right-hand lane, then turn right, almost back on yourself and then go over the railway bridge (Well, there was about fifteen years ago, it's probably got a flyover or a Tesco's Knackers Yard there now.) Just after all this jiggery-pokery there was a little road on the left that took you past the sixth-form college... (What? There's nothing wrong with riding past a sixth-form college on your way to work every morning).

On this particular morning, I decided not to stop at the garage, but to carry on wearing my lid as I went to work. I did the twiddly bits and then turned left down the lane - Although, that makes it sound easier than it actually was, the road dropped away to the left and it was a fairly tight bend, especially if you're going slightly faster than is recommended for the prevailing road conditions. So, I suddenly found myself on two wheels, unfortunately, one of them was the front one.

I sped down the road, under minimal control if I'm being honest, until i clipped a car and took a small, unplanned excursion over the handlebars. I ended up in the front garden belonging to the guy whose car I'd hit, up against the wall, with my face on the ground and my legs in the air.

The guy came out and asked me if I was alright, and we made arrangements for me to sort out the damage to his car. Then I went to check the damage to the trike, it was about as beat up as you'd expect, but the oddest thing was the handlebars, it seems that I was so reluctant to let go, that I'd bent them virtually double as I'd gone over the top.

Seems I didn't know my own strength.

I remember once, being in a bar (The Silk Mill in Derby, for those who are/were local) when a good friend of mine, Paul came up and said,

'Can you do me a favour Dude?'

'Yeah, for you, anything mate, whaddya need?'

'There's this Chinese girl...'

'Right?'

'She won't leave me alone, I mean, she's nice, but... Well... She's not really my type, friend of a friend, too close, pooping on your own doorstep and soforth.'

'And what would you like me to do?'

'Well, can you scare her off?'

'And how would I do that?'

'Well, she likes the idea of the whole biker thing, and I'm currently vehicularly embarrassed.'

'OK...'

'So, could you take her on the back of the trike and hoon it about a bit? Put her off the whole idea?'

'Yeah, whatevs mate, just let me finish this (non-alcoholic *cough*) pint.'

So I finished my pint of weak lemon drink, walked over to the table and introduced myself.

'Alright Paul, not seen you for a while, you been OK? Who's this lovely lady?'

'Awight Dandy! Yeah, fine, this is Lin (I honestly can't remember what her name was, but this will do, as it's easy to type).'

'Pleased to meet you, what you up to?'

'Well funnily enough, we were just talking about you, how your bikes got three wheels and everything, Lin wondered if she could have a look?'

So we went outside, the Silk Mill was one of those places that everyone parked their bikes outside in a line, like you see in Hollywood films, the trike was at the end of the row. Lin looked at it and smiled (At this point I would normally type in a Wishy-Washy stylee Chinese pantomime accent, but that would be racist... And also I had a go and it was virtually unreadable, so you'll have to make it up yourself)

'It's very nice,' she said, 'It's got three seats?'

'Yeah, helps when you go shopping, or for carrying slabs of cans.'

'Are we going for a ride?'

I looked at Paul, 'If it's OK with you Mate?'

'Yeah, sure, knock yourself out!'

'You come too,' She said to Paul,

'Erm, no, I'm OK, I've been on it before,'

'No, you come, I'll put my arm around you and keep you safe.'

Now, I thought that this was embarrassing for him, but bloody funny, so I walked up and whispered, 'So, what do you want me to do?'

'OK, right, carry on with the plan...'

'If you're sure.'

I gave my lid to Lin, put on my shades (even though it was dark), threw my leg over the saddle and thumbed the starter. Paul and Lin got on the bench seat at the back, got comfortable and He slapped me on the back. The trike took off like a scalded cat, Lin hadn't got her feet on the pegs properly and kicked me in the armpit, which sent us swerving briefly onto the other side of the road, even over the engine I could hear Lin squealing. We got to an island near the busy marketplace and did a couple of circuits, the right hand wheel coming off the ground a couple of times, before heading into town, past rows of kebab shops and drunken townies.

I was doing precisely the legal limit (officer) when one particularly booze addled reveller in a Fred Perry shirt, Farrah trousers and loafers stepped out into the road and put his hand out, pretending to be directing traffic. I grabbed a great, steaming handful of front brake, which as you can imagine did not a sausage, and we slid towards him, I didn't want to jam the rear brakes on, as the first thing that would have happened was that we'd have locked up and my passengers would have gone shooting off the front.

Now, you can't lay a trike down and swerve around things like you can on a bike, believe me, I've tried, but if it's got wide bars, you can sometimes get enough leverage to get the back end to break traction if you jam the throttle open, sometimes you can even do this when you mean to. I just missed the guy... Just got around him... and spent the next, hectic few seconds fighting the mother of all tankslappers.

We passed the Island Rock Club (once featured in AWOL, but now a multi-storey car-park), Lin was still screaming and we got a couple of cheers and waves from the guys outside sat on their bikes drinking 20/20. As my anal sphychter was still twitching uncontrollably, I decided that I'd had quite enough excitement for one evening, slowly pottered around the island and headed back to the pub.

I pulled up at the end of the row of bikes, paddled the trike back into her space, cut the engine and got off.

'So, how was that?' I said as I turned around,
'That was great!' replied Lin as she jumped of the seat, bouncing up and down, full of adrenaline, 'That bit where you nearly hit that guy, and when we nearly tipped over, let's go again! Paul, can we go again? Paul?... Paul!'

I looked at Paul, now I'd never seen a dead body at the time, but I remember thinking that that's what one must look like... He was grey, his mouth was open, his eyes were staring straight ahead and his right hand was glued to the mudguard bracket.

'Want a glass of water mate?' I asked
'....'
'Or a brandy? I could run to a brandy maybe... I'll get you a brandy, Lin, here's a quid, get him a brandy will you?'

She wandered into the pub and seconds later came out clutching a tumbler of brandy.

'Here, drink this, you'll feel better.'

As he sipped, the colour started to return to his cheeks, his claw-like grip relaxed, and his jaw started to work.

'Kill.' He whispered
'Sorry Mate, what?' I leaned in closer

'Kill you.'

'What? sorry, still not getting you..'

'I'll F*cking KILL YOU!' He yelled as he launched himself out of the seat, towards my face.

The chase didn't last long, across the road, down the river, into Town, around the marketplace, took him a few minutes to calm down when we both ran out of breath, He eventually saw the funny side... I think it was a couple of years later if I remember correctly; he ended up being the best man at my wedding.

-oOo-

I was in the Vic, the brilliant live music venue opposite Derby Rail Station one night, at closing time, talking to the landlady (oddly called Lin too), when her daughter wandered into the bar.

'I'm off home Mum, I might just get the last bus.'

'Ok, see you tomorrow.'

As she opened the door, we all heard the sound of the last bus driving past. I made the 'Wah-wah-waaaaaahh!' trombone noise and necked the last of my bottle of Newkie Brown.

'You'll give her a lift home won't you Dandy?'

'Ermm... If you like,' I turned and asked, 'Where do you live?'

She told me and it turned out that it was sort of on my way home, but she was blonde, and cute and nineteenish, and her Mum ran a pub, so it could just as well have been in Yugoslavia and I would still have said yes.

'Haven't got a lid though, it might mess your hair up.'

We all trouped outside, and everyone who was still there watched her clamber onto the back of the trike, there was a massive cheer as she wrapped her arms around me, slightly tighter than was absolutely necessary but I can't remember complaining.

We slowly pulled away and drove, very sedately down the street and stopped at the traffic lights. She released her grip slightly just as we pulled away and ended up grabbing on to the waist adjusters of my leather as she shot backwards before managing to claw her way closer until she was pressed into my back and her arms were crossed in front of me (Did I mention I used to be a bit skinnier than I am now?)

It only took about fifteen minutes to get her home, I pulled up by the side of the road and looked at her.

'You OK?'

She nodded,

'Only, I can see all of your teeth.'

'Lips.. Dry...'

'What?'

'Lips... are... Dry...'

Turns out that she'd been grinning so broadly for the entire trip that her lips had stuck to her gums and she couldn't move them.

Now I'm somewhat more worldly, and if I wasn't happily married of course, If a young, pretty, blonde, air hostess (Did I mention she was an air hostess? Or she was training to be an Air Hostess at least, or something) sits on the back of my trike and complains that her lips are dry, there are certain ways that I could remedy the situation, but at the time, I helped her off the back, watched her get her key in the door then went home.

After all, I had work in the morning...

-oOo-

I decided, whilst my current trike was being built, that what I wanted most in the world was a set of stainless steel, straight-thru, unbaffled, drag pipes.

Because I'm a badass, honest.

OK, for the non-exhaustophiles, those things that I describe up there are just really drainpipes that take the noise and noxious fumes away from the engine and deposit them into the radiator grille of the car behind me, or in the lungs of small children minding their own business by the side of the road. There's no boxes like you'd have on a car that take the really poisonous stuff out or baffle the noise.

But, as generations of Badass motorcyclists have always said 'Loud Pipes Save Lives' - And there are many badges and stickers that you can actually buy in real shops that say this, so it must be true.

Anywho, I went to this custom exhaust fabricator guy, who, if I remember correctly, looked a bit like a skinny Thor. He said that it was no problem, seemed simple enough and would probably only take him about week or two. So I went home, enlisted the help of a mate who had a car with a towbar and a dolly (A contraption that allows you to tow something by lifting its front wheel off the ground - Not one of those inflatable things with three holes or the deluxe model with the real hair) and we trundled off down the road, the trike bobbing along behind us like an excited labrador puppy.

Before the next bit, I'd just like to point out that the rear tyres on the trike are 275/75-R15's so they're about 32" (81cm for the Frenchies etc.) in diameter and weigh the same as a medium sized child, or a couple of morbidly obese emperor penguins, or about a fifth of a juvenile Yak.

So, we were going down this hill, towards a mini-roundabout, my mate started to brake and there was a bit of a 'judder' - We both looked at the trike and it seemed fine, so he continued to brake, and as we came to a stop there was this crunch. We turned to look behind us again. The trike was listing at about 30 degrees, so we assumed that one of the wheels had come off... I say assumed... Actually we knew that the wheel had come off because it had just bounced past the driver's side window and made its way down the road, bouncing higher and higher all the time.

By the time it made its way onto the island itself, It was bouncing higher than the cars - There was a lot of beeping of horns, I could sympathise I guess. I'd beep my horn if something like a tractor tyre was flying at my face at 30mph. It made it across the island and swerved into the oncoming traffic. There were many twitching sphyncters on the A514 that afternoon I can tell you. Then it encountered the bus and everything went a bit 'Slo-Mo'. It bounced into the path of said bus, just as it was pulling up at the stop, so the driver slammed his anchors on and all the old ladies that had been waiting to get off were suddenly catapulted forwards and were flattened against the inside of the windscreen. The tyre clipped the front 'wing' of the bus (If buses actually have wings that is) and slammed into the bus-stop. Totally crushing the seating and cracking the glass in the windows.

We both made our way over, saying things like 'Blimey, I wonder who this belongs to?' and 'Well I never, tell you what, why don't I just get this huge wheel out of the way of you lovely people trying to get off this bus?' and 'Goodness Mrs, your nose isn't half flat., want to borrow a tissue?' Grabbed the wheel and had it away on our toes as fast as we could.

There's a nice new bus-stop there now, so I think what I did was actually a good thing for the community, in a way - Don't you?

29 - BOOBS, MELONS AND JUMPER-LUMPS.

This chapter is probably the one that brings most accidental visitors to the blog. The title is intentionally a little bit misleading and though you might think that it's all about the objectification of ladies, it's actually about my love of the popular shop ASDA/Walmart.

Well, I suppose it objectifies women, towards the end.

Just a little bit.

-oOo-

I'm a confirmed ASDA (Walmart) shopper - They're cheap, you often don't get food poisoning from their own-brand range and the opportunity for shenanigans is quite high. I mean, you try the sort of crap that you'd quite happily get away with in ASDA in Sainsbury's and you're looking at being escorted from the premises quick-smart by a security guard with the peak of his hat so close to his face that he looks like a slightly more jobsworth Judge Dredd.

I quite enjoy just wandering around the place and looking at the people - I mean, don't get me wrong, it's no People of Walmart - But it gets pretty close on occasions, you get a few people in their pyjamas and crocs, who I just assume to be escaped mental patients, but most of the time things are pretty sensible.

That is, of course, until LARP season starts...

For those of you who have managed to live your lives without encountering LARP, it stands for Live Action Role Playing - Dungeons and Dragons but with a far higher incidence of personal injury - Rubber swords, people dressed as elves, the whole nine yards. Hundreds (literally) of people congregate in the grounds of the old Leper Hospital up the road and bash seven different kinds of poop out of each other with maces and swords and hammers made of sponge-foam and Duct-tape. It would be all too easy to dismiss these people as boobs, really, it would, but when you see the obvious time and work they put into their costumes and how seriously they take it, they demand a certain respect. Add a bit of cleavage, and a fair smattering of acne cream and shampoo and some of those guys could be classed as cosplayers. (I'm not going to explain that one too - You can't be on the Internet and not know what a Cosplayer is - look it up, it'll be educational) That is, right up until you see them in the cream cake aisle at lunchtime, with a basket full of sausage rolls, scotch eggs and chocolate flavour milk - The studded leather jerkins, ring-mail vest, thigh boots and studded flails lose a bit of their mystique under those circumstances.

But you didn't come here to listen to me opine about people who choose a different entertainment lifestyle, you came to hear about things that caused my physical pain and/or embarrassment.

I show off... A lot... I mean, give me an audience and I behave like a five year old. It's the main reason for this Blog. I'm constantly being told to grow up by my children and I often turn around after shower-juggling a couple of (full) wine bottles in any shop I've not previously been banned from, to be confronted with the rapidly retreating rear-ends of my family as they melt into the crowd slowly repeating their manta - 'He's Not With Us... He's Not With Us...'

One time, I performed a trick that I'd seen in a Calvin & Hobbes cartoon, where you run down a supermarket aisle throwing a watermelon to yourself. You know, that's when I found out that real-life physics and cartoon physics work slightly differently. I don't mean you can't do it, you can, the first three or four throws work perfectly, but as you gain speed, you have to throw the watermelon further and further ahead of yourself...

You've worked out what happens next already, right? I knew I could count on you.

Watermelons make an absolutely brilliant noise when they hit the floor from about 10' up, and the pieces go for miles - I think that I might have actually spread my arms wide, slowly spun around in a circle to the assembled audience and cried 'Tah-dahhhh!'. The look of horror on my wife and daughter's face was worth the price of entry alone. I'd never heard my wife growl before, and it's not a noise I care to get her to repeat.

'Pick... It... Up...' She growled,
'What?' I replied, as innocently as my ear to ear smirk would allow,
'The melon, Pick... It... Up... Now..."
'Yes Dear.'

Did you know: It's possible to fit an entire watermelon in one of those small plastic bags that come on a roll in the fruit and vegetable aisle?

Providing you make the pieces small enough that is. The cashier, when we went to pay, was pretty confused too. She tried to put it through as melon slices rather than a whole watermelon.

My wife made me explain what had happened.

Then she made me apologise.

I felt very sorry for myself.

I have not been allowed to forget this momentary lapse of judgement since, as every time my wife meets someone new she introduces me thusly,

'This is my Husband; he likes to throw fruit at himself in ASDA.'

I think it makes me sound mysterious and interesting.

Another ASDA moment that has entered the annals of Dandy history started with an innocent trip to the shops to get the ingredients for a summer picnic. It was the middle of the kids summer holidays and the store was pretty busy. The weather was hot (well hot for the UK - Maybe 25 degrees Celsius) and most of the clothing worn by the customers was of the shorts and t-shirt variety. In fact, some of the female customers were wearing less, with vests and the occasional bikini top on display.

Mrs Dandy had chosen to wear a somewhat structural top with what are called, I believe, spaghetti straps, which served to accentuate her more than ample feminine charms. I use the phrase 'served to accentuate' here as a synonym for the more vulgar 'struggled to contain', and obviously it was only so long before I resorted to childishness.

I waited until we were surrounded (mostly) by adults, turned to Mrs Dandy and... well... made the action with both of my hands that indicated that I thought my wife's... erm... jumper-lumps were some kind of squeaky-toy.

What happened at this precise time helped convince me of my Super-Villain status.

The 'Honk-Honk' noise actually sounded, in perfect time with the squeezing of my hands. I looked down at my hands as if looking at them for the very first time. The surrounding shoppers looked at me, at the rapidly reddening Mrs Dandy, at my hands, at her upper ladies area - all with their mouths hanging open.

I burst into raucous laughter, which, luckily proved infectious and of course I tried to do it again - But this time I was thwarted, it seemed that this particular Super-Power was a one-time only deal.

It remains a mystery to this day, completely unexplained and unexplainable. We did see a guy dressed as a clown a little further around the store making balloon animals, and he did have one of those old-style car horns with the black rubber ball, but I don't think that had anything to do with it.

30 - SECOND CONTACT CLOSING FAST, BEARING 076!

Another story from one of my many professional roles – As a glorified delivery driver for a Builders' Merchant – Not the most edifying job in the world, but it kept me in chunky Kit-Kats.

And there was rain… So much rain…

-oOo-

In this chapter, I embark on the path to world domination. Testing the feasibility of starting my own land-based navy by turning a normal everyday people carrier and a laser printer into a submarine hunting death-dealer.

Some time ago, I worked for a certain West-Midlands based builders' merchant - who shall remain nameless, but according to their radio adverts, they're 'Where the Trade go'. My job with them, amongst other things, involved the upgrading of the IT at their stores around the UK.

The senior management, in their infinite wisdom had decided that the IT team didn't, at the time, require the use of a van and we were expected to use our own vehicles to transport the equipment to site - The inventory for a single store usually comprised half a dozen tills, cash drawers etc, half a dozen PCs with all their associated doo-dads and gee-gaws - and a number of laser printers.

Now, at the time, I had a Ford Galaxy people carrier, which was nicknamed by all and sundry as 'The Van' - My boss would often say things like;

'Vet, grab a couple of printers, stick 'em in the van and toddle off to install them at <insert store name>.'

(The reason I got called Vet will be covered in a later instalment.)

So, I became the go-to guy for country-wide 'humping and dumping', which I didn't really mind as I got paid mileage, and it got me out of the office, often for days at a time. On this particular day, the first day of land trials for The Chimping Navy, I'd been tasked with delivering some kit to the Reading store, this was just a quick jaunt down the M40, a couple of hours there, a couple of hours eating a fry-up and fiddling about in the store and then a couple of hours back - Simples!

The only jam in the DVD player was that it was raining, not heavily, but wet enough for you to not want to stand out in it, well unless you were a particularly statuesque young lady in a thin, white top. Now, as many of you that have owned a Ford Galaxy will know, they have a couple of little design faults. Firstly, the 'Brain' that controls the central door locks sits in a little cutout, under the carpet, in the passenger-side footwell. Secondly, when it rains heavily, the passenger footwell floods. Either of these problems, on their own, aren't show-stoppers - But taken as a pair... Well, you can imagine the constant hilarity.

I set off down the M40 with a spring in my... erm... step and a song in my heart. Everything was right with the world and the rain was just heavy enough that constant wipe was too much, but intermittent wipe was not enough - I have since realised that the car had variable wash/wipe - But at the time I couldn't be bothered to read the manual. Around halfway down the motorway, I noticed that the footwell was filling with water - I made a mental note to drill some holes in the floor when I got home, I was getting pretty bored with the carpet smelling like a rancid Afghan (That's the breed of dog, not someone from Afghanistan - I have no idea what these wonderful and ancient people smell like when they go off).

Out of the corner of my eye, I noticed a flashing light on the dashboard. Looking over, it turned out to be the 'Your boot is open' warning light - It wasn't doing the whole 'You're running out of petrol' type flash that you get from your petrol gauge, it was more a sort of 'Now it's on, now it's off, no, on, I mean off,' jittery type of thing. I had just enough time to think,

'Hmmm... that's odd!'

When the boot flew open - and one of the Dell laser printers I was carrying, transformed, Bumblebee-like, into a depth charge. Now, I don't know how many of you have ever thrown electrical equipment out of the back of a moving vehicle at 70Mph, but it makes a bloody great noise.

As the scene unfolded in slow motion in the rear view mirror, I saw the printer hit the tarmac and bounce, it then started to spin, and hit again. This time it disintegrated, seriously, there wasn't a piece bigger than my thumb left at the end. The look on the face of the lorry-driver behind me was a picture - He did his best to avoid the wreckage, but he still managed to run over the toner cartridge - Hooo boy, that made a mess. But I had other things to worry about, I was hemorrhaging paperwork all over the rainy motorway, and my boot was still open. I pulled onto the hard shoulder, got out, and slammed the boot shut. I almost missed the feint *click* of the central-locking, but my worst fears were confirmed when I tried to open the door... Locked. With the keys AND my phone inside.

I cursed my choice of wearing a thin, white shirt to work that day and started to walk the half-mile back to the emergency road-side telephone in the suddenly heavier rain. I explained to the nice lady on the phone that 'there was some debris' on the road and that I needed a locksmith, she told me that she'd dispatch someone to take care of the mess, but I was on my own as far as being stranded was concerned.

It took them a good half an hour to arrive, by which time I was wetter than a geriatric dolphin's nappy. They gave me a bit of a talking to about messing up their motorway, and how my employer would get a bill, but they thought that I, personally, had suffered enough and they'd see if there was anything they could do to get me back in my car.

The big chap in the waterproof Hi-Vis walked over to my car, pulled the doorhandle, and the door opened.

'Seems OK to me.' He said, with not a hint of a laugh in his voice at all. 'Want me to close it and try again?'

'NO!' I shouted, possible slightly louder than was strictly necessary.

I thanked him, and wondered how long I'd stood in the rain not trying to get into a car that wasn't actually locked anymore.

Luckily, my face was so wet that they couldn't see my tears as I drove off.

31 - THERMODYNAMICS, IT'S THE LAW!

What you are about to read was the first ever 'Super-post' that I wrote. It rocketed up the charts of my most popular posts and had been viewed nearly one hundred times in the first hour or so after it went live.

I have been asked, by both fetish models and normal human beings whether it is actually true… All I can say is that to the best of my knowledge, every single syllable is amoeba churningly correct. Apart from the last two lines, they might just be folklore – I can't be sure though.

-oOo-

Today's story isn't about me... It's about my dear old Dad - If anything, I like to think it goes to prove that whatever I have wrong with me, I probably got from him.

He's a young 84 year old - He's done a huge number of jobs in his long and happy life, from being in the RAF to working as an electrician on the railways and is blessed with a permanently sunny disposition (apart from the times when he's opinionated, rude and cranky)

This particular tale takes place in the (I think) 1960's and shows the healthy disregard for Health and Safety that made this country great.

It was summer, and hot. Hot enough that you could forget the whole frying eggs on the pavement scenario, and jump straight to the 'nylon trousers melting to your body and your conkers exploding' kind of deal.

At the time, my dear old Dad worked for British Oxygen (BOC), a company that makes and bottles all sorts of interesting gasses for industrial and medical uses. As the company name suggests, one of their biggest sellers was oxygen, liquid oxygen. This was stored in large, white tanks, you might have seen one - They're characterised by the fact that the pipes around their base tend to have a thick layer of frost on them.

On one particular lunchtime, he and his cronies decided to go out into the yard to eat their 'snap' as was the colloquial word for a packed lunch at the time. Finding the sun to be a little warm and direct for their tender, British hides, they found respite in the shade of the big liquid oxygen tank. Halfway through their lunch, one of his friends spotted a pigeon, who had obviously landed on one of the pipes and had frozen, quite solid.

My father, who still has a love of physical humour, went and found some welding gloves and broke the bird free (unfortunately leaving its feet behind) and proceeded to marvel at this wonder of accidental science, it's perfect preservation, how peaceful it looked etc. One of his gang thought that a game of football would be the order of the day until it was pointed out that this might be, in some way, disrespectful.

At that very moment, a young and pretty secretary came around the corner and started to walk across the yard. Thinking on his feet, he grabbed the bird from the aspiring Bobby Moore and cradled it in his hands.

'Awww,' He said, 'Did the little birdie fly into the big nasty tank?'

As he said this, three things happened; He stroked the bird gently, as if it were the most precious thing in the world, his friends looked at him as if he had just had a debilitating brain aneurysm, and the secretary's interest was piqued. She started to walk over, all high heels, miniskirt and bouffanted hair and said,

'What's that?'

'It's a pigeon, we think he flew into the tank and knocked himself out... Didn't you little man?'

'Awwww.' Said the girl, leaning closer.

'In fact, we've been looking after him for a while; he's about ready to be released.'

'Really? can I watch?'

'Of course, Off you go little chap, be safe!'

With that, my Dad pitched the frozen pigeon up into the air, whereupon it arced about fifteen feet then crashed down onto the concrete yard and shattered into a million shards.

It's said, that on warm nights, if you're walking past the old BOC works in Derby... You can still hear her screaming.

32 - AN EYE FOR AN EYE.

So you've had the premiere story of my Father, now I think it's time to tell another story about my Mother, and unlike the first one that you read up there somewhere, She was alive when this one took place.

Very, very alive indeed.

The contents have been described by some as horrific, and we would all probably be arrested for child cruelty if this were to happen nowadays.

-oOo-

Yesterday, I spoke of the awesome bird mutilation skills of my Father. It seems only fair that I now tell you tales of the ocular disassociational episodes that my Mother peppered my younger days with.

If you're a regular reader, you'll be au-fait with my Mother's sense of humour - She definitely mellowed after she died, but whilst she was still alive - Seriously, she'd do stuff even that I'd think twice about - And I can throw fruit at myself.

In the mid 70's, she lost her right eye - I mean, she didn't come home from the shops one afternoon and say 'Oh Bugger! - I must have left it on the bus', there was some serious medical reason for it. I have vague memories of visiting her in hospital and stuff - In fact, one story that she used to tell (she really spun this one out, it could take her hours to tell if someone else was providing tea and/or biscuits) - But it boils down to my Dad redecorating the kitchen, then accidentally setting fire to it, and me running down the ward screeching 'Dad's set the kitchen on fire! Dad's set the kitchen on fire!'

Anywho, after a time of walking around with an eye-patch on, she was fitted with a 'Glass Eye'. For those of you whose total experience of false eyes is Mr Ragetti from Pirates of the Caribbean - I'll let you in on a secret, They're not spherical, they're kind of, well... scutiform (If nothing else happens today, you've learned a new word, it means 'Shield-shaped').

If I go into too much medical detail in the next paragraph, please feel free to skip It - But I feel that it gives some important background info.

For the first few months after the patch came off, she was fitted with a 'training' eye - Much like the oversized bar that they put in when you first have your tongue pierced, only the other way around, in that it's smaller than standard, to make up for the swelling etc. It seems that the way you can tell when you're ready for your 'real' false eye is when your training eye starts to fall out. I poop you not, (Remember this was the '70's, there are probably all kinds of clever scientific ways that they do it now - Anyone with impending eye surgery probably shouldn't worry... Well, not about this... I mean, you should probably still worry, it's your eye, and they'll be poking at it with sharp things... Like, totally, Ewww!)

The first time this happened, I think it was February / March - It was definitely Shrove Tuesday, because we were all sat around eating pancakes. All I heard was a quiet *Tink* noise and my Mother said,

'Oh!'

There, resting on her plate, was her eye... Staring back up at her. The rest of us sat there in stunned silence as she calmly picked it up, brushed the sugar off, and put it back in.

Young Dandy Trauma Level: 2.3

The second time I remember was when she called me into the kitchen and asked her to take stuff out of the washing bowl and pass it to her to dry - You know where this is going, right? I think that I'd given her a few cups, the odd plate and a knife, when I felt something at the bottom of the bowl. I thought it was a piece of broken mug or something as my Mum was famous for washing the crockery overarm - We got through a tea service at least every few weeks - But it wasn't, imagine being a five year old boy holding, what for all intents and purposed was a real, human eye. I just stood there going 'Eye... Eye... Eye... Eye...' Whilst she wept uncontrollable tears of mirth (out of the one eye, obviously)

Young Dandy Trauma Level: 5.1

The third and final time, apart from when it came out into an open package of butter as she was getting out of the 'fridge, was when she dropped it into our old upright washing machine and we had to go through all the pockets of the clothes that were being washed before we found it.

That's an experience that brings a family together, I can tell you.

After she had been fitted for her new eye, you'd have thought that she'd have grown up a bit, but no... They let her keep her old eye (old false one that is, not old real one) which meant she had a spare. Over the next couple of years, I cannot count how many times this 'spare' ended up in my school lunchbox, on friends plates when they came over after school for tea and on the fireplace when she left the room - She would palm it and then pretend to take her eye out, close her eyelid and say something like,

'I'm watching you two,' As she left the room.

When I was maybe eight, I plucked up the courage to ask her what it actually looked like when she took it out... There was no 'Are you sure' or 'No, I don't think you'll like it', she just flipped it out, I was transfixed... If she had held her false eye to her forehead, she would have been the living embodiment of Davros.

Young Dandy Trauma Level: 9.4

She had another couple made over the years, in fact, I seem to remember that her consultant, Mr Farquhar, even made her a 'bloodshot' one as a Christmas present. This just increased the level of tricks she could play on people. One of her favourties was secreting one in her mouth and then slowly opening her eyes and her mouth at the same time - It was like living on the set of The Re-animator at times - Although, in fairness, I did use them in the occasional modelling clay project for school.

I have one at home now, in a little box - I always toyed with the idea of having it made into a signet ring.

I think that would probably go with my Super-Villain persona pretty well.

33 - HAVE YOU TRIED TURNING IT OFF, THEN LEAVING IT?

Yet another set of stories from the early days of my working life. This one goes back to the early 1980's, when I was but a callow youth who didn't know one end of an IT user from the other.

I soon learned though.

I was going to bunch these all together, like the motorcycling stories, but I thought it was better to spread them out.

You'd be shaking your head in disbelief so much that there's a real chance that your head would unscrew.

-oOo-

OK, so you've all had time to formulate your own theories on whether deviant parenting made me the man I am today. I'd like to add more evidence, this time it's not my parents I blame, but my workmates and customers. I have more stories about these people than I have about anyone else.

Except, possibly, myself.

In the dim and distant past, when dinosaurs ruled the Earth and everything was in black and white, I used to work in IT Support - But you still work in IT Support I hear you remark; Ahah!, but no, a common misconception is that everyone who works in IT does what Roy and Moss do in Graham Linehan's excellent program 'The IT Crowd'.

Most of us don't (But it doesn't stop people asking you to give them Facebook hints or asking for your professional advice on what they should buy and then buying something else because it was shinier - You know who you are!) - But at the time, I did. *cough*. You all must have heard those 'Hilarious' stories about people thinking that their CD-ROM drives were cup-holders and wondering why their computers didn't work during a power cut and thought, 'People can't really be that stupid' - Well, let me tell you, a lot of them are...

One of my first jobs, nearly thirty years ago, was in a small computer shop, I was one of the people who they hid in the back room and wouldn't let talk to the customers, ever. Which made it an unusual day when the phone in my cage rang and the girl on the other end said,

'Dandy, it's the Po-leese! Da Five-Oh! They want to talk to you,' and then she put the phone down.

'H-Hello,' I said, 'Can I help?'

'Yes, this is Inspector Momanna Banana Peeyanah from The Derbyshire Constabulary, there seems to be a problem with the printer we brought from you last week.'

'Oh... I'm sorry to hear that, what model of printer is it?'

'How am I supposed to know? You're the computer person, is it not in your records?'

'Well Sir, if you look on the front of the printer, it will say something like - Epson FX something or other, the something or other will be the model number'

He put the phone down and, I assume, wandered over to the printer, read the label and gave me the model number. I had a look around and found we had one over the other side of the workshop. It was just too far away for me to look at it whilst I was on the phone, bearing in mind that telephones had wires in those days and if you had suggested mobile or even cordless phones, you would have been burned as a witch.

'What is the printer doing?'

'Nothing, it's broken'

'Ah, no, I mean are there any flashing lights, or is it beeping?'

'Yes.'

'Which?'

'Both.'

'Fine, which lights are flashing?'

He put the phone down again, walked over to the printer, checked the lights and came back.

'Paper,' He said, as cool as a cucumber. I took this opportunity to repeatedly bang the phone handset off the desk.

'Oh, Sorry, I dropped the phone. Does the printer have any paper in it?'

'Paper?'

'Yes, paper, there should be a box of paper under the printer.'

'There's an empty box that says 2-part, fan-fold, music ruled on it.'

I put him on speakerphone, gestured wildly to my friend Paul, who was busy soldering something and said, loudly,

'Can I confirm that the problem you seem to be having is that your printer has stopped working, it is now making a beeping noise, a light marked 'paper' is flashing and there is an empty box marked 2-part, fan-fold, music ruled underneath it?'

'Yes, that's correct, do you have any idea what it might be?'

'Erm... Yes, I - I do have an idea,' I had to mute the phone at this point, as I was finding it difficult not to laugh, 'I think you might have run out of paper... But that's only a guess - Would you like us to send an engineer out?'

'Yes, that would be great, thank you.'

We did send an engineer, with a couple of boxes of paper, which seemed to cure the problem... For a while at least.

Another time, we had a similar call, but this time it wasn't from Da Five-Oh, it was from a small pharmaceutical company that you probably wouldn't have heard of. We had a deal with the chap who was the IT Buyer whereby he would come to us for everything as long as we occasionally slipped him a free PC game. His latest acquisition was Microsoft Flight Sim V1.0, which at the time, came on and ran from a 5 1/4" floppy disc (which was actually floppy) and was in black & white (Well, black & green). We used to put new labels on the discs for him and everything, so no-one would know. The call went something like this:

'Hi this is Steve from Fisons!'

'OK, how can I help you Steve?'

'Ah.. Erm.. Remember how you guys sent me a copy of the Flight Simulator?'

'Yeah, is everything OK?'

'Not really, no - It's stopped working - I think I might have spilled something on it.'

'Right, not a problem - You know how we suggest you take backup copies of the discs when you get them, and put them somewhere safe?'

'Yes?'

'Did you do that for this disc?'

'Yes, I did, it's in my safe'

'Brilliant, just use that, it should work exactly the same, but I suggest you make a backup copy of your backup and keep that safe just in case.'

'How would I use the copies?'

'Well, you'd just put it in the drive as you would with the originals, just treat it the same as the one we originally sent you.'

'So, should I cut it or fold it up?'

'No... You shouldn't need to do either of those things. Just put it in. close the door and start the software as you normally would.'

'Ah.. No, I don't think that'll work, the copy is bigger.'

'Bigger?'

'Yes, it's A4.'

'A... 4... ?'

'Yes, I photocopied it, just like you guys suggested.'

I slowly put down the phone, went over to the emergency toolkit, took out the revolver and shot myself six times, in the face.

34 - BUT WILL IT FLY SMICK?

You remember my friend Scots Mick? The one with the chilli recipies and the trike stories? Well we had a few summers in the early nineties when we formed a bit of a dynamic duo, touring our local hostelries and getting up to no-good in an Enid Blyton, jumpers for goalposts kind of way.

Here's one about us getting needlessly mechanical for financial gain.

And then it all just went a bit wrong, and there were some quite serious injuries, which oddly, we found funny at the time.

-oOo-

We've all heard stories about people who've found wonderful things in the most unlikely of places. Antiques Roadshow is full of people who have found original Picasso sketches in their Aunt Mabel's loft or there are those despicable people who find an original, fully working, 1920's Brough Superior in a neighbour's garage which they buy for a fiver as 'It was our Derek's and he never used it, even when he was still alive'.

So, imagine my excitement, when everyone's favourite Chilli cook and professional Scotsman, my good friend SMick, arrived at my front door with news of a 'vehicle' that he'd found out about, just lying in the mud in a farmer's field just around the corner. It was, quite literally, just around the corner, as in those days you could spit the distance from my house to the wonderful British countryside - You had to check no-one was in the way of course, things like that didn't go down well with the residents' association, but a well-hawked loogey would land on grass, or in a tree, or on a sheep.

So, dutifully, I clamboured into his Peugeot and drove the 100 yards to the farm. I walked around to the outbuildings, through knee deep mud, in my white Status Quo style white hi-tops (It was around this time that I changed my footwear of choice to second-hand army boots) and said to SMick.

'OK, where is it?'

'There,' pointed SMick, proudly

'Where, is it behind that scabby P.O.S. Mk1 Ford Transit Luton?'

The slow grin that swept across SMick's face told me all I really needed to know.

'You've got to be... erm... flipping joking, I'll be in the car...' I said, and started to squelch away as fast as I could.

He convinced me that it would be a good idea, a nice little project, something to do during the day when the pubs were shut. And if we couldn't get it going, then the box on the back was aluminium (Not Al-OO-min-um) and we could weigh it in and get some money out of it.

I honestly cannot remember how we got it out of the field; I think I blocked it from my memory the same way that victims of alien abduction do, I'm fairly sure it involved lots of sheets of wood, many, many bottles of Newcastle Brown Ale and an almost Olympic quantity of swearing.

Eventually, it found itself on my drive. It didn't actually look all that bad with a large proportion of the mud washed off. It also turned out to have a V6 engine which was a bonus, which on its own started a selection of trike/go-kart fantasies. After the battery was left on charge for about six weeks, the engine would successfully turn over but not 'catch', dutifully we did what any men confronted with a failing engine would do, we stood staring at the engine and scratched our heads.

'I think the carb needs priming,' SMick suggested, sagely.

'Right you are, how do we do that?' I replied - I wasn't then the mechanical whiz that I'm still not now.

'Well, we just take the air filter off, put something flammable down the carbs and see if it will start then.'

'Flammable?' I asked, nervously, not quite liking where this was going, 'Like what?'

'Like... petrol!'

'Like petrol, or actually petrol?'

'Actually petrol, we've got petrol, and it's what you'd expect to find in the carb anyway, should be fine.'

I bowed to his greater knowledge and we poured, what turned out to be significantly too much, petrol into the top of the carburettor and turned the engine over.

Now, I've never seen a real giant lightsaber, but I can imagine it looking something like what came out of the top of the carb - a nine foot high column of flame and noise which existed just long enough to drive my eardrums into my rectum and blow my eyebrows over to the other side of the road - It's a good job, in hindsight that we'd taken the bonnet off else it would have bounced off it and cut a neat porthole in the garage door.

'I think we might scrap it,' Said SMick, batting at his still smouldering sweatshirt.

'What?' I shouted as I was still mostly deaf and over the other side of the road looking for my left eyebrow.

Over the next few weeks we set about stripping down the van to its component parts. Many interesting and fun times were had during the project.

Do you remember when I talked about our friend 'Gullible' Steve? The gentleman who ate of the baby-carrot and Rottweiler chilli? Well, a couple of incidents involved him:

He was stumbling about in the back of the van, seeing if there was anything of any worth amongst the rotting hay and mud. When there was a cry, a protracted coughing fit, a torrent of expletives directed at myself, SMick, life in general and birds in particular. I turned to SMick, who was sat next to me in a deck-chair and said,

'Didn't think to tell him about the nest full of rotten blackbird eggs we found yesterday then?'

'Nope,' replied SMick, taking another gulp of his beer. 'But I did put it right near the side door so we wouldnea forget to throw it in the bin.'

The roof of the Luton box was made of fibreglass, which is not as weigh-innable as aluminium sheet, so we asked Steve to have a go at taking it off. We assumed (Which taught me that you should never assume) that he would get a ladder, and maybe a saw and cut the roof off. But no, he clamboured up onto the roof with an axe and a hammer.

'Is that a good idea?' I asked SMick, knowing full well that it wasn't

'Idea? No... Opportunity to laugh? Yes.' He replied, reaching down into the crate for another beer.

It took him a good fifteen minutes to fall the eight feet or so into the back of the van as he smashed the roof out from under himself. Thinking about it now, we really should have thrown that blackbird nest in the bin.

I didn't remain completely unscathed through the project, I had countless fibreglass splinters pulled out of my arms with pliers, cuts, bruises and boo-boos of various kinds.

And I understand that SMick still bears the scar of his particular mishap. We had got to the stage of trying to flatten the aluminum enough to get it in the back of the car and take it to the scrapyard and SMick was belting away with a lump hammer at a piece of metal that he was stood on.

Well, he missed... And hit his shin... He went completely silent, looked at the group of grubby schoolchildren that were hanging around watching us, looked at me, said, very quietly,

'Excuse me.'

And then threw the hammer at my face and went inside the house.

The flow of profanity lasted a good half an hour and featured words that I didn't think could be used in that particular context. It left seven local dogs paralysed down one side and a further three pregnant. He'll show you the scar now if you ask him nicely, it's quite impressive.

I'll never forget that summer - And neither will the person whose drive we dumped the still-burning remains of the van on.

35 - AND THEN, I SHOT MYSELF.

Here we go… Firstly yes, you read that right. I did, indeed, once shoot myself.

Yes, it hurt a lot, no I won't be doing it again in a hurry, yes I learned a valuable lesson.

And hopefully you will too kids – If you ever get given the choice, say 'No thank you' when anyone asks you if you'd like to shoot yourself.

For although it makes for a good story, I can sometimes go a bit wrong and you'll end up a bit dead.

-oOo-

I have yet again had the subject of this chapter chosen for me. This time by my dear daughter, who told everyone on her Blog that I had once shot myself - And said that I would probably tell you all about it, as you seem to enjoy stories of my misfortunes.

Firstly, I'd like to take a few moments to look at the whole 'accidentally shooting yourself' issue.

Weaponry is a lot more widespread and more easily available over the pond, and as a large proportion (over 25%) of the visitors to this site hail from the Grande Olde US of A, I am expecting all kinds of safety advice is going through their heads right about now, and they're just itching to post it. I'll save some of them the trouble:

- Never play with a loaded weapon.
- Always make sure the weapon is unable to fire if you're cleaning it.
- Never point a weapon at yourself, loaded or not.
- Never point a weapon at anything that you don't want to make go away. (And by 'Go Away' I mean, to shuffle off this mortal coil and join the choir invisibule)

People shoot themselves a lot more than you think, there's no end of stories of people shooting themselves in the foot, and losing fingers or being hit in the ass by a ricochet *cough* Mrs Dandy *cough* but you don't get many stories that pan out the way that mine did.

I'm hoping that this particular story will act as a cautionary tale, but I'm also pretty sure it will make you laugh - I mean, who doesn't like to see over-confident idiots getting it really, really wrong and hurting themselves quite badly?

I know I do.

So, just sit back, relax, turn your schadenfreude dial up to eleven, and listen to the tale of:

The Day The Chimping Dandy shot himself.

It was only a few weeks after the events of the last chapter, still summer, still hot, still lazing around the house drinking beer and being irresponsible. These were the times that I refer to, in conversation, as 'The Good Old Days'. SMick and I were sat, as was our custom at the time, in the front garden of my house enjoying the sunshine. We were drinking beer and thinking of things to do that were a) possible and b) within our somewhat limited budget. The list wasn't particularly extensive if I'm honest and it often contained the words beer, sun, nothing and more beer. And we were in grave danger of spiralling into another day, which whilst not exactly wasted, certainly wasn't turning out to be particularly productive.

Suddenly, the day took a turn for the... ah... well, not exactly better... More sort of... erm... odder, as Gullible Steve pulled up, got out of his car and asked us what we were up to. Steve's presence seemed to act as a catalyst and I decided that rather than just lying in the sun all day, I'd do a bit of target practice.

Now, I wasn't drunk, as such... I mean I'd never, well not very often at least, I'd say it would be quite unlikely that I'd choose to handle a weapon of any kind whilst drunk - I'd at least think about it for a second or two before doing it anyway... Probably.

So, I suddenly found myself lying in front of my open garage door, on the bonnet of (somebody's) car, with my head on the windscreen, taking aim at the door into the house from the garage (which was a firedoor - I'd assumed that it was in some way 'toughened'). The first shot flew between my outstretched feet and took a decent sized chunk out of the back of the door - The noise was considerably louder than I thought it would be, the garage walls acting as an amplifier, to the point where I thought it might attract the attention of the neighbours. I decided that I'd take one more shot and then call it a day, before the Five-oh turned up.

I looked down the sight, lined up the centre of the door and sent the signal to my fingers to fire. Now, a number of things happened at the same time…

SMick shouted 'Steve!'

Steve, who had wandered into the garage to look at the damage I'd done to the door, moved into my field of view and started to bend down and pick up the chunk of wood that had detached itself.

I pulled my arm up and to the right to try and not shoot Steve in the head.

I fired.

Luckily, the shot went wide, but I still only missed Steve's head by about three inches. It took a fair chunk out of the brickwork around the doorframe and came straight back at me.

It hit me in the left forearm, and it bloody hurt - I've still got the scar, it's about three inches long and pretty feint, you have to bear in mind this was twenty-five years ago. Another thing to bear in mind was that my left arm was tight up against my chest, due to me lying on the bonnet of the car, so if I'd got hit four inches to the right, you wouldn't be reading this...

And then there's the other thing... Most of you reading this will have assumed that I was firing some sort of gun, possibly the .50AE in my timeline picture - This is not, however the case. I was using a 5' Flatbow and I had three feet of wood sticking out of my arm, Oh, yes, and I was holding the bow with my feet.

The arrow was removed in the traditional style, i.e. with uproarious laughter from everyone but Steve. And bandages were amateurishly applied.

Steve stayed frozen to the spot, bent almost double, for a good few minutes, and the garage floor stood silent, wet, testament to the fact that he'd been really, really scared.

So, now you know, you have a new story to tell your friends in the pub - about a guy who shot himself - With a bow and arrow (That he'd been holding with his feet).

(Feel free to pass any of these stories on - If you think to credit me then that's be great, even if it's just 'There's this weird guy in this book called the Chunking Monkey or something and he did this really stupid thing')

36 - OPINIONATED ISN'T EVEN A WORD.

Working in IT, you'll often hear people say things like 'I only every buy Dell' or 'I only ever buy NVidia'. You'll sometimes hear people say 'I only ever buy Apple' but luckily those people are few and far between and we tend to ignore them as they usually have more money than sense.

But Brand Loyalty is a real thing – but so are blinkers and dice, doesn't mean that you should base important decisions on them though.

We've covered bigotry in most of its forms before, right at the front of this book in fact But there's one type that I left out. If I were trying to sound clever, I'd say 'I left it out on purpose so that I could cover it now, when I had a bigger fanbase,' but actually - I've only just thought about it.

It's not a recent invention; people have suffered this particular ailment for at least the past hundred years, if not more.

I'm talking about the bigotry that masquerades as 'Brand Loyalty', this is most prevalent in whatever the current emergent technology market is of course - In recent times for example hordes of fan-bois throw insults at each other about their choice of mobile phone operating system –

Android being for the Geeks,
IOS is for the hipsters,
BlackBerry is for the pay-as-you go Jeremy Kyle watchers,
Windows Mobile is for the hard of thinking.

I mean it can get pretty brutal at times, well, as brutal as people who fixate on electronics and their firmware can get, I mean - You might get a Chinese burn from one of them maybe, if they'd known you for a long time, and as long as your Dad wasn't bigger than their Dad. No-one's going to stab you for having an iPhone, well actually, there is a chance that you might get stabbed if you have an iPhone - But it won't be because of your choice of operating system, it's more likely that the stabbist will be chemically imbalanced and he'd like to sell your phone to his mate, Honest Brian (Unlock any phone for a fiver - No questions asked, Very clean Sister, you like her?), down the market, for £15.

Psychologists, or at least people who are currently doing the first year of their Sociology Degree will say that this is all to do with the Homo-Sapiens tribal urge, strength in numbers, social stratification etc. And will point you at the collected works of Max Horkheimer (Mainly to get rid of you for a while, as his stuff's a bit off the wall).

I say that it's a lot simpler than that, and that most first year Sociology students are only doing that subject because Media Studies or Sports Marketing was over-subscribed. I reckon it's because everyone thinks that their own, personal opinion is worth about a bajillion times more than anyone else's. I don't mean their professional opinion, I wouldn't take my car to the garage and ask the opinion of the oily chap who'd been fixing cars for the past twenty years, wait for him to look it over for an hour and when he says,

'Your head gasket's gone, it needs replacing,'

Reply, 'No, I think you'll find that the oil and water in the engine have had a bit of a chat and decided to co-exist in a shared living space, embracing their cultural differences and going halves on the shopping.'

I mean that'd be nuts, people are called professionals because they do something as a profession; they get paid for it - The clue's in the name.

But your Brand Loyalist only has a personal opinion, it's subjective and often completely wrong - But that doesn't mean that he (because it's invariably a man) won't defend this opinion up until the point where he foams at the mouth, jumps up and down, grabs hold of his feet and tears himself asunder, leaving only a smoking beaie-hat with a post-it note on it that says 'HTC's are the best phone to buy because I've got one.'

I'm exactly the same, not with phones as such, because I've got an ancient 'Candy-bar' phone that does me just fine when I remember to charge it. I have a work-provided BlackBerry that mostly gets used for playing Texas Hold'em during my 'alone time' at work and an iPad, also work-provided that I use to... erm... well, get my email when I'm not at work.

It's the iPad that causes me the problems, the only reason that every single person in the free world doesn't have one is because they're guinea pig meltingly expensive. Mine was free, and therefore has become (In My Humble Opinion) the single greatest piece of tech the world has ever seen

It has bad points, don't get me wrong, but I don't talk about them, so for all intents and purposes they don't exist. The interface is a bit clunky, even hit and miss sometimes, but that's because I've got old, fat fingers, not because it's a thrown together triumph of form over function. It's sleek, blank visage evokes mystery and familiarity at the same time, it's not just a magnified iPhone at all (You can tell by the way that the old iPhone charger fits into it, but it won't charge it very well - that's a feature to remind you how different it is, and how different YOU are for owning one).

The first thing I think when I see people with a tablet that isn't an iPad is:

'Oh, poor you, couldn't you afford a real one?'

Which is odd, because the first thing I think when I see someone with an iPhone is:

'Dude, you seriously have more money than sense, they're not even that good, functionality wise, compared to other Smart-Phones'

And I will react in exactly the same way, right up until I get my new iPhone when work replaces my BlackBerry.

(Since writing this chapter, I was given a shiny new iPhone 5 and my BlackBerry was consigned to the bin… iPhones are now, like, completely the Shizznit dudes)

37 - IT WAS LIKE THE SOMME!

I injure myself quite often, it's usually no-one's fault but my own, I'm monumentally clumsy. I trip over stuff, put hot things down on non-existent tables, trap my fingers in doorframes and generally spend a lot of my time saying 'ouch'

Even when I go for 'a walk in the park', something that's supposed to encompass everything that is easy, I manage to do myself a grave injury.

A long-time friend of mine once shared my Blog on Twitter/Facebook with the words...

'Do you ever feel like you're a massive walking disaster? Well spare a through for The Chimping Dandy, who really is.'

And in a way, he's right - I do have a fair collection of stories that involve gross physical harm taking place on or about my person. Many involve motorcycles, some, such as today's, involve a lack of care or attention, fewer still involve paint, but they're all true and up to a point, educational - I do idiotic stuff to myself so that you don't have to.

-oOo-

I'm a bit of a rambler, in most senses of the word, obviously, you all know that I could quite happily drive an echidna to suicide with my opinionated diatribe about the true meaning of Ridley Scott's Bladerunner, but in this case I'm talking about wandering about, in the Great British countryside, with a packed lunch and a flask of weak lemon drink. It doesn't take much to convince me that I need fresh air and I am more than happy to drag my progeny with me (Mrs. Dandy never requires much convincing, of anything really, she what we used to refer to, in the Olden Days as 'a game old bird').

This particular day we had decided that it would be a great idea to walk the three or so miles to a nice country pub, have a spot of lunch, maybe sample the steeped fruit of the hop and get the charabanc home. So far, so; start of the Enid Blyton book entitled 'Five get drunk and upset some cows'. As has been recounted previously, we used to live a lark's belch from the 'Cundry' so I loaded the Micro-Dandy into his papoose, hefted him onto my back, gathered the clan and we set off.

We'd just left civilisation and started trudging across farmland when the terrain got a bit lumpy, then it became bumpy, and after a while we had to invent a new word, so we chose 'Rabbity', as in –

'I say Muriel, look at all the bally holes in this meadow,'
'Yes Tarquin, it's distinctly Rabbity'

So, we wandered on, through hedges and ditches, honouring the country code at every turn, right up until the point where I put my foot down a rabbit hole. I started to fall backwards, but realised that I had a small person, effectively in my rucksack, so I turned right to try and land on my side. Well, I say I turned, most of me turned, about 97% I think.

My right foot took the unilateral decision to stay pointing in the same direction. It didn't 'really' hurt when I hit the ground - I mean, it hurt, don't get me wrong, and there was definitely a wet *crunch* as it happened, but it was more of an 'Oww! you Bugger' than a 'Quick! call the Air Ambulance'. With some assistance, the papoose was removed and the Micro-Dandy checked for ouchies and boo-boos, of which there were, luckily, none.

We continued the walk, at a slightly reduced pace, and finally made our way back to civilisation. The discomfort in my ankle was increasing slowly (I was wearing proper, supportive, walking boots though, which helped) and decided that maybe, it would be for the best, if we cut the walk short and just went home.

Walking home (as it was a Sunday and the buses were once every nine hours) did my minor injury no real favours and I spent the rest of the afternoon lying on the sofa feeling a mixture of nausea and self-pity. Every moan was answered with:

'If it hurts so much, go to the hospital.' Louder and louder, with more and more exasperation behind it every time.

I finally thought that the only thing that could take my mind off the pain away would be a catering pack of Cadburys' Minstrels. Obviously, I was much too weak to make it the three yards to the kitchen, so Mrs. Dandy was dispatched on the provender run. She gave me (threw) the chocolates with more force than was strictly necessary, and I ate them, one after another until the oversize bag was empty.

Eventually, it was time for bed, and Mrs. Dandy went to the door, opened it, turned on the stairs light and said,

'Are you coming?'
'I don't think I can get up,'

After a series of exasperated sighs, she came back and helped me up - I was really quite uncomfortable at this point, and she helped me up the stairs. About halfway up, I fell to my knees, suddenly feeling dizzy.

'Come on,' Said Mrs. Dandy, 'You're nearly there.'

And she was right, in a way - With a noise that has since been likened to a herring giving birth to a rhinoceros, I threw up the entire packet of Minstrels, my breakfast, and a selection of things that, to this day, I don't remember eating. This all managed to just miss my Dear Wife, but did mean we had to redecorate the stairs. Her reaction to this was priceless, she said;

'Oh my God. I'm so sorry - I didn't think you were really in pain, I thought you were putting it on!'

38 - AND DAVID ATTENBOROUGH WAS NO-WHERE TO BE SEEN.

Ah, here's a diamond from the archives, another one where I experience excruciating pain, this time through no fault of my own.

I blame a certain fish-eating bird, and a red haired purveyor of processed meat products. But I think I'll not bother with any kind of litigation.

-oOo-

It started like any one of a thousand other Saturday evenings, the kids had gone to bed, there was a half-decent film about to start on Sky Premiere (other broadcasters are available), dinner had been successfully eaten and all was right with the world. Apart that is, from one glaring omission...

The whiskey, and its partner in crime, the slightly oversized glass, were still in the kitchen - a whole floor away, rather than being on the table next to the sofa - within lunging distance. I stretched out my hand and concentrated reeeeaaaaly hard... But unlike Luke, in the Wampa cave, with the lightsaber, it didn't spring into my outstretched paw. I asked Mrs. Dandy if she was thinking of going down to the kitchen for anything in the near future, but the withering look she gave me told me that I was actually going to have to get up and service myself.

So I struggled to my feet, trudged the length of the lounge and started downstairs (Dandy Towers, as the name implies, manifests itself over multiple floors, time-zones, and states of being) - The thought of impending alcohol the only thing keeping me going. It was this momentary lapse of concentration and premature ribaldry that led to my, quite literal, impending downfall.

We've all trodden on things going down the stairs haven't we? Especially those of us lucky enough to be blessed with children. But how many of us can say that we've trodden on things that are roundish, possessed of small, almost fur-like injection moulded feathers, usually found in the Antarctic and of a piscavorian persuasion? Contrary to millions of years of evolution, the penguin (for it was he - But I was unaware of this fact at the time) flew across the stairwell, bounced off the clock and disappeared into a boot that I wear very infrequently.

I however, performed an almost perfect vertical triple salchow and finished with an impressive three point landing, the points being the heels of both hands and my left buttock - The assembled audience of the downstairs bookcase, my cashmere crombie and my amusingly ironic cowboy hat all gave me 6.0 for execution, but minus several million for good thinking*.

I proceeded to slide down the remaining stairs in the style of a dimensionally blessed Homer Simpson, complete with the '*bang* Ah... *bang* Uh... *bang* Sunnova... *bang* d'oh...' soundtrack, belting my wrists and behind on every single step. When I came to rest, in a heap, at the bottom of the stairs, I noticed that my left forearm looked a bit 'funny' and was flopping about to the point where, apart from the excruciating pain, I could have quite easily done the David Brent, floppy arm-y dance without relying on the optical illusion.

I cradled the offending limb; in much the same way as my Father did the frozen pigeon and let out a distress call to alert Mrs Dandy that her assistance was required. She came to the top of the stairs and peered into the gloom.

'Are you OK?' she asked, 'Only, I heard a noise'

'I'm fine,' I replied, calmly, 'I could do with a hand in the kitchen if you've got a second.'

'The film's due to start, shall I pause it?'

'Yes, that'd be for the best, it might take a few minutes.'

I stood up, gingerly, and walked to the kitchen, opening the door with my good shoulder, I turned to Mrs Dandy and said,

'I need you to hold something for me and not let go.'

'Oh, really?' She replied, smiling, grasping the wrong end of the stick entirely.

'No, not that, this.'

I proffered the limb in question. which took this opportunity to flop alarmingly in the wrong direction. Mrs Dandy's visage took on an ashen colour and she backed away.

* © Douglas Adams 1978

'Erm... nope,' she squeaked, quite sensibly, 'Go to the hospital.'

'Casualty? On a Saturday night? With my reputation?', I quipped, trying desperately to make her feel more comfortable, 'Look, all you have to do is hold on, it's a really simple dislocation, as it swings, I can feel it wanting to go back in.'

On the whole, this didn't have quite the calming effect that I'd initially thought, and Mrs Dandy's complexion went from grey to white.

'OK, really, just grab my wrist, I'll try and pull it out of your hand, but don't let go - It'll pop back in, then we can go and watch the film.'

'Erm... I don't know.' She said, reaching for my wrist.

I contemplated yelling out as she touched it, but thought better of it. She took hold, braced herself against a cupboard, and closed her eyes, pushing aside the obvious similarities to our wedding night, I gritted my teeth and yanked my left arm back. Apart from a few stars appearing behind my eyelids, and having to resist the urge to invent a couple of new expletives, nothing happened. It seemed that Mrs Dandy hadn't been quite prepared for the violence on the movement involved. My arm waved around at my side like a particularly boneless octopus.

'Shall we give that another go?'

'No, just go to the hospital...'

'Look, really, it will only take a second; you just really need to hold on.'

So, my wrist was dutifully grabbed, the slack was taken up, nods of implied readiness were exchanged and I threw myself backwards. This time Mrs Dandy was ready, she kept hold of my wrist, my humerus and ulna separated and relocated with a loud *schlock* and I swore, loudly and earthily.

'I'm just going to have a bit of a sit-down,' I said as I slid to the floor, quite dizzily.

The rest of the evening passed without incident, the occasional twinge perhaps, but nothing more than that. The bruising came out nicely and the story joined the ranks of those that get told when anyone mentions falling down the stairs, whisky, dislocations, stairs, McDonalds, hats, trees, carpet or the number 43 bus (i.e. any time I can shoe-horn it in)

In actual fact, nothing was really mentioned about it until a couple of weeks later when I decided to wear a particular pair of boots. Giving rise to a phrase that I have only uttered once, but may well have printed on a T-Shirt one day;

'Why is there a penguin in my New Rocks?

39 - WE DON' NEED NO STEENKING DIPTHONGS.

Now, occasionally, I like to write stories based on real life events, but kind of 'sexed up'. This is one of them.

It's about my son and It'll help to improve your Danish if nothing else. Caution, may contain Vikings.

(Originally published in three parts – Currently unfinished)

This chapter was suggested by my good friend @PedroVader1138 - The basic premise that is, not the theme. I mean, he's not mad or anything.

It's the (almost completely) true account of the Micro-Dandy's first, confirmed, lone kill. Only the setting, era, style, state and type of target, age of hunter, language and most of the other salient facts have been changed to maintain its artistic merit.

-oOo-

The hunter lay in the snow, looking over the ridge at the village below. All was quiet, the snow lay in deep blankets and the only movement, apart from the curl of smoke rising from the long-house chimney, was the sullen dawdle of the single huscarle on guard outside. The full moon caught the boss of his shield, and brought the raised kraken motif into sharp relief.

'Alfrun Krakensdottir... I am here,' Breathed the hunter, rising slowly from his prone position and brushing the snow from his furs.

He moved around the ridge until the huscarle was directly between him and the main building, not wanting his approach to look like he was trying to sneak and cause alarm. It took the man on guard a few minutes to notice his approach.

'Stoppe der!' He yelled, slowly raising his sword.

'I am here to see the Krakensdottir,' shouted the hunter, the snow deadening the echo so that his voice sounded flat and emotionless, 'I have heard of your problem, I am here to help.'

The sword was lowered, equally slowly, to be replaced with an empty hand,

'Vent her,' ordered the guard, pointing at the spot where the hunter was stood, his Norse was rusty, but he knew enough to stay where he was.

The door opened and closed, leaving the hunter alone with his thoughts. He looked up into the night sky, the constellation of Orion directly over his head, he laughed, if that wasn't a good omen, he didn't know what was. He could hear the grumble of conversation from inside the long-house, the few words he could pick out made it plain they were talking about Him,

'Jaeger... Frysning... Daemon... Ubevaebnet...'

The last one confused him... He was a Hunter, he was Freezing, he was here about the Demon, but Unarmed? He wasn't unarmed, he looked down at the hilt of his sword, Lyssvaerd, at his belt. Stroking the smooth length of sky-Iron he smiled, he was about as far from unarmed as it was possible to be.

The opening of the door and a beckoning hand drew him back from his remembrances of past hunts. He entered the long-house and was immediately blinded by the sheer number of torches that lined the walls and the size of the bane-fire in the middle, he was surprised that any snow survived within a mile.

'Hvad er dit navn?' Asked an aged man, clad in wolf fur and strips of studded leather.

'My name? My name s Mal Ak'hai, I am a hunter from the south, I heard that you had a problem with a d...'

'Pschh!' spat the old man, putting his hand in front of the hunter's mouth.

He turned to look at a figure that was barely visible beyond the fire and called,

'Hans navn er Mal Ak'hai! Han er en jaeger fra sid!'

'I understand the language of the south, bring him to me.' The female voice, though obviously strong, conveyed notes of tiredness and stress.

He was led, by the elbow, around the fire towards the voice. The heat seared his face as he passed, close enough to see the pile of bones at its heart. He looked up, into the face of Alfrun Krakensdottir, new leader of the Kraken clan, ever since her father had died on their last raid to Vinland,

She had led the hundred or so remaining Norsemen to times of plenty and prosperity. Until, that is, they had come upon their current trouble.

'Failures,' she said, noticing where he had been looking.

'Failures?'

'Yes, we recover the remains of people like you and burn them, it speeds their journey.'

She stared deep into the fire.

'Yours will be the 17th body that we burn.'

She looked at him with sadness, and a certain amount of longing. She thought that he was handsome in the style of the south, but his hair was blonde and he would have had no problem passing for a Norse prince, if he survived.

'What makes you so sure that you'll be burning my remains? If you don't think anyone can succeed in this quest, why have you had your men travel the country asking for help?'

'We were looking for a hero, one that we could write sagas about, one who's song would be passed down through the ages, that is not you, you come unarmed to the fight.'

'Unarmed?' He looked down at Lyssvaerd, hanging unnoticed at his side, then back up at the warrior queen, 'I will do this thing for you, I will not be more fuel for your fire.'

'You will go alone, to the clearing in the forest to the east of here, which is where the demon makes his home. You must stop him, he raids our farms and kills our children, we find our animals frozen when the sun comes up and the well is solid ice. We cannot last much longer, there will be a bounty... and more'

The hunter bowed, turned, gave the bane-fire one last glare and walked out into the night, ignoring the shaking heads of the assembled Norsemen and the hushed mumblings,

'En modig mand gar til hans dod...'

It took two hours to reach the clearing, the moon shone down, creating short shadows which could serve only as hiding places for rabbits, the demon was not there. The recent snow had covered the tracks of previous heroes, but large patches tinged gently pink showed where they had met their end. He walked slowly, but confidently out into the moonlight, took Lysswaerd from her thonging and called out to his prey.

'Come and face your end, demon, I have come to save the people of the Kraken clan, leave them in peace or die!'

His words echoed around the forest, but apart from a fall of snow triggered by a bird roused from his slumber, there was no reply.

'Filth! come and face me, stop hiding behind your mother's skirts and fight, I am your doom!'

With the sound of a calving glacier, the snow behind the hunter began to rise, climbing into the night sky one hundred feet or more. Its features slowly resolved into those of a demon, with a goat's head and human body.

'Jeg er Hati, der spiser manen!' it howled, it's voice like the tumbling of thunder.

'You are Hati, and you eat the Moon?' Shouted the hunter, 'Why would you eat the Moon?'

The demon paused, looked down, and replied with a swipe of his giant claws. The hunter jumped aside at the last moment and pressed the stud on the side of Lyssvaerd. A shining blue blade spung from the hilt and severed the demon's paw at the wrist, as it fell, it turned back into pure, virgin snow. The demon howled even louder, shaking the snow from the trees, and spun around to find his rapidly circling foe.

'Last chance!' Screamed the hunter, and held his glowing sword high above his head.

The demon lunged, changing form into a giant dire-wolf with its maw open, breathing a plume of hoare-frost. The hunter jumped back, just out of range of the freezing blast, but tripped on a root hidden under the snow and fell heavily, stunning himself. The impact jarred his sword from his hand and the blazing blade disappeared with a hiss.

Sensing that the game was nearly over, Hati reared once more. He inhaled deeply, intending to freeze the hunter to his very core and stamp him onto shards so small that his bones could never be burned. The giant wolf's head fell towards the hunter, its icicle teeth bared, the howl of the coming ice-storm reverberated from the far foothills and his eyes closed as the strike came. The hunter rolled, grabbed his sword, loosed the blade, and severed the demon's head with a single stroke. With a sound like the breaking of a thousand glass pianos, the demon exploded into chunks of ice and fell to the ground.

The hunter lay panting in the debris, trying to get his breath back. He looked around the glade, trying to find some proof that the battle had actually taken place, if someone happened across the scene now it would just look like he'd been smashing a block of ice, and none too expertly at that. His eye chanced upon a glinting object, slightly brighter than the surrounding snow. Levering himself to his feet, he picked it up, it was a diamond, the size of a watermelon, when he held it up to the sky, he could see the feint impression of a wolf's eye. This would be his proof, and his dowry, Alfrun Krakensdottir would be his queen, and his saga would be told until the Earth froze.

(OK, what actually happened was my son knocked the head off the snowman we'd all built with a stick... But who'd want to read about that?)

The hot sun beat down from the clear, blue sky. He'd stripped off most of his leather armour and was watching the tower intently from the small grove of scrub and trees that was the only shade on the entire plain.

'Tror du han kan se os?' Asked Algot, the leader of his guard; Alfrun had made sure that he took reinforcements with him this time. Since their marriage two months before, they had become inseparable; she wasn't going to lose him to some stupid quest.

'Yes, I'm sure he can see us, if nothing else, these damn helmets reflect the sun like signal fires!'

The helmets that they were forced to wear had no substance, their thin metal wouldn't stop an arrow, never mind an axe, but they did stop you losing control of your own mind and slaughtering your own men if the Magus turned his attention to you.

'Ewald, Algot, you two circle around to the right, stay as low as you can, Jarne and Razmus, to the left, follow the line of the rocks, Runar...' He shook his head, not agreeing with the tactics that he was being forced to use, 'Prepare the pigs.'

They had 'liberated' the pigs two days earlier from a village baron who had too many and refused to sell his surplus. Though he would have been even less inclined if he had any idea what their fate was to be. Runar tried to calm them, they were not enjoying the heat and there would be no respite for them in the few minutes of life they had left. He tied large bundles of straw to each of them and then delicately attached the vials of græsk-ild, being careful not to break the fragile class vials.

'Ready?' Mal Ak'Hai looked at Runar questioningly, almost hoping that he would say no, and that the pigs would get a reprieve.

'Ja herre, de er klar til at brænde.' The plan had been Runar's idea, and he was sure it would work.

'Very well, light them up...'

Runar nodded and applied a burning torch to the straw bundle nearest the rump of the pigs. As they realised what was happening, they started to squeal and panic, trying desperately to get away from the heat. A leather clad boot kicked them in the direction of the tower and the pigs ran. Palls of black smoke plumed from them as they crossed the scalding sand to the tower.

As they got within a hundred yards, the rain of arrows started from the ramparts.

'Go... Go...!' Yelled the hunter, 'Stay in the smoke, but keep away from the pigs until they've done their job!'

The six men ran into the thick smoke and made their way towards the castle, eyes streaming as their lungs filled with the smell of burning pork. Despite the reduced visibility, they could still see arrow after arrow hitting the pigs, a gout of flame signalled a lucky hit on a vial of græsk-ild, which only made them run faster and created more covering smoke. They finally reached the cavernous rock that served as the foundations of the tower.

'Get Down!'

The mix of græsk-ild and rendering pig fat detonated with a deafening roar that shook loose stonework from above.

'Into the cave, now!' His five guards followed him into the burning darkness, the smell of roasting pork causing his mouth to water against his better judgement, 'Find the entrance, it must be close-by somewhere, but be careful, I think they know we're here..'

The Norsemen grinned at each other and split into two teams, searching the twisting caverns for a way into the stronghold. It was only minutes until the sound of fighting alerted the hunter to the fact that the other team had found the entrance. They ran towards the noise and got there in time to see Rasmus swinging his battle-axe around in circles and cleaving defenders in two at the waist. Jarne picked up two more, stoved their skulls together, and threw them to the ground.

Mal drew Lyssvaerd, extended her blade and plunged it into the chest of the nearest enemy - bringing the sword up so that its burning tip exited the top of his head in a fountain of blood. His guard roared as they saw this, finally sure that their new Lord was a fighter.

'Push them back, we need to get to the tower!'

Too busy to reply, the small force responded by action, redoubling their efforts and cutting down anyone that stood between them and the door. It took an age to make it to the armoured door, and as they cleared the last few guards, it started to swing closed.

'Runar! Don't let them close the door!'

Runar reached into his pocket and pulled out the last vial of græsk-ild, he hefted it to gauge its weight and then threw it through the rapidly narrowing gap. It sailed through the air, hit the doorframe and smashed. The sticky liquid spraying through the opening and finding its way to one of the wall torches.

The explosion blew the door closed and the screams of pain from behind it echoed through the cavern. As the noise died down, they tried to open it but the hinges had been bent by the force of the blast, and it took the combined strength of all of them to force it open. The scene that confronted them was a glimpse into the mouth of hell, burning, shattered bodies lined the walls and unidentifiable chunks littered the floor.

'ved Grabthar's kølle...' whispered Ewald, as he surveyed the scene.

'Up... We need to go up!' Mal rallied his troops and started to climb the stairs into the tower.

They were halfway to the top when an ethereal voice echoed around the stairwell. 'INVADERS... LEAVE NOW, STAY AND YOU WILL DIE HORRIBLY.'

'Yes, he definitely knows that we're here.'

They encountered light resistance for the rest of their journey, the Magus having committed the majority of his forces to the defence of the cavern. At the top of the stairs there was a small anteroom, decorated with occult symbols that seemed to creep slowly across the walls and change shape as they went. Skulls of various animals languished on shelves and tables and stacks of parchment, decorated with unknowable sigils littered the floor.

'Magus! We have come for you!' Mal Ak'Hai declared, 'You will pay for your crimes...'

A low growl came from the stairs behind them, Rasmus swung his axe without turning and separated the owners head from its shoulders. The rest of the half dog-half lizard thing slid to the ground and bubbled into a toxic slime.

'Du bliver nødt til at gøre det bedre end det.' called Rasmus.

'I've a feeling that he can do better than that my friend,' replied the hunter, 'Else there wouldn't be such a price on his head.'

With the violence of a hurricane, the ornate door at the other side of the room flew open and a gust of wind threw them to the floor. They were held there until the gale subsided, as they rose, they saw their target silhouetted in the doorway.

'YOU WERE GIVEN A CHANCE!' The Magus bellowed, 'NOW DIE!'

He closed his eyes and made a complicated gesture with his hands.

'I'm afraid that your tricks won't work on us, we're protected,' The hunter indicated their flimsy metal helmets.

'ALL OF YOU?

Rasmus yelled, raised his gargoyle-blood caked weapon and charged at his clanmates.

'Jeg kan ikke hjælpe mig selv!' He screamed, unable to control his own actions, his helmet had been blown from his head by the wind.

Ewald ducked under the blade and brought his sword up to block it, 'Uanset hvad du vil gøre, gør det nu!' The sinews on his arms tightened as he fought to keep the dripping axe blade away from his face.

The sweat poured for the Magus' brow as the force of trying to control the straining bulk of Rasmus started to tell on him. Mal sprung, holding the hilt of Lyssvaerd in his fist, as the Magus sensed his approach he opened his eyes and screamed. in a split second, Ewald rolled to one side, the now dazed Rasmus fell to the ground and the hunter pressed the button that released the blade.

It extended through the Magus' temple, through his skull and out of the other side; and as the light slowly faded from his eyes, he smiled. 'Run...' he whispered.

The heroes looked at each other and smiled. 'See what you can find to supplement the bounty, we'll need to...'

The room started to shake, dust and skulls, parchment and elixirs started to fall to the ground... One by one, the stones of the tower were winking out of existence...

'Run!' Yelled Mal Ak'Hai, 'Run as if your life depended on it!'

Which, in hindsight, it did.

(I wrote the above as,my son asked me to make him, without a trace of irony, a tinfoil hat... So I did, and that was the adventure that he could have had, in another place. I continue it below)

They lay, panting, against the rocks. Behind them, all that was left of the Magus' tower was the huge rock that it had originally sat on, a few fluttering pieces of paper and the smoke from the still smouldering pigs.

'der var tæt...' Breathed Rasmus.

'Close? I'd say it was a damn site worse than close!' Exclaimed Mal, they all looked at each other and laughed.

They had only got down as far as the second floor when they were forced to jump by the accelerating magical disintegration of the blocks that made up the tower.

'Thank the Gods we were jumping onto sand.'

'Jeg ville foretrække at springe i vandet.' replied Ewald.

'Yes, jumping into water would have been even better, but there's not a lot of that around here, in case you hadn't noticed.'

They all looked around, to see the unending, shifting sand in every direction, 'although, whilst we're on the subject, we'd better start heading back to the boat. Alfrun will think that we've been having a holiday.'

His new wife, Alfrun Krakensdottir, had been the head of the Kraken clan since her Father had been killed. She was known for her beauty and her fairness, but not necessarily for her patience. She didn't agree that he needed to continue his Bounty-hunting, instead believing that he should be at home, defending the clan and making babies.

He recovered his leather armour and pulled the compass from his pack, pointed at the southern horizon and started to trudge towards the horizon.

It took them two days to reach the coast, as they climbed the dunes towards the landing, The Hunter held up his fist, the group stopped and knelt silently in the sand. He sniffed the air and listened.

'Can you hear that?'

'Jeg kan ikke høre noget...'

'Exactly, a longship full of Norsemen, sat on a beach, waiting for us, with enough heather ale to drown an ox. Shouldn't we be able to hear the screams?'

'ja du har ret...'

'I know I'm right, that's why we're still alive.' He slowly craned his neck and looked over to top of the dune, down towards the ship, 'Bertrum has a green shield and a handaxe, right?'

'Ja?'

'But he doesn't have black hair does he?'

'på, rød.'

'Then that's not Bertrum.'

They all lay along the ridge of the dune and one by one identified that none of the people stood next to the longship were actually their men. They were wearing their clothes, but that's where the similarity ended.

'hvad skal vi gøre?'

'I tell you what we'll do...' He thought, and then thought again, and try as he might, he couldn't think of a way that they could get around twenty enemy soldiers, take the ship and get it into deep water before losing a kidney or an eyeball to an accurate arrow. And then it hit him.

'Algot, Runar tells me that your mother entertains rabid badgers in her bed, is that true?'

Both Norsemen turned to him incredulously, 'Hvad?'

'Yes, and Ewald, Jarne says that both he and Razmus have enjoyed the charms of your sister, both together and separately, many times, and she enjoyed it too most of the time.'

Ewald launched himself at his kinsmen, screaming, 'Du har vanæret min søster, jeg vil afskære dine testikler!'

The scream, obviously, attracted the attention of the men guarding their ship, and within seconds they were charging up the other side of the dune, all pretence at stealth thrown to the winds.

'Look, they're coming!' Yelled Mal, as he pressed the button that extended the blade of Lyssvaerd. Immediately the berserking Norsemen saw their enemy howling towards them and forgot their fictitious petty differences and descended to meet them.

The clash as the two sides met could be heard all the way to Svalbard, or so it seemed. Instantly the Norse warriors started to hack blindly at their foe, arms were lost to axes, hammers were dodged and Lyssvaerd flew through gaps between armour and shield with clinical precision. In minutes they were knee-deep in gore and the berserker rage had hold of them all.

They had fought their way down the dune and across the beach, Jarne had sustained a wound to his forearm that would need attention before the day was out and Runar was bleeding from a deep cut above his eye. Other than that they were completely unscathed. The few defenders that were left guarding the ship were easily dispatched. Algot even managed to pin one to the bow through his neck, luckily above the waterline.

As they clamboured onto the deck of the ship, the smell hit them. It wasn't the remains of the crew, it seemed that they'd been dumped into the sea, Then they saw it, in the bilges of the boat was an oily scum, it was moving against the rolling of the sea and slowly gathering towards the bow. As the heap grew, it took on the features of a slouched human with a pointed head and long, grasping fingers, at least eight feet high and getting taller all the time.

'hvad i al helveder er det?' gasped Razmus.

'I don't know,' Replied Mal, 'But let's see how easily it dies!'

They screamed out a battle-cry and charged towards the giant, teeth bared and weapons ready.

And I'm afraid that's where it ends for the time-being; maybe I'll finish it one day. I'll let you know if I ever do.

40 - THEN I POSED, AND HE TOOK MY PICTURE.

The story is another two-parter about a party, or show that I went to a number of years ago, when I was younger and fitter.

It was like no party I've ever been to before or since. Give it a read, it'll broaden your mind, amongst other things.

-oOo-

Some of you, mainly the people who've known me a while, or worked with me, or attended a formal event that I've gone to, or helped me celebrate a birthday, will know that I occasionally make and wear kilts. Not for any real ancestral reason, although the Dandy line is almost certainly blessed with a bewildering array of Scottish blackguards and jackanapes.

I just like messing with people's heads, and, as has been mentioned in multiplicity before, I am a massive show-off - And there're few things more likely to get you noticed in public than having your knees out and not wearing any underwear - You ask any woman between the ages of 16 and 40.

However, there are times when even wearing a kilt sees you fading into the background, Highland events for instance, or weddings of whacky and/or self-important people. The thing to wear on these occasions, for the fashion conscious Dandy at least, would obviously be something like full Roman Imperial battledress or the rear half of a pantomime horse. This situation vexes me greatly, the Chimping Dandy does not do 'fading into the background' easily.

Which is bizarre really, because on one occasion, I was in a room with over a thousand, like-minded, people - And I was probably one of the most conservatively dressed people there, and I had a marvellous time.

Many, many, years ago, I used to work with a young lady, quite pretty, moderately shy, and very efficient at her job. If you looked up the phrase 'Butter would not melt in her mouth' in a dictionary of phrases (if such a thing exists) there would be a picture of her. After we both left the company, we kept in touch by email, as Facebook etc. did not exist at the time.

One day, I received an email from her that said something along the lines of, 'We're going to a show in London and can get you some cheap tickets if you're interested'. Now, not being blessed with children at the time, both Mrs. Dandy & myself jumped at the chance and immediately started to prepare.

Prepare? I assume that you're asking, 'Why would you have to prepare for a London Show? Unless it was Rocky Horror? Was it Rocky Horror?'

No...

It wasn't...

The young lady in question, and her significant other of the time, had developed certain... erm... Shall we say 'Peccadillos'? That made them very popular with other, like minded, couples (Don't get excited, that's not where this story is headed - Not exactly anyway) - And the show in question was: Skin-Two Magazine's Rubber Ball.

Google it... But probably not at work...

It's a jolly get-together for people who enjoy dressing up and pushing the envelope, or being naked and being sealed in an envelope. And they really won't let you in if you're wearing 'Smart-Casual'. So I put on my Seamstress' head (The one I keep in the freezer for situations just such as these) and knocked up a couple of costumes. I made a PVC hobble-skirt for Mrs. Dandy - Which was more zips than PVC. And for myself, I made a kilt, also out of PVC (Which, for those who wish to replicate the experience, is a right, royal, bitch to iron pleats into).

We booked a VERY nice hotel in London, a couple of First-Class train tickets, and waited.

On the night in question, we'd all agreed to meet in a pub around the corner from the venue in, I think, Hammersmith. Of course, when we got there, they were nowhere to be seen (Turns out that they'd 'bumped into some old friends in the hotel' - repeatedly, in several different positions, I'd imagine), but the place was full, almost to bursting, of clinically odd people. We found a table with a couple of spare stools and proceeded to wait.

We shared the table with three giant transvestites, I don't mean they were really, really, transvestite... I mean that they were all just shy of 7 feet tall. I really wish that I could remember their actual names, but I'm just going to have to make them up, they were great... guys?... And introduced themselves with both their male and female names - 'I'm Patrick-Mary, He's Brian-Fifi and that guy at the bar's Steve-Tracey'.

One was dressed in an outfit completely made of car-mats, which gave... him... a distinctly Female Klingon vibe, one was dressed as a bald Nun, with a PVC habit (the clothing item, not the lifestyle choice), but with the buttock area cut out, and the other was dressed in sort of a neon Flashdance ensemble which left very little to the imagination for either his male or female 'identities'.

We spent a happy couple of hours, swapping stories, such as we could with our limited knowledge of this type of thing - it turned out that we'd all turned up unfashionably early. And 'Patrick-Mary' was just telling us about the time his wife came home early and found him dressed in her wedding underwear and pleasuring himself with the toilet-brush when I felt a hand on my shoulder and a German voice said,

'Excuse me, may I haf a vord?'

I looked up and saw a bald, stocky gentleman, with a magnificent handlebar moustache, wearing a tight white T-shirt and a significant amount of rubber/leather.

'My friends unt I noticed vat ju are vearing vhen you vent to ze bar, ve vere vonderink if you minded us takink a few photos?'

I looked at Mrs Dandy, she shrugged, I looked at our new found friends, and they grinned and excitedly gave me the thumbs-up. I stood, and then followed the German chap to the other side of the room, where a table of similar gentlemen, clad in various wipe-clean outfits were sat, along with a collection of suspiciously professional looking cameras.

'Ju stand zere und ve take a few photos, yes?'

I nodded, still not 100 percent comfortable with the situation, but did my best to strike a pose that didn't make me look like I'd stepped from the pages of the Littlewoods catalogue.

'Nein, nein, nein... More... er... GRRRRRR!'

I did the 'Hulk-Smash' pose, you know where you grit your teeth, and sort of bring your arms into your chest and bend over (towards the camera, before you ask).

'Jah, Jah, ist gut... Now er... More sidevays!'

We were starting to attract a bit of a crowd, and if I'm honest, I was well out of my comfort zone, but it was all in fun and no-one seemed to be taking themselves too seriously (apart from one of the photographers, who REALLY looked to be enjoying himself) - It probably didn't take more than five minutes, it felt like a lifetime though.

'Gut, jah, I sink zat iz enough... Can ju just sign zis?'

They handed me what I assume was a model release form and offered to buy us all a drink, which we accepted. We were there for about another hour before we decided to head off to the event proper. As we left, the chap with the moustache waved and called,

'The magazine should be out next month!'

So, if you ever find yourself rambling in the German countryside, and happen across a gentleman's art pamphlet, designed for one-handed reading, lying unloved in the bottom of a hedgerow, and think you recognise someone in a two-page photo-spread...

You might not be wrong.

Some time later, we wandered from the pub, which was virtually next-door to the venue, The Hammersmith Palais (Sadly, no longer with us) and joined the queue of deviants. I remarked to Patrick-Mary, or possibly Brian-Fifi that there were a number of people there who weren't exactly 'dressed for the occasion', he smiled and nodded, as if to a child who had just asked why the sky was blue, and replied,

'Ah, a lot of the more hardcore types can't, or won't, really wear their gear out in the real world, there are changing rooms inside,'

I pondered on this for a while, I was still a little bit vanilla at the time, but thought it was odd that these people would be embarrassed about, well, anything really. We reached the front of the queue in short order and after being given a quick look up and down by the security staff and a read of about a thousand signs that explained what would happen to you if you were found taking pictures without a press-pass, we entered the hall proper.

What would be the best way to describe the scene? Have you seen Blade 2? There's a party scene in that film that is about the closest to my first impression of that room. Except that there was slightly less gunfire and the attendees of this party were significantly cooler, to the point of being, well, not exactly indescribable - Because there wouldn't be much point in me trying to describe them I guess, but they were certainly 'unusual'.

I'll describe a few of the more memorable guests:

I'm not sure how many of you are conversant with the work of Thomas Gainsborough, the 18th Century painter? But there was a couple there dressed in costumes inspired by his work. However, instead of being made of richly coloured silks and velvets, they were made of PVC, with a giant, yellow and black, hound's-tooth check pattern, and they were full coverage... As in they were wearing gloves and Luchador style (gimp) masks (with hats on top). I later found out that these were one-piece costumes with a long, single zip up the back from... Erm... crotch to top of the head - Please don't ask me how I found this out...

There was a young lady with an incredible powder blue crinoline shepherdess costume, also made of PVC, complete with white PVC underskirts - Odd you'd think, but not out of the ordinary, you might even just get away with it at a normal fancy dress party. She did have a lamb with her too... Well, I say a lamb; it was actually a hairy gentleman, on his hands and knees, being led around on a collar and lead... He wasn't the only one of these, but he was one of the few wearing pants.

An unusual gentleman, who seemed to have a very particular, I hesitate to use the word fetish, but I probably should. He was wearing a suit made of what I would describe as 'dummy' rubber - That thick, yellow tinged clear rubber that babies dummies are made of... It had no separate arms, these were constricted by his sides, and his legs were similarly constrained (I think, although I may be wrong - I remember wondering whether he'd been placed there by a friend or he'd shrugged his way there like 'The Very Perverted Caterpillar'). He spent the entire night lying in the doorway of the Ladies Conveniences, occasionally thanking the people who took the time to tread on him, with stilettos. And you'll notice I said people, not ladies, as both the wearers of the footwear, and the gender of toilet user were fairly mix and match.

The last people who particularly stick in my mind were a very accommodating couple... We went to have a sit down, after an hour or so of being bombarded with Dutch Techno music and performers taking angle-grinders to their codpieces and found a seat opposite them. The young lady was sturdily built and topless. I will not even try to estimate her cupsize, but I'm fairly sure it was at the end of the alphabet where the high-scoring scrabble tiles live. She was providing a service for her boyfriend, normally reserved for hungry new-born babies and nowadays, for some reason, frowned upon in train carriages.

Once he'd had his fill, as it were, he stood up, thanked the young lady, shook the hand of the almost skeletal gentleman sat on the other side of her. (Which I thought was the most insanely British thing I had ever seen in my life) and walked off. It turns out that the skinny chap was her boyfriend and the gentleman with the brand new milk moo-stache was simply a fellow partygoer. He looked at me, raised his eyebrows, and pointed at his partner. I shook my head, waved my hand in a negative fashion and patted my stomach - Immediately thinking that me not wanting to suckle from his girlfriend/wife because I wasn't hungry was probably not the reply that he was expecting.

We made our excuses and left.

The rest of the evening (Well, early hours of the morning to be exact) passed without many other major incidents, we bumped into our friends a few times, we were 'halloooed' and flashed from the balcony by our new-found transvestite horde, we talked to some people who I've since found out were 'famous' in that particular scene and through them, got invited to a couple of after-parties.

We didn't attend them unfortunately, the thought of getting a cab halfway across town, partying until lunchtime and then doing the walk of shame back to the hotel didn't sound that appealing - And I was pretty tired. But given the chance again... I'd be there like a shot, and you should too. And I now fully understand why a significant number of people there were virtually naked...

PVC's bloody hot to wear...

41 - ARE YOU EXPERIENCED?

Remember in the Foreword, where I said that I was opinionated and loud and got upset with people who posted ineffectual, passive aggressive status updates on Facebook?

Well, you're a better man than I am, 'cos I didn't say anything like that at all – Aha! Gotcha.

But I am and I do, I can't remember what had actually been said, maybe it was many different people complaining about their life online in different ways, but it led me to post this little number, which became quite popular.

-oOo-

What're the two most infuriating words that any parent will hear from their children ever, in their lifetime? I don't mean the really scary ones like 'I'm pregnant' or 'It's broken' or 'On fire'. I mean the ones that you hear every weekend and every school holiday and every advert break during an otherwise immensely exciting program?

Yes, that's right, 'I'm boooooored!'

The little cherub, who you not so long ago bought the entire collection of Moshi Monsters for? Who you queued for at 07:30am a week before release day to make sure she was the first of her friends to own the new One Direction CD that detailed not only their tour dates, but a scratch and sniff sampling of their underwear drawer? Who has demanded, and received, every type, style and colour of Nintendo games system past, present and future?

We must have spent the GNP of Lesotho on toys etc. for the Dandies, both Mini and Micro, over their respective lives. But both of them would much rather sit in front of a PC or Laptop or iPad and watch YouTube videos. If for some reason you temporarily take away this dubious privilege, say they've been zoned out for six hours solid, or you actually need to use the device yourself. You get a selection of sighs that could extinguish an Australian forest fire and the occasional theatrical flounce onto the sofa.

There are cries of 'I'm bored!'

To which my normal reply is, 'No, you're lazy!'

And then I go on to enumerate all the things that they could be doing instead, which in fairness gets more and more ridiculous every time - It'll start off as 'Play on the Wii, or the PlayStation, watch a DVD, walk the dog, wash the pots, draw a picture...' and ends up with, 'Shave the cat, iron a herring, translate Harry Potter into Klingon, laminate a duck...' By this time they've usually stopped listening, wandered off or slipped into a narcoleptic coma - All of which, I consider to be a win.

But I realised recently that it's not just kids that do this, maybe it's my particular group of friends, but for every Facebook update I see on my timeline that says 'Today I got up, felt great, walked the dog, took an artistic photo of a thing, made something tasty for lunch and did stuff with a person until my eyes rolled back in my head when I OD'd on the greatness of it all,' there's twenty seven that say, 'Aren't people rubbish, I'm staying in bed, there's nothing to do, it's raining, everybody stop picking on me, it's everybody else's fault, wah-wah-wah!'

For Gods' (yes, pedants, that apostrophe IS in the right place) sake people DO SOMETHING! If your life is crap, do something about it, find out what's wrong and change it. There's no situation that anyone is in that is insurmountable. Then again, you might counter with any or all of the below;

'But I've got depression!' To which I would reply 'Me too!' diagnosed and prescribed for, but the one thing I took to heart is what my Doctor said just before signing the green slip that I took to the pharmacist, 'Mr. Dandy, this isn't a cure, this is just to make life easier for you whilst you figure out what's wrong and sort it out.' - Which is exactly what I did, and I'm proud of myself for doing it. I know it's often easier said than done, and I know that a lot of people's triggers are more difficult to sort out than mine, but you're never going to feel any better unless this happens. (P.S. if they offer you CBT, even if there's a long waiting list - Say 'Yes please' - I've seen this really work well... If you go to your CBT appointment and they ask if you need to borrow a helmet and gloves, don't panic, it just means they've booked you on Compulsory Basic Training, not Cognitive Behaviour Therapy - Just go with it, fewer people who can ride motorcycles are depressed - That's a fact... Probably.)

'But I'm missing a leg!' Life's harder with a disability, I truly appreciate that and I've not experienced it first-hand myself, so I'm not really qualified to judge. (Unless you count an inability to stop correcting people on their pronunciation as a disability - It seems the people who give out the Blue Disabled Parking badges don't... Fascists!) But you hear stories every day of people who have conquered seemingly insurmountable odds to achieve what their doctors said was impossible... Be one of those people. If you need a bit of a lift in this department, Google a guy called Taylor Morris, and then try keep a straight face whilst you tell the Dole Office that you can't make it to the shops because you've got a bit of a dicky ankle.

'But I'm thick!' Well, that's as may be, but you can't let lack of education hinder your dreams, book yourself on a course at your local school. Learn about something you're interested in to start with - just to get you back into it, then try learning something that might help you take the next step towards happiness. You never know, you might be lucky and those two things are one and the same. If you can't do this, due to having to look after your young or similar, become a member of your local library, borrow books and actually read them - There are, quite literally, worlds to discover.

'I'm in the middle of nowhere with no transportation!' Walk, no... Seriously... walk. There's nowhere (OK, barring islands etc.) on the mainland United Kingdom that isn't accessible by you leaving your house, locking the door behind you and walking in the right direction for long enough - It might take a while, you might need to take a snack and maybe a thermos with you but seriously, you can do it. We've only had the Infernal Combustion Engine for the past hundred and thirty years. What do you think people did before that? It wasn't bitch and moan and lie in their own filth watching repeats of Jeremy Kyle all day I can tell you.

'I'm broke!' Me too, again, sorry. I sit around all the time going, 'I could just eat a raisin and biscuit Yorkie, shame I'm broke!' I normally say this in my living room, surrounded by CDs I don't listen to and DVDs that I'll never watch again. If you can't afford to buy the stuff you need (not want, don't waste your money on things you want, spend it on stuff you need, you know, carrots rather than beer and stuff like that) then sell something that you don't need quite as much.

'But!' - This is, without doubt, the most invidious word in the English language, people usually use it to explain why they're not going to do something. Examples include 'I'd take the dog for a walk, no problem, BUT I've got some completely fictitious stuff that I've already arranged to do' and 'Yeah, I realise that this is a very important issue, BUT It doesn't affect me directly, so I don't care.' Do me a favour people, if you feel the need to use this word at all, use it in a positive way, as characterised by the axiomatic T-Shirt slogan 'I'm not a gynaecologist, BUT I'll take a look at it for you.' - Embrace the chance to do things, even if they're new, scary and have a medium to high risk of you getting slapped by a complete stranger. At least you'll be meeting new people.

I know that this has all been very flippant, because that's what I do, this is ostensibly a humour book after all. I do try and keep it light even when I rant.

And I understand that there are those people who are housebound due to circumstances beyond their control, for whom there is no available assistance, this was not directed at them in any way.

BUT, The rest of you, seriously, grab your life by the nuts and shake every single, solitary experience you can out of it - I'm fat, lazy, bald, not particularly attractive and don't have a huge circle of friends and even I've had enough experiences that I've thought are interesting enough that people would enjoy hearing about them here. (Rightly or wrongly).

Just imagine what things a svelte, vigourous, hirsute, beautiful person like yourself could get up to! - Don't hold yourself back with insecurity, propel yourself forward with childishness and a blindness to your own inadequacies.

Just like I do!

If you do do this, feel free to tell me all about it via email and you never know, I might include your success story here, in these very pages.

42 - PIRACY ON THE HIGH WINDS. (THE EDWARD TEACH STORIES)

Now, this is a biggie, a life changer (for me at least). You remember the story that was based in truth but totally fabricated about my son being a Viking Hunter?

Well, I tried a similar thing with something that happened to my Daughter, and it grew, and grew and grew into a Steampunk-lite Sci-Fi epic.

It grew so much in fact that it turned into its own book, which will hopefully be published sometime in 2014.

I think that I originally posted these stories in seven or so instalments, and whilst they bear some resemblance to parts of the story in the book, the details have definitely changed. For instance I have removed a large percentage of the blatant plagiarism and ideas/names stolen wholesale from Games Workshop, Douglas Adams and George Lucas (I'm a fan you see). I include it only so scholars examining my work in hundreds of years' time will have the whole story.

If you're interested in the finished work, (which is written significantly better) whether reading it or indeed publishing it, drop me a line at TheChimpingDandy@Hotmail.co.uk and I'll be in touch.

-oOo-

'Frobisher!'

'Ma'am?'

'Which hat? The flying helmet?' She tugged on a shiny leather and brass B6 of uncertain vintage, squinted into the mirror , and removed it, 'or.. The riding hat?' she picked up a miniature top hat, decorated with lace and black roses from the table, and perched it on her head at a jaunty angle.

'I'm... Sorry... I...'

She sighed, sometimes being the corsair captain of your own fighting airship didn't leave time for the finer things in life.

'Access weather control and see what they have planned for all points between our current position and the Straits of Madripoor.'

'Working...' The lights on Frobisher's brass face dimmed slightly as he rerouted power to establish a secure, untraceable, link with The Great Cloud, 'Winds light to moderate from the South West, point seven percent chance of tropical rain, dependant on local humidity, light cloud cover beginning at nine thousand feet, temperature ranging fr....'

'Enough! Riding hat it is! Have the detailed report for the area around Chandra Island fed to my screen on the bridge, after that, put in a request to maintenance and get your contacts cleaned, you're starting to clack.'

'Ma'am.' The construct replied.

The captain fixed the hat to her elegantly coiffed hair with a selection of ornate pins, and strode from her quarters directly onto the bridge. The crew stiffened as she entered, suddenly taking a much deeper professional interest in their respective screens and readouts.

'Dr. When?' she called.

'Aye Ma'am?' He replied, the creaking of her first officer's aged leather overcoat not quite managing to mask the twang of his strange, half Cornish, half Centauri accent.

'Set a course for Chandra Island, Eastern Madripoor, best speed but keep us below detection altitude,' She sank into the command chair and started to digest the information displayed on her screen, 'Notify me at fifty miles.'

'Aye... Alright you dogs, you heard the captain, rig the gasbag for best stealth speed, ramp up the fusion engines, seal all external hatches and report when ready!'

The deck shook as the engineers stoked the huge nuclear engines into life, and the captain could feel the vibration in her bones. She closed her eyes and listened to the creak of the connecting chains tightening around the bags of gas above her. One by one the tell-tales on her panel turned from red to green. As the last one lit, she looked towards Dr. When.

'Stations reporting ready Ma'am, we move on your word.'

'Take us out nice and easy Dr. no showboating this time, Another punctured bag and I'll take it out of your share.'

'All jets ahead one quarter, when we see clear sky take her up to two thousand feet and engage fusion drive.' When turned to the captain, grinned and bowed, 'All hands - prepare for acceleration in ten! Hold on to anything you don't want to be looking for in the stern later!'

The shock of the nuclear reaction always caught her by surprise, its limitless acceleration took them from twenty-five to four hundred miles per hour in an instant. There was a cacophonous noise that rang through the ship, followed by gurgling screams.

'100 credits says cook forgot to secure his pans again?' When commented, hanging on to the guardrail behind the helm.

'200 says it was the kniferack,' The Captain replied, thumbing the switch for the shipboard Intercomm system, 'Medical team to The Galley on the double, patch up the cook and check the Galley for damage - He does a day in irons for every smashed pot.'

The ship settled into its cruising configuration as the gasbags finally caught up with the main hull, she was a beautiful ship, her hull built to resemble an early 18th Century Barque, the sails replaced by the voluminous gas-bag and the bowsprit replaced by a bronze and copper Ion Cannon, nicknamed 'Daisy' by the crew. She was, rather confusingly, named the Edward Teach, for reasons best known to her Captain.

'Captain!' Barked the Sensor Chief, 'We have a contact, bearing 076 degrees, speed 300, distance 20 miles, closing fast.'

'Identify!'

'Looks to be mechanised, showing no lifesigns, minimal biological mass, but plenty of movement. Wait! We're being scanned!'

'Dr When, secure us from best speed, bring Daisy to bear and fire as she rolls.'

'Aye Ma'am!' The Doctor pushed the Helmsman from his seat and took the controls himself, he locked off the engines and threw the ship into a tight turn. The hull slewed viciously under the gas-bag as the chains tried to compensate for the rapid change of vector. The Captain peered through the viewscreen as their foe came into view.

'Spiders!' She called, 'Blow them out of my Sky When!'

The Captain had tangled with the Spiders before, they were a completely mechanical life-form, developed by the military for jungle and urban warfare. Of course, as is the way of such things, they had become too good at their job, finally turning against their controllers and setting off on their own journey, attacking cargo ships and corporate supply balloons, stripping them of their power sources and taking scalps as trophies.

Daisy barked, a glittering beam of blue energy shot from the prow of the ship and hit the Spiders' vehicle amidships, deactivated spiders fell to the ground like metal snow, but the main body was still aloft.

'Hit them again!'
'Recharging!'
'They're closing!'
'Nearly there!'
'Doctor, now would be a good time!'
'Firing!'

The Spiders' were almost within boarding range as the next blast hit them. The remaining Spiders bounced off the side of the hull and fell the two thousand feet to the ground. There was a moment of furious action as everyone checked that there was no damage to the ship.

'Resume course and speed,' Ordered the Captain, finally breathing out.

The rest of the voyage went without incident, and the crew was just settling back into their normal routine when the fifty mile alarm sounded.

'All stop!' Called When.
'Take us up to fifteen thousand feet and continue on jets only.'

The sudden silence as the fusion drive was taken offline was almost deafening, the ship slowly began to rise as air from the still hot exhausts was fed into the bags to supplement the already buoyant Tritium gas. They broke through the cloud layer and started towards the island. The Captain beckoned When towards her.

'Once we are directly over the island we will be storming the base using two drop-pods, pick a team of seven and take one, I'll do the same with the other.'

'Base? What're we after?'

'Whatever we can get our hands on, as usual.'

When grinned, grabbed his chainsword and hit the intercomm,

'Khan, Russ, Guilliman, Jonson, Curze, Corax and Vulkan - Report to the podroom, we drop in 60.'

As her pod fell, the Captain looked at her assembled team; she saw in the eyes of her crewmen the glint of impending action, the lust for new booty...

'Landfall in five... Four... Three...'

The landing rockets fired, almost doubling everyone's apparent weight and the Captain instantly regretted putting on her corset and kneeboots before boarding the pod. The doors fell open as soon as they touched down and the crew jumped out of both pods, screaming like banshees. A wave of construct guards poured from the main door of the building and ran into When's whining chainsword, cogs, gears and oil sprayed in all directions, covering the ground like glistening brass snow. Their cries of 'Invaders must die!' silenced by the churning teeth.

'We bounce in ten minutes, take what you can!' Yelled the Captain, 'Split up, we'll cover more ground!'

As the flow of guards died down, her crew entered the base and scattered in all directions. She made her way through strangely quiet corridors towards the base commander's office. The trip took minutes longer than she expected and when she arrived at the door, she was faced with an ornate lock of an unknown type.

She reached into her pocket and pulled out the small glowing sphere that had cost her a month's share from the Dentrassi trader at Long-Pig station. He'd said that it was guaranteed to undo any lock that could be undone, although he did look like the sort from whom it might be difficult to extract a refund.

The Captain did not care, after a few seconds of melodious humming, the door clicked open. As she entered the office, she noticed how tidy it was - She realised she was in the right place and searched the walls for an entrance into the commander's private quarters.

'Where are you? Where are you?'

'Where is who?' Commented a voice from the doorway.

The Captain froze, turning away from the slowly opening cupboard that she had found. She was confronted by perhaps the most beautiful woman she had ever seen, long, red hair, delicately chiselled features, a classically proportioned body and a flowing, black, spiders' silk dress. She stood, brushed herself down, cleared her throat and asked,

'And you are?'

'I am Belinda Von Messier, I command this base, who are you and why are you in my office?'

'Well, I am Dorleith Ahralia, countess of Minidandia, Corsair, Pirate and occasional rabble-rouser, I have come to relieve you of your wardrobe.'

'My?...'

Her sentence was cut short by the timely arrival of the Doctor, his repeating siege bolt gun and two explosive shells to the head.

'We need to leave now Captain!'

'But...'

'No, now, one of the men thinks that he might have accidentally triggered some sort of self-destruct mechanism, it said 120 when I left, but it was counting down. Grab what you came for, we have to leave.'

The Captain looked across to the now, fully open cupboard and saw:

'Shoes!'

'We're leaving!'

'But... Shoes!'

When picked her up by the waist, threw her over his shoulder and ran. The sound of huge explosions getting closer and closer. By the time they reached the exit, the wall of flame was right behind them and he could feel his ponytail starting to shrivel. He threw himself into the pod and hit the launch button. He was deafened by the roar, but not before he heard the Captain say.

'Shoes... Lovely Shoes... All gone!'

(OK, much like the story about my son knocking the head off the snowman - My daughter went into Town and saw some nice boots, which she couldn't afford, only I, like, sexed it up a bit.)

The flight back from Chandra Isle to Long-Pig station had been surprisingly quiet, they'd had to avoid some company interceptors that had been sent to investigate the explosion, but it seemed that the base had either not had time to get off an alarm, or had not wanted to for some reason.

The Intercomm buzzed,

'Captain, this is Torville, Dorys' bed hasn't been slept in.'

Dorys was one of her finest marauders, she hadn't had time to do a headcount in the drop-pod when they had bounced back to the ship as the base was exploding.

'Are you sure she's not just gone landside?'
'No, no-one can remember seeing her since we made way.'
'Right, get the crew back aboard, we're going after her!'
'But Ma'am?'
'Now, Mr Torville!'
'Ma'am...'
'What!'
'It's Dr When's birthday, he'll be celebrating.'

The Captain disconnected the Intercomm and performed a sliding face-palm, her first officer was known for his somewhat salacious personal life, finding him on Long-Pig was bad enough normally, but the chances were - he wouldn't want to be found.

'Frobisher?' She called, addressing the brass head in the corner of the room,

'Aye Ma'am?'

'Is When's locator functioning?'

'No Ma'am, it appears to be disconnected.'

'You mean turned off?'

Frobisher's immovable features still managed to look slightly embarrassed.

'I don't suppose we can use the station's security cameras to locate the good Doctor can we?'

'I will try to connect.' The lights on his face cycled through the colours of the rainbow and settled on red, 'I'm afraid the security systems are significantly tighter than the last time.'

'Remind me why you're still connected Frobisher?'

'Ma'am, it's because the output from the old fusion engines that you insist on using fluctuates so rapidly that without me to correct the baffles, you would all die in a massive thermonuclear event.'

He was right, the engines were rated for a much smaller boat, that's why they had twice as many, but they were the only brass ones she could find, and they were beautifully engraved.

'I'm going landside,' She announced to the bridge-crew, 'If When comes aboard whilst I'm away, contact me immediately.'

The cries of 'Aye Ma'am!' were still ringing through the walkway as she reached the external door. Pressing the opening stud caused an alarm to sound and a recorded warning message to be played in Frobisher's voice,

'Danger, docking arm is currently located on the port side of the ship, attempting to open this door could cause personal injury or painful death. To reach the port docking area, please follow corridor A-24 to...'

'Override.'
'Warning, over-riding thi....'
'OVER! RIDE!'
'Acknowledged, opening starboard doors.'

The cargo doors opened with a squeal of protesting metal, she would skin the maintenance team alive when she got back aboard. She took a step back, breathed in deeply, and jumped through the still opening doors.

'Geronimo!'

The ground was around two hundred feet below her, giving her about six seconds before she became an unpleasant greasy stain on the floor. She continued to fall in a graceful swan-dive until there was less than fifty feet between her and a sudden stop, she grabbed hold of the steel hawser that connected the Edward Teach to the ground and engaged the grip function of her power-gloves. As he slowed, she could see the upturned faces of the roustabouts below her. At ten feet, she disengaged the gloves, back-flipped off the rope and landed, like a cat, on the deck.

She turned to the assembled men, gently blew the smoke from her palms and said,

'What? Have none of you swabs ever seen a lady get off a boat before?'

'Y... Y... You jumped!', said one of the dockworkers, a solid lump of off-green muscle. He pointed upwards, 'From up there!'

'Yes, yes I sort of did, didn't I? Anyway, have you seen my 1st Officer? Solid looking fellow, hair in a ponytail? Centauri accent?'

The assembled throng slowly shook their heads, or whatever they chose to keep their primary sensory organs in.

'He's in the Queen and Scorpion,' Said a tired voice from above, 'Behind the Governors building, follow the stream of tuppenny doxies, you can't miss it.'

'Thank you, Mr....?'

The wiry man perched on top of the tall pile of packing cases regarded her closely from under the brim of his hat , and replied,

'Preen, Criven Preen.'

'Thank you Mr. Preen, a credit for your trouble.' She tossed a ten credit piece up towards him, he raised his hand, the coin stopped dead in the air and fell to the ground.

'No thanks required... Ma'am,' He pulled the brim of his hat down over his eyes and his posture made it clear that that was the end of the conversation. She gave him one last look, sighed, and set off for the bar.

Preen was right, it was easy to find, there was an almost constant stream of 'ladies of negotiable virtue' flowing in both directions, both towards and away from the establishment. The latter looking significantly more flushed than the former, although they also looked to have fuller purses.

Arriving at the main doors, a quick glance towards the sign above her confirmed the building's identity. It portrayed a buxom female wearing a tiara, presumably the titular queen, her armoured suit mostly torn away apart from a few choice pieces that protected her modesty. She was standing on top of a construct in the shape of a scorpion, whilst tearing one of its legs off with her teeth - A nod to some half remembered skirmish with the Spiders perhaps?

'Where you go?' A grey reptilian paw grabbed her shoulder.

She slowly looked up, and then looked up some more, and saw a face that could only be described as belonging to a lightly furred T-Rex with rotten teeth and a single, long eyebrow.

She pointed around him, as well as she could, 'In there?'

'Nope, men only, no little girl allow in there, you be in big trouble.'

The Captain, shuddering, plunged her hand into the Doorman's cloaca and squeezed. The reptile dropped to his knees and he started to cry, 'You go... go inside... no charge... please... let go... Try the... Veal... come... back soon...' She left the giant reptile rolling around on the floor and walked into the gloom.

'When!'

'I got your When right here Bayb*urgh*' The stool caught the prurient patron under the chin.

'When! Where are you, you stinking pile of kraken guts?'

'In there...' replied a familiar voice, 'Through the door marked Whore-Pits.'

'It seems that I owe you thanks again Mr. Preen.'

With a deep bow, he disappeared back into the shadows. She turned towards the door, took another deep breath and turned the handle.

Even though she'd known When for many years, the sight of him naked, apart from some welding goggles and an odd pair of suspender socks, surrounded by over twenty women, in various states of undress, whilst what looked like a cross between a marmoset and a bagel played the harmonica in the corner was too much.

She unholstered her Sutter and Aitchinson Compression pistol and shot out the lights one by one.

The discordant music stopped instantly and When turned towards the source of his interrupted reverie.

'Who the... Ah, Captain, I...' He tried to cover his shame with a sadly undersized one hundred credit note.

'Find your drawers, pay anyone who needs paying and get back to the ship, we've got a rescue to organise!'

(The story continued the next day)

'Cheek'

The assembled bridge crew turned slowly to look at the Captain. She looked at When, the corners of her mouth pointing upwards in a barely noticeable smile.

'Dr. When, you have something on your cheek and I pray to the Gods that it's lipstick.'

'Aye Ma'am I'll see to it, erm..' The first officer patted the pockets of his waistcoat until he found one containing a silk handkerchief, which he produced, furtively, and wiped away the waxy mark.

'When?'

'Yes Ma'am?'

'When did you start buying handkerchiefs with gussets and waistbands?'

The hirsute privateer looked down at the scrap of silk in his hand, noticed the embroidered cog on the front and realised that he must have picked it up accidentally in his hurry to retrieve his clothes in the whore-pit. He quickly stuffed it back into his pocket.

'Frobisher, connect to The Great Cloud and look for reports of our little shopping trip to Chandra, specifically anything about prisoners.'

'Working...' The lights on the bridge dimmed slightly, 'No mention of the raid on normal channels, boosting power to access the Company network.'

'Be careful, this doesn't feel right...'

'Lines secured and encrypted, I am invisible to their security measures Ma'am.'

'If only you were inaudible too,' The Captain whispered, in a strangely good mood for someone who had recently lost a valued crewmember.

Frobisher's head turned towards her, paused petulantly and said, 'I have a report of a single captive, found unconscious at the scene with minor burns. She has been taken to the secure hospital aboard the Company ship Hellingly, currently en route to Nukuoro'

'Cut the connection!'

The lights on the construct's metal face resumed their normal cycling and the captain took a deep breath. Nukuoro was just outside the jurisdiction of the Democratic People's Republic of Australasia, it was a Company supply base during the first trouble with the Spiders. She'd visited there once, a long time before she was Captain of the Edward Teach, on a resupply raid. It was a barren ring of rock and sand barely four miles across, a few buildings, a fuel dump, and strangely, a small school.

'Helm, plot an intercept course for the Hellingly, take us high and quiet.'

'Course set, range just over a thousand miles, less than three hours at best speed,' the helmsman barked the numbers at they appeared on his display.

'No, take us slow, three-quarter speed at 20,000 ft. Make us look as much like a cargo barge as you can.'

When took a deep breath, opened the Intercomm and barked out his standard string of orders, 'All hands make ready to leave port. Secure all lines and hawsers, we will be breaking dock in 30 seconds, anyone still on board who's not on my roster'll be thrown over the side the second I find 'em, let me remind you that water's as solid as concrete from the height we'll be cruising at. All Doxies, Merchants and Pox-Doctors, off the ship now! Repeat - We are breaking dock in 25 seconds.'

The deck below them shifted as the docking cables were reeled in and the sudden release of pressure on the gasbags lifted her higher into the air. The station slowly receded into a small dot below them, as they reached 20,000 ft, the fusion engines started and the ship leaped forward like a scolded porpoise. Everyone waited for the traditional thundering crash from the Galley, but this time it seemed that the cook had finally learned his lesson.

'Blades out, make us look fat and non-threatening.' Called the Captain.

All over the hull, molecule-thin carbon-fibre sheets flowed out from between the hull plates, they billowed briefly, then caught the wind and took on the impression of solidity, what had once looked like a traditional buccaneer's ship now looked like a bloated, unarmed cargo barge, painted in an independent haulier's colours.

They sailed westwards for nearly four hours without incident until suddenly the Helmsman called that they were approaching the position where the Hellingly should be.

'All stop!' Called When, 'Scan for the big shiny bitch.'

'Nothing on scanners sir, nothing for 200 miles.'

'Sky's empty Captain, she must have changed course, we've lost her.'

The Captain stood, reached under her chair for her respirator, looked at When and said, 'Get your mask, we're going on deck.'

The air rushing from the pressurised door helped the reluctant Doctor out onto the deck and the cold atmosphere caused condensation to form on the outside of his brass respirator. He stayed well away from the guardrail as heights were his least favourite thing, next to sobriety, celibacy and hunger.

'Out of the way you bloody Jellyfish', called the Captain, her voice sounding muffled through her mask, 'Pass me the Glass!'

When passed her the magnifier, and she put it to her eye, the view was slightly blurred through the fabric of the blades, but she could see well enough to spot the Hellingly, two thousand feet below them and floating in the sunshine as bold as a halibut.

'Sky's empty?' Asked the Captain, 'Weren't those your exact words?'

'Aye... Well... Maybe the scanners need an overhaul?'

'Maybe you're lucky and they're cloaked or maybe we're being jammed.'

'Why would a hospital ship be cloaked?'

The Captain shrugged, 'I have no idea, but I mean to find out, let's get below before we have to insulate ourselves with layers of your stolen underwear.'

The Doctor's face reddened and he quickly made his way back below deck. The Captain paused to take a long look at the large silver airship below them.

'Hold on, we're coming for you...'

Back on the bridge, the Captain settled back into her chair, cracked her knuckles and opened a communications channel.

'Company Airship, this is the Cargo Ship... ah...' The Captain looked desperately at When,

'Tydirium?' Suggested When with a shrug,

'Tydirium. We have a minor medical emergency and request succour.'

There was no reply.

'Company Airship, I repeat, this is the...'

'Tydirium, this is the Company Hospital Ship Hellingly, we received your transmission but are unable to assist.'

'Hellingly, we have a crewman effected with what we believe to be an unknown toxin, we require immediate assistance as per Company regulations, Book thirty-six, subsection eighty-seven..'

'I know the regulations Captain! Hold for further instructions...'

The Captain muted the channel and turned to her first officer.

'When, you need to start acting sick, well, sicker...'

(And yet another day went by)

When sat in the operating chair in the middle of the Med-Bay, looking worriedly at the magnetised trays of medical instruments on the walls.

'What does that one do?' He asked, pointing at a curved, spiked blade around fifteen inches long.

The med-construct turned his head around to see where When was pointing, 'That's a Quanari birthing scoop, it holds open the...'

'Ugh... Doesn't matter, what about that one over there?'

'That's a number eight bifurcated Trunquor press, we won't be using that one, your species don't have a Trunquor, well, not one of any great size at least.'

'And that one?' When's voice was slowly rising in pitch and had almost reached the point where only bats could hear him. He pointed at a wickedly pointed lance, which was connected to the wall by a thick cable.

'That's the one I use to give myself high-voltage shocks when no-one's looking, it keeps my pincers steady,' He turned and whispered to the Captain, 'It's not Ma'am, it's an emergency defibrillator for people wearing body armour.'

The Captain shook her head, turned to When and said, 'Look, we won't be needing any instruments, we're just going to give you something that will make you look like you've been poisoned,' She turned to the construct, 'That can be reversed instantly?'

'Yes, in this,' he produced a syringe full of poisonous looking green and orange liquid, 'Is a mix of a weak synthetic Tubocurare and Variola, I can mix in an emetic if you require projectile vom...'

'No, thank you, the mild paralysis and boils should be enough I think.'

'As you wish. I will implant the curative in a capsule in his chest, a brisk blow will trigger it, he will be completely free of the toxin within ten seconds.'

'Excellent,' replied the Captain, 'I'll leave him in your capable hands.'

As the door slid closed behind her, she glanced back to see four of the Med-Construct's arms holding down the Doctor, whilst another waved the syringe, mockingly, around his face.

'Need to get that one's personality looked at when we get back to base,' she thought to herself as she headed back to the bridge.

'Mr. Landry, have we heard anything from the Hellingly?'

'No Captain,' Replied the young Communications Officer, 'Nothing since they told us to await further instructions.'

The Captain opened a channel, 'Hellingly, this is the... Tydirium, our crewman seems to have taken a turn for the worse, we respectfully request urgent medical assistance!'

'Please hold,' Replied an obviously synthetic voice. The channel went silent for fifteen or so seconds and then a human voice said,

'This is-a Gianni Eduardo of de Company Medical Corps - What eez eet dju need?'

'One of our crewman seems to have been bitten by an unknown insect, he's come out in boils and he seems to be paralysed from the neck down, we don't have the facilities to diagnose it, we wondered if?..'

'Djess, eet would be simple for us, we haff de top of der range medical equipments, I vill clear it wiz our Ceptain now. Prepare to brink djour man aboard, dockink bay six.'

She smiled as she switched the Intercomm to internal, 'Mr Russ? Prepare an aggie for Doctor When, load the hidden compartments with our standard boarding kit, don't forget the Doctor's chainsword - He'll never forgive you.'

'Aye Captain, I'll meet you in the Med-bay.' Growled Russ, still getting used to speaking around his newly implanted tusks.

'Aye Mr. Russ, and can we try to dress a little more like merchantmen this time? No longknives, no siege weaponry, no high-explosive grenades?'

'As you say.' The suddenly dejected marauder replied, in the background the Captain could just hear the sounds of dangerously shaped pieces of metal dropping to the floor.

The Captain turned to the Helmsman, 'Bring us alongside her, extend the docking tube to bay six and keep the engines spun up ready for a quick exit, and for the Gods' sake, try to remember that as far as they know, we're merchantmen!'

In the Med-bay, Russ was assisting the Med-construct in placing the unmoving Doctor onto the aggie, the already overloaded anti-gravity motors of the floating stretcher groaned as they took his weight.

'Could do with laying off the Suckling Pigs,' He commented.

'His Body Mass Index is well above the recom...' Replied the Med-construct

'Thank you Gentlemen,' Interjected the Captain, striding into the room, 'Can we not speak ill of the almost dead? Let's get him down to the docking bay.'

As they moved through the tube towards the Hellingly, The Captain turned to Russ, 'We're merchantmen remember, but be ready, the signal is me punching When in the chest.'

Russ nodded; As the door opened, they were confronted by six construct guards armed with pain sticks and a remote floating drone, effectively just a set of scanners and a speaker.

'Follow me, we will take you to Dr. Eduardo.' said the drone, turning away from them and moving towards the interior of the ship.

The Captain and Russ shrugged, and pushed the whining aggie in front of them. As they followed the drone, the construct guards fell into formation, three either side of them. They walked down a number of well-lit corridors and finally stopped outside a secure medical unit. The drone sang a short string of modulated beeps and the door opened. The group entered the room and the guards took up defensive positions around its perimeter.

'Zis iz der patient?' Asked Dr. Eduardo, pointing at When's prone form on the aggie.

'Yes, he's my First Officer,' Replied the Captain

'He looks very bat,'

'Erm... yes, he's been getting slowly worse over the last few days.'

'Ve vill soon haff him up and about and doink whateffer it is First Officers do!'

'Good... Oh no!... He's going into cardiac arrest!'

'Cardiac? No, my instruments clearly show zat...'

'No! he's dying!' The Captain hammered on When's chest 'Don't leave me, you're the best First Officer I've ever had!'

'But, dear laydee, he iz not haffink a heart atteck!.. Oh!'

Dr. Eduardo's exclamation was caused by Russ reaching underneath the aggie, pulling out an Ion Sprayer and de-activating all the guards and the surveillance systems with extreme prejudice. When eased himself upright and took his chainsword from its secret compartment, the boils on his face and hands quickly shrinking, but his head was still fuzzy.

'Where's my crewman you filthy patient molester?' Yelled When, waving his chainsword at the blurred shape in front of him.

'He's over there,' Whispered Russ, turning him to face the Company Doctor.

'Right, yes,' mumbled the Doctor, his vision clearing.

I... I... Don't know vhat... Please... vhat are djou talkink about?'

'You picked up a prisoner at Chandra, she was one of my crew, we want her back.' Explained the Captain.

'Prisoner? I don't know about zer prisoners, I'm an immunologist!'

'Damn!' breathed the Captain and delivered a blow to the side of his head that cleanly knocked him out, 'When, find out where Dorys is, Russ, clear us a route.'

When accessed a nearby computer terminal, 'She's in secure storage, just down the corridor, although we're about to have company.'

Russ grinned and pulled a blaster from the aggie, 'Follow the noise!'

He laughed and jumped out into the corridor.

(This is about the point where people started saying 'You should write a book')

'When? how do you feel?' Asked the Captain, her hand resting on the recently cured First Officer's shoulder.

'A bit groggy still, and itchy, very itchy, but I'll live Ma'am.'

'You'll need to do a damn sight more than that if we're going to get out of here, we need to catch up, Russ sounds like he's having far too much fun on his own!'

They raced out of the room and into the corridor, following the sound of blaster fire and raucous laughter. When restarted his chainsword, revved it a couple of times and ran headlong into the fray, sweeping it to and fro at waist height, chopping guards in half with gay abandon. The Captain stayed back at the junction, where she had a clear view down three corridors and contented herself with putting holes into the skulls of any constructs that came into view.

'When! Russ! Stop playing soldiers and clear me a path to Secure Storage!' The Captain yelled, so that she could be heard over the mechanical mayhem.

The Brigands looked at each other, grinned hugely and pushed forward. When's chainsword became stuck in the gears of a particularly large construct, four of its six arms continued to try to crush the life out of him as the toothed chain snagged and the engine stalled.

'Ooof! - KillIt!-KillIt!-KillIt!' Yelled the Doctor.

Russ reached under his Wolf skin cape and pulled out a siege bolter, which most people require two hands to use, and aimed at the construct's head.

'Hang on, let me get out of the...'

There was a deafening noise and the construct's head simply disappeared, along with part of When's luxuriant moustaches and a significant portion of the bulkhead in front of them.

'Which part of no siege weapons didn't you understand? How about Sudden loss of buoyancy? or Plummeting to a watery grave in a mass of tangled metal?' Barked the Captain.

Russ looked sheepishly at the Captain and then back to When, who was still trying to put out his smouldering facial hair. He holstered the siege bolter and continued forwards just using his blaster to clear a path. A mass of constructs was building up behind them and the Captain was doing her best to hold them off, but they were closing through sheer force of numbers.

'How many damn guards do you need on a medical boat?' She asked the empty air, whilst shooting a hole in the head of the nearest enemy.

'Door's locked Captain!' Yelled When from around the corner, 'As you'd expect I s'pose in somewhere called Secure Storage!'

She reached into her pocket, grabbed the Dentrassi lockpick and threw it over her shoulder. She heard it hit the wall and roll, then the familiar musical chirps as it started to work.

'Russ! come here and give me a hand whilst the Old Man does the technical stuff!'

The reply came in the form of a dozen blaster bolts whizzing from behind her into the broiling throng of mechanical defenders in front of her, exploding faces and shattering bodies into clouds of brass and copper, which seemed to buy them some breathing space.

'Thank you!'

'Captain, I've found her, she seems OK.' Said When's voice in her ear.

'OK, get her back here, we'll make our way to the docking bay.' The Captain thumbed the switch on her communicator, 'Teach, this is the Captain. We are making our way to the docking bay now, prepare for departure at best speed once we're aboard.'

'Captain, this is Landry, as soon as you started the rescue, the Hellingly severed the docking tube, we're holding station about 50 feet below the port bow.'

'Frak!'

'Captain?'

'Nothing, hold steady, we'll come to you.'

'Aye Ma'am, Landry out.'

When chose that moment to come into view with an unconscious Dorys draped over his shoulder.

You're making a habit of that Doctor,' Smiled the Captain, referring to her unusual forced exit from the base on Chandra Island.

'Aye Ma'am, I'm a sucker for a lady in distress, or dat dress, or any dress for that matter.'

'Mr. Russ?' Announced the captain, ignoring the Doctor's gallows humour, 'Make me a hole in that wall there, We need a way out'

Russ, slowly raised his blaster and aimed at where the Captain had pointed.

'No Mr. Russ, I think that something with a little more bite is required.'

He grinned and pulled out the siege bolter from behind his back, braced himself against the wall and started to fire repeatedly into the bulkhead in front of him. The explosive shells made short work of the wood panelling and the steel behind it. The sudden drop in pressure signalled that he had breached the hull, he stopped firing and spat on the glowing barrel.

'Now we go - Teach, this is the Captain, can you see the new hole in this nice shiny boat?'

'Yes Ma'am, on our way.'

'Good, position yourself as close as you can get, we're going to jump.'

'Aye Captain!'

'We're going to what?' Said When, looking at the limp form of Dorys.

'Russ goes first, you throw her, he catches her, then you jump and I bring up the rear - simple.'

They made their way through the damaged section of the ship until they reached the outside skin. The Edward Teach was just taking up position, ten feet away and five feet below.

'See you on the other side!' Yelled Russ and then he jumped. He managed to catch hold of one of the chains connecting the gasbag to the hull, slid down it hand over hand and took up position on the deck. He beckoned to the Doctor, 'Toss her over!' He yelled, trying to make himself heard above the wind.

When moved Dorys from his shoulder and held her in his arms, 'Lovely Theya, I'm going to apologise in advance... I never was very good at throwing, I was always picked last for the cricket team. Here she comes!' He took a run-up and launched her across the gap to the waiting marauder. As he let her go, her eyes opened, she looked at the hospital ship, and the sea far below her and started to scream, a scream that didn't stop until she landed in the paws of the fanged monster, braced on the deck.

A shot rang off the steelwork next to the Doctor's head, 'We need to get going!' He yelled to the Captain, who was busily laying down covering fire.

'You first, I'll follow you.'

'But, no you should...'

'When, if you don't jump now, I'll shoot you myself and use your liver as a parachute!'

'See you onboard!' He replied, flinching as another shot took a chunk out of the floor. He jumped the distance, landed heavily on the deck and rolled to a stop. Looking across at the massive bulk of the Hellingly, he watched the Captain firing shot after shot into the depths of the ship until her blaster ran out of charge. She threw the now useless weapon at the oncoming constructs and jumped.

She sailed through the air for what seemed like hours, and was only a few feet away when she realised that she wasn't going to make it.

'FFFFFFFUUUUUUuuuuuuuuuuu................!'

'NO!' Yelled When, forgetting his vertigo and rushing to the side-rail. But the Captain was nowhere to be seen. He stood there, unbelieving until Russ grabbed him by the shoulder.

'We need to get underway now, there are interceptors coming, don't let all this be for nothing!'

When nodded, took one last look over the side and went below.

'Full reverse, hit them with Daisy a few times to slow them down and then set a course for home, best speed,' Commanded When as he took the vacant Captain's chair.

'Where's the Captain?' Shouted Landry as the Helmsman scrambled to obey the Doctor's orders.

When looked at him and slowly shook his head. The forward viewscreen lit up as the shots from Daisy found their mark and the lights started to go out all over the Hellingly.

'Bring us about and rig for best speed.'

'Belay that!', came a feint, crackly voice from the Intercomm, 'Send someone to haul in the remains of the docking tube, which happens to have your Captain tangled in it and THEN rig for best speed. Oh, and When?'

'Aye Captain?'

'Get your arse out of my chair!'

(I had started the first draft of the first paragraph of the book here, it was very difficult writing two different stories about the same characters at the same time)

'Intruder Alert! Intruder Alert!' Yelled Frobisher, the lights in his face flashing from an angry red to a vile suppurating yellow, 'Unexpected lifesign detected in engineering! Intruder Alert!'

The captain jumped from her bunk, still groggy from the celebration after the successful rescue of Dorys, and her own return from an implied watery grave, 'Shut that damn alarm off you bag of rusty cogs! Security team to engineering deck, immobilize the intruder, whatever it is I want it alive!'

She pulled on her jodhpurs and kneeboots, rescued the crumpled linen shirt from the floor, buttoned it up and suddenly noticed the tousled hair of

Torville poking out from under the covers. The sound of his gentle snoring now obvious as the alarm had been silenced.

'Bugger!' She said, slowly lifting the covers and confirming that he was, in fact, naked, 'And double bugger!' She looked for slightly longer at the taut muscles on his back than was strictly necessary, then sighed and exited to the bridge.

The crew of the morning watch turned and saluted, 'Captain on the Bridge!' a crewman whose name she couldn't remember at the best of times yelled. The noise made her wince more than the alarm had, but she resisted the temptation to raise her finger to her lips and shush him.

'Why is there an intruder on my boat?' She asked the assembled throng as she sank into the command chair, 'Anyone?' A sea of blank faces was her only reply. She thumbed the Intercomm, 'Security team, have you found it - whatever it is?'

'Baju-Merah here Ma'am, engineering's clear, no-one here who shouldn't be here. We've checked everywhere!'

Frobisher chose that moment to voice yet another alarm, 'Intruder Alert! Intruder Alert! Unexpected lifesign detected in the Forward avionics cabin!'

'What?' exclaimed the Captain, 'That's at the other end of the... How? Frobisher, check the logs, was the intruder detected anywhere between Engineering and Avionics?'

'No Ma'am, the signal disappeared from Engineering and simply re-appeared in Avionics.' The emotionless brass face still managed to radiate an air of abject confusion.

'Mr. Baju-merah, report to Avionics, bring our unexpected guest to me now! Frobisher, perform a diagnostic on the internal scanners, if you've woke me up because you've gone defective I'll have When reprogram you, overarm, with his chainsword.'

The pattern of lights on Frobisher's face skittered as he performed the self-diagnostic, 'All sensors performing within prescribed parameters, zero defects found, my assumption is that my log entries are correct.'

'Then how the hell is something jumping from one end of this boat to the other without passing through all the points in-between?'

'I have no...'

'Rhetorical!' Shouted the Captain, 'Look it up.'

'I am fully aware of...'

'Ma'am, this is Baju-Merah. Avionics is clear, in fact, I don't think there's actually enough space in here for anything larger than a chicken.'

'Frobisher, is our intruder larger than a chicken?'

'Yes Ma'am, scans indicate that it is of standard dimensions for a humanoid male. And he is also no longer in Avionics.'

'Has he re-appeared somewhere else? The galley? Up on deck? In one of the Gasbags perhaps?'

'No Ma'am.'

'No, he hasn't re-appeared or No, he's not in the Gasbags?'

He has re-appeared, but it is in none of the areas that you suggested.'

'So, where is he pray tell?'

'In your quarters.'

She turned, along with the entire bridge crew, to face the door to her quarters. Activating the Intercomm she whispered, 'Mr. Baju-Merah, to the Bridge, as quick as you like.'

It only took the security team minutes to get to the Bridge, but in that time the Captain had armed herself with a compression pistol and a longknife. and was stood by the door.

'I'll go in first, you take up covering positions, stand close so the door doesn't close.'

'Ma'am, may I suggest that I...'

'Mr. Baju-Merah, I appreciate your concern, but the interloper hasn't shown any degree of hostility as yet. If anything, his antics seem to be designed to confuse us - He could have simply appeared behind any member of the crew and shot them in the back of the head if he'd wanted to.'

She took a deep breath and stepped through the door as it opened. The second her heel cleared the frame, it slammed shut at ten times its normal speed and locked. She spun and banged futilely on the door, then turned back to scan the room, her eyes slowly getting used to the gloom. The automatic lights had failed to turn on and even Frobisher's head was dark and silent.

'Torville!' She called, looking towards her bunk, 'Frobisher!' There was no reply from either of them. She felt her way forward, holding the pistol out in front of her. 'Where are you? Damn your Argh!' She rubbed her shin where it had rapped off one of the ornate castings on her iron bunk.

'Allow me,' Said a mellow voice from the far corner of the room, 'Lights!'

Instantly, the wall lights came back on. The Captain blinked, and turned towards the voice.

'You!' She raised the pistol and pointed it the wiry man sat in her easy chair, 'What are you doing on my ship?'

'At your service Captain,' Criven Preen raised himself from the chair, removed his hat and bowed deeply, 'I apologise for the dramatic means of my entrance, old habits die hard.'

'I'll say it again, only more forcefully... WHAT are YOU doing on MY ship!'

'There's no need for unpleasantness my Lady, nor should we have to worry about unfortunate accidents,' He waved his long fingers and the compression pistol slowly faded out of existence.

'Whu?' She looked down, the dull tingle in her fingers the only evidence that the gun had ever existed at all, 'How did you..?'

'A simple parlour trick, the weapon is back in its rightful place, in the arms locker, on the bridge... Your, ah, friend is also back in his rightful place, asleep, in his cabin. I took the liberty of removing the last twelve hours from his memory, saves any later discontent in the ranks.'

'What do you want?'

'Want? I want to deliver my message and go home, these things worry me,' He indicated the ship around him, 'If the Gods had meant us to fly, they would have given us gasbags.'

'Message? What message? Who is it from?'

'My Lady Dorleith Ahralia, Countess of Minidandia, In Nominate Ruler of the Open Lands, High Voort of the Shattered Spire and Keykeeper of the Pewter Army - I bring greetings from your Illustrious Father, Massimo Lohlephel, Baron of...'

'My Father? My Father fell at the Battle of Tromega, I saw his ship explode! He's dead!'

'Not... anymore...'

(The penultimate part, which comes next, has elicited real tears from some of the people that the characters were based upon – Which goes to show something, I think, probably.)

She stood on the bridge of the Grabthar's Hammer, next to her Mother's heavily decorated command chair. The battle had been raging for nearly an hour now and the sky was dark with Spiders.

'Alexander! Report!' Baroness Bhin-dhee of Minidandia yelled at the battleship's ancient AI.

'We are currently outnumbered five to one, we have Spider interceptors inbound on bearings zero-four-two, one-two-four, three-five-eight and…' Replied the ornately lit brass and copper head in the corner of the bridge.

'Enough!' She turned to Dorleith, 'let's see if we can find your Father shall we? He'll probably be needing a hand about now?'

The eleven year old girl looked up at her Mother and smiled, she knew exactly where her Father would be, right in the middle of the biggest, thickest ball of Spiders that he could find, tearing them out of the air with his bare hands if he had to. It was hard for her to understand why he hated the Spiders so much, even back at the Roost, before she was old enough to come along with her parents on the raids, every story he told ended up with his knife being plunged into a tabletop, or a crystal goblet of brandy being thrown into the fire, and him stomping off hurling obscenities at whoever got in his way.

'DiGriz, this is The Hammer, Where are you, you old goat?' The static from the speakers indicated that they were out of range, 'Alexander, what was the last known position of the DiGriz?'

'Our Cruiser, the James DiGriz, last known position bearing two-six-four, distance four miles,'

'Show me.'

The main screen changed from the tactical display to a map showing Northern Macedonia, the flashing red dot indicating the last known position of the James DiGriz was hovering over the mountains to the west.'

She opened the shipboard Intercomm, 'All hands, this is the Captain, we're rendezvousing with the DiGriz, any gunner that has a Spider in their sights, take it out now and make ready defensive positions, keep those mechanical scum off my hull,' She turned to the helmsman, 'Lay in an intercept with the DiGriz, let me know when we're in communications range.'

'Aye Ma'am, course laid in... Captain!'

'Aye?'

'We're going to have to fight for every yard, that course'll take us through a cloud of Spiders a mile thick,'

'Gods damn it Mr Hadleigh, bring Mary online, divert power from the engines to her and fire as you get a target.'

The deck thrummed as power poured from the great fusion engines at the rear of the airship, to the Ion cannon that occupied almost the entire front half. The Grabthar's Hammer had been built around this big gun, it was designed to kill the Spiders' electrical systems and render them inoperative en-masse but unfortunately, because it was so powerful, they could only fire a few shots before they needed to cool and recharge.

The first blast took nearly one hundred spiders out of the fight, their systems fried as their lifeless husks fell onto the ruins of what used to be Kumanovo.

'Well Ma'am, that certainly seemed to have got their attention, we have fifty... No, sixty targets inbound, five seconds before we can fire Mary again!'

'Fire as she becomes ready, Helm, then as soon as she fires, hard a-port, bring us broadside to the cloud. All starboard guns, be ready to fire as you acquire a target!'

Mary barked again and the sun-bright blue flare carved another chunk out of the cloud of chittering limbs and spines. The Helmsman dragged the ship hard to the left, airbrakes and scoops deploying all down the port side, the connecting chains to the gasbags groaned with the sudden tension as the deck slewed drunkenly below them.

The Captain grabbed hold of her chair and held onto her Daughter with her other hand.

'You alright?' She shouted, over the blare of the bridge alarms.

'Aye Ma'am,' replied the little girl, attempting a salute,

'Good Girl, strap yourself in, it's going to get bumpier before it gets calmer. Mr Hadleigh!'

'Aye, Ma'am?'

'Keep us headed in the direction of the DiGriz, but initiate a Crazy Ivan, let's clear ourselves a gap.'

'Aye, All hands! Prepare for violent manoeuvres, we will be initiating a Crazy Ivan in five seconds, tie yourself to something solid and find yourself something to be sick into.'

The ship slewed hard right, as Mary pointed towards the enemy she fired, scooping great swathes of Spiders out of the cloud, then the Hammer came full broadside to them and the deck guns fired another cannonade. The left-right movement continued for two miles until the Helmsman cried,

'Captain, I'm getting a signal from the DiGriz!'

'Onscreen!'

Through the interference on the viewscreen, the unmistakable silhouette of her Father appeared, he had his favourite monomer edged cutlass in one hand and a repeating ion pistol in the other, he was in mid-flow.

'… Damn your eyes, man if I thought for a second you were running from your post I'd show you your own liver before making you eat it…' The picture faded and then snapped back into sudden clarity, 'Get off my bloody ship!'

He had the head of a Spider impaled on the end of his sword and was rapidly beating it against the bulkhead.

'Massimo?'

'I'll kill ye, I'll kill every one of ye, you'll wish you'd never been riveted…'

'Massimo!'

'I'll hunt down where ye wuz made, an I'll kill everyone there, then I'll find where the constructs that made ye wuz made, and I'll kill them, then I'll…'

'MASSIMO! – I think it's dead!'

'Aye, Whut?' The bear of a man that was Baron Massimo Lohlephel blinked the red mist from his eyes and looked at his screen, 'Ah, hullo my Sweet Flower, Mist of my Midsummer Morning! Ah.. I'm.. a bit busy at the moment, I'll pull out your eyes you clanking contraption… No, not you Dear, I'll get back to you in a wee while…' He turned away from the camera and yelled, 'Get that bloody million legged abomination off my bridge Mr Cotterill!' And with that, the connection went dead.

'Alexander, can you contact the Slut?'

Dorleith giggled, The Slut was her Mother's pet name for Angelina, the AI on board her Fathers ship.

'Aye Ma'am, connection established.'

'Get a status report on the DiGriz's systems.'

'They have multiple hull breaches, Spider boarding craft cover the entire fore-section of the ship, there are more mechanical lifesigns on board than the internal sensors can reliably count.'

'Damn! Are we close enough to fire on the Spiders without hitting the DiGriz?'

'Not with any degree of certainty Ma'am, no.' Replied Hadleigh.

'Take us in, weapons free, fire at will!'

The Hammer lurched forward, Mary and the other cannons killing Spiders in all directions as they went.

'Erm, Captain?'

'Yes?'

'We're slowing down!'

'What?'

We're slowing, I've lost control of the throttles... We're... We're in full reverse?'

'Alexander, what in the seven hells is going on?'

'The James DiGriz has invoked remote access; they are controlling us for the moment.'

'What? Can we over-ride the signal?'

'No Ma'am, Angelina has locked me out of my own control systems; I will be having stern words with her when we get back to the Roost... Ah!'

'What now?'

'I am detecting a tritium leak in the the DiGriz's starboard engine, there are signs of an impending cascade event.'

'Get them onscreen... Now!'

The main viewer sprung into life, Captain Lohlephel was sat, calmly in his command chair. The bridge was swathed in smoke and the sound of gunfire could be heard in the distance.

'Hullo my Jewel, I'm sorry about pushing you away..'

'What're you doing Goat?'

'I'm saving your life...'

'I don't...'

'Angelina informs me that my engines are just about to go critical, and the lifepods are covered in Spiders, so I'm going to take as many of these mechanical monsters with me as I can.'

'No!.. I... I fought my way here, I've come to save you... We can...'

'You know this is the only way, Is Dorleith there?'

She nodded and beckoned her daughter across, 'Daddy wants to talk to you.'

'Hello Daddy!'

'Hullo Beautiful Girl, hope you're OK. I'm sorry, I've got to go now, but I know you'll keep on fighting... Don't let the Spiders win, try to stop 'em any way you can.'

'I will Daddy, I promise!'

'I know Baby. I love you both so much.' He put his hand on the viewscreen, 'I…..'

A freezing globe of tritium gas rapidly expanded from the rupturing engine, which then ignited in a ball of fire two miles across. The main windows of the bridge exploded into shards which spread across the room like knives, narrowly missing the dumbfounded crew.

'DADDY!'

'I beg your pardon?' Criven Preen's calm voice brought the Captain back to the present, she slowly looked around and realised that she was once again in her cabin on the Edward Teach.

'Nothing… I just remembered…'

'Yes, indeed, nasty business, your Mother has the details, if you wish to help.'

'Help?'

'Yes, your Father needs rescuing.'

'Rescuing?'

'Yes, rescuing, you have been following my conversation haven't you?'

'Well, no, I…'

'I see, well, I suggest you talk to your Mother, she has the details. Now, I need to leave, I have other errands to attend to.'

'Can we drop you anywhere?'

'No, that won't be necessary, thank you.' He doffed his hat, stepped back into the shadows, and was gone.

'I…' She turned and re-entered the bridge, 'Set a course for Minidandia, best speed, and get the ship tidied up, we're going to visit The Baroness.'

(And here's where this story winds up for the times being, I hope you've enjoyed it)

'Roost traffic control, this is the Edward Teach, requesting landing clearance.'

'Good morning Edward Teach, you are expected, please make your way to dock four. Five knot speed limits apply and will be enforced.'

'Understood, dock four, thank you Roost traffic control, you bloody officious pile of scrap tin and frayed wires.'

Everyone on the bridge turned to look at When.

'What? No damn construct's telling me how fast I can pilot my own boat in friendly airspace!'

'Whose boat, Mr When?' The Captain asked as she strode through the door from her quarters onto the Bridge.

'I... I mean, we... That is, obviously, she's your boat Captain... I... I just meant that...'

'Calm down man, when I'm not on the bridge, better yet, when I'm not actually on board, feel free to think of the Teach as your own. Although I'd like to think that you'd treat your own ship better than you treat this one sometimes. You still owe me a new boarding tube.' She sat in her command chair and surveyed her screens, 'Which dock has she put us in?'

'Erm... Four.'

'FOUR?' She jumped back up and stormed towards the main viewer, 'Four is the bay where the garbage cutter docks on a Friday morning!'

'Lucky for us that it's Wednesday then,' Commented Landry, the Communications Officer, with a smile.

She turned slowly towards him, and the colour drained out of his cheeks, 'Mr Landry, who are we exactly?'

'Captain... I don't...'

'Let's start with something a little simpler, Who are you?'

'Carter Landry, Ma'am, I don't see...'

'Ah-ah, and what do you do?'

'I'm... I'm the Communications Officer,'

'Where?'

'On board the Edward Teach?'

'Yes, well done. What kind of ship is the Teach?'

'She's a Corsair...'

'And who is the Captain?'

'You are Ma'am, obviously. I meant no disrespect!' He looked at When, with a growing glint of panic in his eyes.

'Don't look at him, he can't help you. Next question, where are we?'

'At the Roost, your family home... But...'

'Ah! Finally, there we have it! We're at my family home, where my loving Mother and Brother will no doubt be waiting for us with open arms and a twelve course banquet.'

When stifled a laugh.

She shot him a look made of knives and thunder, 'Can you see why I'm upset that they're making us dock in what is, effectively, a garbage chute?'

'Yes Ma'am, of course, I completely understand. I'm sorry...'

'I'm glad we all understand each other. Frobisher!' She shouted, not taking her eyes off the quivering young officer.

'Aye Ma'am?'

'Connect to traffic control and get us a better berth will you, there's a good disembodied head!'

The lights flickered on Frobisher's face as he inveigled his way into the Roost's network.

'Edward Teach, this is Roost traffic control, please cease and desist you efforts to connect to...' There was a loud crackle as the communication signal was cut and reconnected, 'Edward Teach, please make your way to dock two. Fifteen knot speed limits apply but will not be enforced.'

'Fifteen knots, but not enforced?' Mouthed When to the Captain.

'You expressed a concern that five knots was too slow for our purposes, so I took the liberty of increasing the dock speed limit and disabling the pressor emitters whilst I was connected.' Replied Frobisher, an air of smugness radiating from his expressionless face.

'Very good, Dr. When, bring us into dock two, try to keep us below fifty knots and if you take any more paint off the hull I'll skin you and use you to patch that slow leak in the number three gasbag.'

'Aye Ma'am!' Grinned the First Officer. He opened the Intercomm, 'All hands, prepare for docking at the Roost, this will be a...' He looked at the Captain questioningly, she shook her head slowly, 'A short visit, grab what decent food you can and if you need equipment, Ask for it, don't steal it, these people are our friends'

The airship turned majestically and made headway towards the Roost. The stark cliffs of the Captain's home coming into view piecemeal through the mountain mist, showing the vast extent of the ancient estate. She missed her home and her family, but her Mother's disapproval of how she made her living made these visits few and far between. They were less than five hundred meters away when the green landing indicators lit up around the entrance to dock two, and the huge steel doors started to grind open.

She sat back into her seat and braced herself, When always showboated his way into the Roost and she was sure that this time was not going to be any different. He took up a position behind the helmsman and cracked his knuckles.

'Roost traffic control, this is the Teach, we're having difficulty with our landing automatics, we will be docking manually.'

'Acknowledged Edward Teach, dock two is cleared for approach. Emergency services have been advised.'

When cut the connection and pouted, 'I said that we were coming in on manual, not on fire...'

'They've seen you dock before, obviously.' Grinned the Captain.

He glared as he took the controls, gunned the engines and aimed the ship straight at the broad, glass windows of the traffic control centre. The Teach jumped forward, her tethered gasbags struggling to keep up with the sudden acceleration.

'Ramming Speed!' Yelled When over the squeals of the over-stressed connecting chains.

He waited until he could see the screaming faces of the traffic control team through the armoured glass, and the heavy shutters of their collision screens starting to deploy before he turned abruptly and headed for the docking bay. Cutting the engines, he allowed the ship to turn around completely so that it was facing backwards and applied full burn on the manoeuvring thrusters. She entered the bay stern first and coasted slowly to a halt just as the docking tube engaged on the hull.

The Captain turned to the bridge crew. 'Secure engines and thrusters, rig the gasbags for neutral buoyancy and for gods' sake lock the cargo bays, we don't want any inquisitive members of the Pewter Guard nosing about in my booty.'

The crew dissolved into fits uproarious laughter.

'What? Why are you all laughing?'

They all turned towards her, and seeing her reddening face, started to laugh even louder.

'What are you laughing at? Mr Landry, When, stop laughing! I'll keelhaul the lot of you if you don't stop laughing.'

Luckily, they were laughing so loud that they didn't hear the Pewter Guard Commander on the viewscreen, demanding to know why they'd docked their sloppily patched, scab ridden junkpile of a corsair in the Baroness' personal dock.

Else there'd have been a massacre.

43 - YOU DO KNOW HOW A BUTTON WORKS DON'T YOU? NO, NOT ON CLOTHES.

Time for a few more IT Hijinks. You'd think that the kind of people who use computers on a daily basis, as an important part of their job, would have some basic idea of how they work, or at least how to do what they use them for day in and day out?

You'd think that wouldn't you..

I wanted to use a quote from 'The IT Crowd' as a title, and I just got caught up reading through the quotes from Series One, and then I had to have a bit of a sit down and a rest because I couldn't breathe properly because I was crying with laughter - I couldn't even tell my workmates what I was laughing about, I was, quite literally, unable to speak.

Anyway, as you've probably guessed by now, this chapter is IT related. In it I will relate a few more of the things that have happened to me over the years. During the time when I had to resist slamming peoples' foreheads onto their desks on a daily basis.

The following few 'incidents' that happened whilst I was working for the popular Midlands Builders' Merchant 'Where the Trade Go'. And are all, as ever, completely hamster-fondlingly true.

The thing you don't want to have happen when you've just got into the office after a two and a half hour drive, is to be told that one of the London stores cannot trade because their server has crashed. Do you know how most Back-Office server crashes are fixed in Midlands based Builders' Merchants? Yes, that's right, you turn it off and then back on again.

So, after someone had made coffee for the team, I called the store, with the intention of talking whomsoever answered the phone through the aforementioned task. The sales desk phone rang out... The office phone rang out... Then I took a deep breath and called the Manager's phone.

Now, before we go any further, let me just say that most of the Store Managers we had at the time were pretty good, they knew exactly as much about computers as we did about selling screwdrivers, and that was fine - We understood each other's limitations, but this particular guy was a bit... special. Imagine Del-Boy's mind in a Bond villain's body, but with the vocabulary of Father Jack Hackett. He was also known for having a lot of temper, but not a lot of patience.

He picked up the phone.

'Yeah?'

'Oh Hi, it's Dandy from IT...'

'Yeah?'

'You've got a problem with your system, you can't process any sales?'

'What?'

'The computer, that runs the tills, has stopped working.'

'Why?'

'Well, we're going to take a look at that in a minute, but we can't log into it, we need you to restart it.'

'What?'

'The big computer, in the metal box, in the office... We need you to turn it off, is that OK?'

'Yeah,' then he dropped the phone, and it went dead... For about ten minutes, then he picked it up again, 'It's not working.'

'Right, OK, Sorry, what exactly do you mean when you say that it's not working?'

'It won't turn off.'

'So, you're pressing the round button on the front?'

'Yeah.'

'With the little green light?'

'Yeah.'

'And it won't turn off?'

'No.'

'OK, can you hold it in and count to ten for me, see if it turns off then?'

'Yeah,' He dropped the phone again, this time, I had time to go and get a sandwich, when he came back he said, 'No, doesn't work.'

'OK, what I need you to do now is...'

'I'm too busy, send someone to fix it.'

'Well, we just need to...'

'Too busy, Bye,' Then he put the phone down.

So, we were stuffed, 'someone' had to drive to London and get the store working again. OK, it was only about a 200 mile round trip and it was a nice day, but I had been nominated as the 'someone'. (Like you hadn't guessed that already). The trip down the M40 took a couple of hours, but on this occasion no laser printers were harmed.

I wandered into the cavernous store and made myself known to the guys there. I went behind the counter and knocked on the door of the manager's office, which was duly opened by the man in question.

'Yeah?'

'Alright? I've come to see why your computer won't turn off.'

'Right.'

I went into his office, where the little rack was sat in the corner, covered in dust.

'Can you show me what you did?'

'Yeah,' He wandered over to the cabinet and pushed the button, 'Doesn't work, see?'

'Ah, I think I've found your problem, the round thing that you're pressing is actually the Dell badge, the power button is the 'other' round thing on the front, with the green light...' I held in the button, powered off the server, turned it back on and service was restored.

I then had a fry-up for my lunch, got back in the car, and drove the 100 odd miles back to Birmingham...

Funnily, the remaining two stories are also about a London store, the same one in fact, well, not the same one as the one above, these two stories are about the same one. (That made a lot more sense in my head) However, this one was managed by a wonderful guy, He was an ex-mountain, I don't mean Mountain Rescue, or Mountaineer, but an actual honest to goodness mountain. He was computer literate, outspoken and he knew how to motivate staff, usually by causing a small avalanche to form in their general direction.

Anyway, we'd just installed the new system at his store and we were going through the basic training. The tills that we had installed were touchscreens, but you need to remember that this was in the days where phones didn't have them, but PDAs (remember them?) did.

So our training guy had given the sales assistants their standard half-day's training and was spending the afternoon going from till to till, with the manager, watching them putting sales through and answering questions. I was tagging along, just for the hell of it really, I should have gone back to the office, but I was trying to spin it out a bit and then go straight home.

We came to one young lady, who was fastidiously using the keyboard and mouse rather than the touch screen, we looked at each other, looked at her, looked at each other again, and the manager said to me,

'You did check the touchscreen was working didn't you?'

'Yes, definitely.'

'Then, why isn't she using it?'

'You're asking the wrong person Dude, sorry,' I said, and pointed to the assistant.

He sighed, waited until she'd finished serving her customer, walked over and asked,

'Why aren't you using the touchscreen? We pay a lot of money for them you know'

'I'm waiting for the thingy'

'You're doing what to the who-now?'

'The thingy, the pokey thing, you know?' She mimed the stabbing scene from Psycho.

The manager turned to me and shrugged in a very accusatory fashion, which is fairly difficult if you think about it, 'Pokey thing? Do we supply pokey things?'

'I think she means a stylus'

'Yeah! stylus, I'm waiting for the stylus,'

'Oh! the Stylus, why didn't you say,' He beamed, 'They each come with ten, and they're pink, you'll love them!'

'Really?'

'Oh yes!' He exclaimed as he reached down and took hold of her wrist, 'Here they are look, one.. two.. three.. four.. five... and the rest are on your other hand!'

The store had been trading for a while, and everything was both Hunky and Dorey. We were well into the business as usual phase and we'd handed the support of the store over to the Helpdesk. One day I overheard a conversation that one of the girls was having with the store.

'I just need you to press 'Escape'... No, that's 'Return'... Escape is the one in the top, left hand corner... No, not F1, next to F1, it has E.S.C. written on it... It's definitely there... You are using a computer aren't you?... Well, what's in the top, left hand corner then?' She pressed the mute button on her phone and asked me,

'Dandy, do we give the stores keyboards without an escape key?'

'Not to my knowledge, no, ask them if their keyboard looks the same as another one there.'

'OK, good idea,' She took the caller off hold and asked, 'Can you see another keyboard? Right, has that got an 'Escape' key? No? Can you check another? What about the one in the office? Yeah, I'll wait... What? That hasn't got one either? I don't really understand...'

'Why don't you just log into her computer remotely, do what you need to do, and we'll look at it later?' I suggested, which is what she did.

We thought it was odd, and had a laugh about how stupid you'd have to be to not be able to find the Escape key on a keyboard, but eventually we forgot about it.

Until, I was visiting the store some weeks later, about something completely unrelated when I suddenly had the need to get my email. I went into their little office, logged on, started my email and chanced to look down at the keyboard. Where the Escape key should be there was a hole, no key, no spring, no button, just a hole. I collared one of the guys behind the counter.

'Are all your keyboards like this?'

'Yeah, the Manager did it.'

'Why did he do that?'

'Well, someone from IT said that if we hit Escape while we were doing a Credit Card transaction, it'd muck it up and the sale would go through but the customer wouldn't be charged.'

'OK...'

'So he decided that the best way to make sure we didn't do that was to take the key away.'

'Did he use a drill?'

'Yeah, I think he did...'

'I'll order you some new ones.'

So, it seems he wasn't quite as IT literate as I'd initially thought, although I guess it was lateral thinking on his part.

44 - TITLE *REDACTED* FOR SECURITY REASONS

First of all, let me explain the title of this one, I was hurrying so much to get this particular page posted that I forgot to give it a title. One of my many loyal readers called me on it and I made a huge joke about MI5 having to vet all of my posts, or some such nonsense.

It's actually a rant about the prostitution of peoples' good names for the sake of fashion… And I sort of go off on one, but still worth a read I think.

-oOo-

So, a quick one today on a subject dear to my heart, and one I find myself infinitely qualified to talk about...

Yes, you've got it...

Fashion.

What? stop laughing at the back... I'll have you know that I'm very fashionable, perhaps not in the sense of 'current' or 'accepted' fashion, but I'm a dapper Dandy when you get me down to my nitty-gritties, (as more than a few people have).

My specific gripe (today) is the bastardisation of things that are inherently cool by big business, purely to make money out of the ill-educated herd. You've all seen the Christian Audigier clothes branded with the 'Ed Hardy' and 'Von Dutch' logos right? Generally worn by the sort of people you would actively cross the road to avoid, I think I might have labelled them as Gits in a previous Chapter, a description I wholeheartedly stand by.

If there wasn't the danger of the person turning out to be a confirmed multiple stabbist, I would go up to people wearing an Ed Hardy T-shirt and ask probing questions like:

Who is Ed Hardy? (He's a retired tattoo artist from California, Taught by Sailor Jerry)

What was his first name? (Don)

Why are you wearing a shirt with a person's name on that you don't know? (Because I'm a member of the herd and a guy on Jersey Shore told me to)

If they could answer any of those questions I would give them a shiny five pound note. The likelihood is of course that they will look at me askance and drool slightly out of the corner of their mouths.

Thinking about it, Von Dutch is even worse, the guy was a genius, Kenny Howard (Von Dutch's real name) was a Bike-Builder and painter from the '50's, he's acknowledged as one of the fathers of Kustom Kulture, along with people like Big Daddy Roth and he finally joined that hallowed rank of people who have drank themselves to death - And a more typical Rock-and-Roll exit would be difficult to orchestrate (Unless it involved a Hot-Rod, painted like a flaming devil's phallus, being driven off the rim of a volcano, into the lava, playing Little Richard songs, but exploding before it hit in a quiff shaped explosion that smelled of Brylcreme)

There are people out there of course, who wear Von Dutch gear completely non-ironically, but they are the people who drive restored Chevy Stepsides and attend Rock 'n' Roll weekenders all over the country. These people are great, you should buy these people beer and/or ice-cream whenever you see them. (I am not one of these people before you ask, my involvement in this scene is restricted to respecting the work done by Betty Page, but most of them are pretty Gorram cool)

The reason this particular subject came to mind is that Steampunk has been identified as the next mainstream style 'trend' - OK, it's going to be watered down, as these things tend to be. I don't think we're going to see people wandering around in brown leather top hats with goggles permanently attached to them, or Dorothy Perkins selling Victorian style ray-guns in their accessories department. But I do sense a definite increase in things with cogs on them (because when you get down to it, that's what people who've heard about Steampunk, but don't know about Steampunk, think Steampunk is).

I'm not afraid to admit that like things a bit Steampunked-up, I'm a dyed in the wool anachronist when it comes down to it. But the first time I see someone on TOWIE wearing a brown leatherette corset, adorned with an ammunition bandolier and a scattering of diamante cogs, I will go to my hand-made, Ugandan Teak carcased, purple velvet lined, gun cupboard, take out my brass trimmed Fortune & Sanderson Discomnervulator 5000 and go on the rampage.

I truly will - And no-one without a handlebar moustache, impressive décolletage or pith-helmet, worn unironically, will survive.

45 - DANNY IN THE WOODS.

This chapter is another story I'm afraid, it's a kind of sequel to a piece of Flash Fiction that I wrote that was included in Volume 1 of the James Josiah Flash Project Collection. Which is also available from Amazon on your Kindle.

The story was called Danao, which is sort of the Chinese word for 'Brains'.

Zombie apocalypse fiction was very popular at the time, and this was my contribution to the genre, as well as it being another one of my 'sexed up' real life stories – See if you can figure out what happened in the real world before I tell you at the end.

-oOo-

The old Landrover bounced over the uneven ground, its ancient leaf springs making some very concerning noises.

'How far Ranth?'

'I don't know, that survivalist guy we found said that we just had to follow the river and we'd trip over them, you know exactly as much as I do.'

They'd been following the river for hours, there was nothing indicating that a settlement was nearby, no smoke, no signs, no nothing.

'Do you think we'll find him there?'

'Ellie, I don't know, but it seems that this is the only settlement for miles, can't think where else he'd run to.'

Ranth was starting to get sick of Ellie's constant questions, She'd found him hanging from a tree, luckily by his wrists not his neck, about a week ago. He said that it'd all been a big misunderstanding with a group of outlaw survivors that he used to run with, she wasn't so sure that they hadn't just got sick of his incessant talking.

'Wait! What's that?' Ellie pointed into the trees, 'I saw something move!'

Ranth stopped the 4x4 and looked into the trees,

'Where?'
'Over there, by that big rock, it's a shambler, I know it!'
'I can't see anything.'
'Look, between the rock and that dead tree, you can just see its head.'

Ranth took the binoculars out of her pack and looked again, scanning the treeline for the rock,' I see it, ' She said, 'It's not a shambler, not any more at least.'

'What is it then?'
'It's a skull, on a stick.'

They looked at each other, Ellie paled; Ranth started the engine and turned the car towards the grim totem. The skull wasn't that old, and it looked as if the local wildlife had been helping themselves to whatever choice morsels they could find.

'Looks like we've found the settlement then,' Said Ellie,
'Unless someone's got very interesting ideas about garden furniture,' Replied Ranth, 'Whoever they are, one of them's a decent shot, blew the top of the head clean off,' She poked her fingers into the hole where the cranium used to be. 'We'll continue on foot, get your gear.'

They'd only been travelling for a few minutes when a disembodied female voice sounded through the trees.

'Stop where you are, put your hands in the air.'
'Do as she says,' Whispered Ranth, she raised her voice and shouted, 'We don't mean you any harm, we're looking for someone!'

A rustling of leaves above their heads made them look up, to be greeted by the sound of snapping twigs and the silhouette of someone making their way through the branches, towards the trunk of a huge Elm tree. They looked at each other again, and shrugged.

'Don't move, we have you covered!', said another, younger, voice from behind them.

The tree-creeper dropped to the ground and immediately drew a Desert Eagle handgun, that was obviously much too heavy for her. She was about thirteen years old, with matted blond hair and about six weeks' worth of mud covering her face and arms.

'What do you want?' She growled, never taking her eyes off them.

'Like I said, we're looking for someone.'

'Who?'

'Well, I don't exactly know, but he stole something from us whilst we were asleep a couple of days ago and we think he came this way.'

'Nobody comes this way, not if they've got any sense at least, not since Danny came.'

'Danny?'

'Yeah, he lives in the woods, we hear him at night sometimes, stumbling around.'

'A Shambler?'

'No, he kills shamblers, that's where we get the skulls from.'

'The skulls?'

'We use them to mark our territory, the shamblers mostly stay away, I don't think they like their own dead.'

'Can you take us to your settlement, so we can ask about the man who stole our stuff?'

'Settlement?' She laughed, 'There's no settlement any more... Not since Danny came.'

'Well, where do you live?'

'Here,' replied the girl with a smile, 'In the trees, we don't bother Danny, he don't bother us.'

'Can we talk to Danny?'

Both of the children started to laugh, 'You can try, but he doesn't say much.'

'What do you mean?'

'He mostly just says his name, we think he might be simple, but we don't want to get close enough to find out, he's too big and funny looking - You can try if you like, he's in there somewhere,' She pointed into the forest.

'Come on,' Ranth turned to Ellie, 'Let's see if we can get some answers out of Danny.'

Picking up their packs they started off into the jungle, being careful not to make too much noise as they trod through the heavy undergrowth. they were starting to lose the light when they both stumbled and fell to the ground with a shout.

'What the?'

'I think we're getting close... What was the guy who stole the gear out of the Landrover wearing?'

'Erm... Brown leather jacket, cargo pants... I think.'

'Like these?' Ranth held up a scrap of brown leather and some beige canvas, both covered in blood.

'Exactly like that... Should we leave?'

'When we've got what we came for, it must be around here somewhere.'

'Seriously?'

'Do you have anything left to barter when we run out of diesel next?'

Ellie shook his head.

'Well then.'

They started to poke at the grass, avoiding the bloody mess that had once been the thief, trying to find the box of trinkets that was their only remaining currency in the world.

'Did you hear that?'

'Don't tell me, a shambler?'

'No, there's someone talking, shamblers don't talk... Do they?'

'Nope, that's the one thing I like about them,' Ranth gritted her teeth as she lifted the remains to search underneath.

'Maybe it's the kids, it sounds weird though, too deep.'

'Ha!' Shouted Ranth, as she held aloft a gore spattered box, 'Right, let's go!'

They both stood and started to make their way back to the path, when there was the noise of splintering wood from behind them. Slowly, they both turned, to be confronted by the oddest thing that either of them had ever seen.

'You can see a panda, right?' Ellie breathed.

'Unfortunately, yes...'

'There's good eating on a panda, probably,' Ellie slowly reached for his gun.

'Maybe it's Danny's pet,' replied Ranth, 'I think he'd be upset if we shot it and ate it...'

'Danao.'

'What?'

'I didn't say anything.' Ranth whispered, pointing at the panda and backing away,

'But, panda's don't...'

'Danao!'

'That panda spoke!'

'Back away, very slowly.'

'What's he saying?'

'I don't know, I don't speak panda, but it sounds awfully like Danny to me.'

'He wants Danny!', exclaimed Ellie, 'Maybe you were right about him being his pet.'

'No, I think this is Danny, who's been killing all the shamblers, and scaring off the settlers.'

'DA-NAO!' Screamed the panda, dropping his head and charging towards them.

'RUN!' Yelled Ranth, 'Make for the Landrover!'

They both ran until they could feel their hearts beating in their mouths, but the panda was still gaining.

'I can't... I can't run any... any more...', choked Ellie.

'Just a few.. more... yards...'

When the explosion came, it deafened the pair of them and they fell to the floor. They looked up to see the little girl, sat on the ground, with the smoking gun on the ground behind her.

'Owwww,' The girl said, massaging her swollen wrists, 'That's a big bear!'

'That's not a bear Baby, that's a panda.' Remarked Ellie, who had suddenly got his breath back.

'Whatever it is, I goddit - Right through the heart!'

'You did, nice shot, OK - let's get out of here, you kids coming with us?'

'I don't know... It's nice here.'

'I've got a feeling that the shamblers won't be leaving you alone as much now, think they might have been scared of this guy all along.'

'OK then,' said the girl, 'C'mon Mal!'

A little boy, no more than eight years old, climbed out from behind a thorn bush, walked over to the panda, kicked it and started off down the path towards the car.

'Let's try and find some food, but not anywhere around here,' Smiled Ranth, as she got into the Landrover and slammed the door.

Far behind them, on the forest path, the panda slowly rose to his feet, stared at the receding car and wailed, 'Daaaa.... Naooooo?'

(And in this instance, my wife lost her purse, which had my petrol money in it, and we all turned the house upside down looking for it.)

46 - WAITING FOR GOD-OH!

Now, without wanting to get all metaphysical on your collective asses, I'm a firm believer in evolution. But, (Gods how I hate that word!) there are so many weird, wonderful, badly designed animals out there that there must have been an over-arching designer involved, probably on a Friday night, on the way home from the pub, in some celestial Kebab shop somewhere, and I like to think the conversation may have gone a little like this:

In all seriousness though, someone actually reported me to the Pope about this story, calling for my immediate excommunication.

God1: Dude, nice work on that hoppity thing you did, with the long tail and all the (mimes foxy boxing) stuff!

God2: With the pouch?

God1: It's got a pouch? Where Man? What for?

God2: Totally on its stomach, It puts the babies in there, I put the boobs in there and everything.

God1: Wait, what? you put boobs in a pouch?

God2: Yeah... Awesome!

God1: Aww man, I spent ages on boobs, took me weeks to get the shape just right - (Mimes squeezing imaginary boobs) Honk-honk! shame to hide 'em really, they rock! - (to kebab shop owner) Yeah mate, two tandoori chicken / shish mixed, loads of chilli, no onion.

Kebab Shop Owner: Chicken? we don't got chicken my friend, what chicken anyway? ees kind of fish or somefink? Got plenny fish!

God1: *Paff* And on the eighth day, I did create tandoori chicken, and saw that it was good (Bucket of tandoori chicken appears in a cloud of Dogma)

God2: LOL! But, seriously man, I'm having, like, major trauma with my new project?

God1: What you workin' on Brah?

God2: Well, the kid wanted something cute, on the same island I did the hoppity boxing thing on, you know to kinda like balance out all the bitey snakes and spiders and stuff.

God1: Man, you and your fangs and your venom... You gotta remember to get rid of those things before we let those naked two-leggedy things loose, got a feeling they might wander about a bit. So what did you do?

God2: You remember that wombat thing you did? Where you mucked up the guts and it ended up taking it like, two weeks to eat anything?

God1: Yeah, I should totally look at that when we release the next set of updates.

God2: True Dat! So, I took that, streamlined it, made it semi-aquatic and gave it poison spurs.

God1: Poison?... Spurs?... You make a little furry thing, supposed to be cute, then give it poison spurs, You're sick dude, LOL! Totally off the hook!

God2: I know, right! Anywho, I give it to Iesu, and He just looks at me like I'm an idiot, shouts 'More Cute!' and goes back to making towers out of his Lego.

God1: Man! Kids today, don't know they're created... Whaddya gonna do?

God2: I'm, like, totally outta ideas, tried making it furrier, but the damn thing just sank to the bottom every time I put it in water, had to get my resurrection freak on a few times that day, I can tell you!

God1: Ha! I would have paid good sheckles to see that (Mimes drowning animal) Bloop-Bloop Help Me! I'm melting!... LOL! Have you tried mixing it with animals that can float?

God2: What, like cows?

God1: Man, cows don't float, I mean like ducks or something.

God2: I am totally giving that beeyatch wings!

God1: You want flying aquatic wombats stinkin' up the place? Nah, I mean, like, waterproof feathers or some shizzle like dat.

God2: Feathers? s'a mammal dude, it's got nipples and stuff, you can't do feathers on mammals, s'against the law or something, probably... 'Member we tried that with those flying mice things, with the fangs and the Scooby-Doo eek-eek-eek noises? We got that memo saying we had to put the fur back on before we released 'em.

God1: Yeah, I remember, those skin wings gave me the heebie jeebies, I made the big ones eat fruit though, just to mess with their heads!

God2: Way to stick it to the man!

God1: Yah! (The two Gods high-five) Why don't you give it a beak?

God2: A beak?

God1: Ducks have beaks, and they float... Maybe it's that that does it, I don't really unnerstan' it completely, I'm not technical at all.

God2: Yeah, that might just work dude, what if it laid eggs too? An internal floatation device, eggs float, right?

God1: Probably, you'd have to test it I guess, try it on the spikey anteater thing that was in the newsletter last week.

God2: Do they swim?

God1: Not very well, that's what'd make it a good test.

God2: Right! Yeah, oh-Oh! I know, I'll give it a big-ass tail too, flat like a beaver's

God1: Hahahahhahaahahahaaahhahaha!

God2: Whut?

God1: Hahahhahahahah *sob* HahaHahaahaHAHAHahAha!

God2: Seriously dude what? Don't make me smite you.

God1: *sniff* You said beaver!

-oOo-

So there you go, the complete story about how the Duck-Billed Platypus got it's singular good looks. Just as possible as any other explanation I think you'll agree?

LOL

He said Beaver!

(Dedicated to Maurice and Heinkel, my imaginary platypus doorstops)

47 - THE BARNEY STINSON OF THE ANIMAL WORLD.

And here's when Seedy the Pangolin, mascot of The Chimping Dandy and star of our Merchandise was born, in the very chapter we talk about how wonderful your average pangolin is and why we should all bow down before them…

I mean, they actually poop actual acid. And who amongst us can say that they do that?

I messaged Neil Patrick Harris about this, and asked him if he minded me using his character's name in this. He didn't reply as such, but minutes after I sent the message, someone in Los Angeles read it… Which is as good as proof as far as I'm concerned.

-oOo-

I'd like to take a few minutes to talk about my most favourite of those weirdo, throwback, Friday afternoon type animals...

The Pangolin, specifically the Giant Pangolin of Central Africa.

If you've never heard of the Pangolin, you're not alone, they're not widely advertised, I don't think there have ever been any famous Pangolins. None have ever saved a burning bus full of children from going over a precipice into the ocean as far as I'm aware.

They're just so Gorram odd!

Firstly, they're a scaled mammal, their scales are made of the same stuff as fingernails and hair (and therefore Rhino-horn - BooYah!), they're also sharp on the edges, and it rolls into a ball when threatened, kinda like a pinecone made of razor blades - Awesome!

Secondly, should you try to threaten a Pangolin and fail, because you are not awesome enough, it will excrete stuff from its butt that smells like skunk spray, but just happens to be acid - ACID? Who thought this up? - Doesn't matter - Awesome!

Thirdly, it walks on its fists, ON... ITS... FISTS... Because it is so hard! - And because its claws are so long and sharp that they make walking difficult - Again - Awesome!

Fourthly, it only eats ants, OK, so that's not so awesome, and it doesn't have any teeth and can't chew... however, it does have a tongue that's over a foot long and covered in glue - And if you don't think that's Awesome, well, obviously you need your head examining by an expensive professional!

It can be mistaken for a house eating alien monster from beyond the stars! In July of 2011, a small village in India saw a Pangolin crawling out of a building that had recently fallen down. Instantly, they decided that it was, and I quote, 'a dangerous and strange animal' and that the best thing they could do would be to tie it up and beat it to death with rocks. Then to prove their bravery, they hung it up (once it was safely dead), beat it with shoes and then took its picture before cutting it down and dumping it for feral dogs to eat. OK, maybe they do occasionally claw their way through the walls of insubstantially built houses looking for termites, but I mean, who among us can say that they've never done that after a night on the sauce?

Really? Just me then...

I've decided that, to honour this poor animal, I will make a humble Pangolin (whom I have dubbed Seedy) the official mascot of The Chimping Dandy - She will no doubt be gracing the huge range of Chimping Dandy merchandise that will, possibly, soon be available via mail order to selected clients at vastly inflated prices.

-oOo-

And so it came to pass that you can get all sorts of Chimping Dandy gear (T-Shirts and mugs and so-forth) by getting in touch with the nice people at Hash Togs, via Facebook -www.facebook.com/hashtogs1 and they will, quite literally, take your money off you and send you wonderful things that have Seedy's picture on them. You can even choose your own slogans (Within reason)

48 - A BUCKET FOR MONSIEUR.

I was sat in the pub with a very good friend of mine one evening and something appeared on the TV in the bar that brought up the subject of 'Bucket Lists'.

A Bucket List, for those of you who've never heard the term, is a list of things that you'd like to do before you die. It usually comprises of things like 'Swim with dolphins' or 'Write the next Great, British novel' - Generally a list of things that are possible, but very unlikely.

Mine, as you can probably imagine, doesn't contain those things... It does however contain one that appears on a lot of people's lists, even though it's more of a wish than an activity. It's the 'trigger' that would enable many of the others to come to fruition, so I'll start with that one:

- Win more than £100 million on the National Lottery. This one causes a bit of contention in the Dandy household, Mrs Dandy is a great believer in the idea of 'having enough' - She'd like to win the lottery, but just win enough to live comfortably and never have to worry about money ever again. Maybe just a couple of millions. I however would like to be so obscenely rich that it caused fish to spontaneously combust if they swam within 500 yards of me.

- I want to own a house, with a private lake, that had a Captain Nemo themed, Victorian cast-iron conservatory under it. So I could sit in a sunlounger, watching my killer whales swim by overhead.

- Ah, yes, I want to own a breeding pair of killer whales (Maybe this should have been higher up the list.)

- Over the years, I've developed quite a list of people I'd like to go for a beer with, these include, but are not limited to: Nathan Fillion, Sir Patrick Stewart, Kevin Smith, John Rezig, Robert Carlisle, Danny Trejo, Denis Leary, Hugh Jackman, Richard Dean Anderson, Jason Bradbury, Adrian Edmonson, Rufus Hound, Al Murray, Felicia Day, Peter Dinklage, Samuel L Jackson, Rob Brydon, Neil Patrick Harris, James May, Henry Rollins, Anthony Bourdain, Ron Perlman and obviously, Guy Martin - If any of you know, or indeed are, any of these people - feel free to get in touch. (You'll notice that there is only one young lady in that list, this is because I said 'go for a beer with' not 'Git jiggy wit' in a Hall Pass stylee.)

- I want an 18th century pirate ship, and crew, with which I would sail around the pacific firing broadsides of chocolate and cream cakes at passing cruise-liners. I would call it the HMS Old Jamaica, and operate under a letter of Marque personally given to me by Bertie Bassett.

- Have a fully working F302 (Google it) and use it as my day-to day transport.

- Buy a brand new Lamborghini, in cash, from the dealership on a busy Saturday afternoon, then chainsaw it in half on the forecourt whilst dressed as Pennywise from Steven King's IT and laughing maniacally.

- Build a branch of Domino's Pizza in my house.

- Have a set of bespoke combination spanners made and tuned so that they played different notes when struck, I would then hang them in my twelve car, centrally heated and carpeted garage and have Sir Patrick Moore brought back from the grave holographically (Like Tupac) so that he could teach me to play the Imperial March from Star Wars on them.

- I would buy a horse, a narwhal and a marabou stork and have a repatriated Nazi scientist combine them to make a unicorn Pegasus (or Alicorn), which I would then name Teal'c and train to stand on my F302 and act as a kind of 'lifeboat' in case I ever got into trouble whilst in the air. He would also have to be trained to say 'Indeeeed' and wear a space-helmet (presumably with some kind of hole for his horn).

- Have a combat - ready AH-64 Apache attack helicopter, painted in the Louis Vuitton brown & gold luggage pattern and provide a vigilante traffic enforcement service, whereby I would blow up any car that seemed to be driven badly, by a chav, or pink...

- And lastly, the thing I saw on the TV that fateful night, that started off this whole mad idea - I would like to render a midget unconscious with a single karate chop to the side of the neck. (Maybe Peter Dinklage could help?)

There are many other things that I have thought of that might one day make their way onto this list, but a lot of them will probably never happen, so I thought I'd just put down the ones that were most sensible and achievable.

49 – ALL THAT AND BROWN SAUCE?

I like my food, a lot, and one of my favourite things is the traditional Full English Breakfast.

The thing is, there are so many combinations of things that can be thrown together to still make up something you can call a Full English, that I felt the need to make a list to end all list, a definitive list, one that you could set in stone.

People still disagreed with me though. But I don't talk to those people any more.

Not without a Ouija board at least.

-oOo-

I was driving to work this morning, through the drizzle and the greyness and the occasional four-car pileup, wracking my brain for a subject for this chapter.

Then it struck me, why not write about something incredibly close to my heart, a subject that has helped to get me through the bad times, and helped the good times feel so much better.

Then I realised that adult ladies gyrating whilst wearing Catholic schoolgirl uniforms probably wasn't very politically correct, so I quickly switched to the Gods given taste explosion that is the cooked breakfast.

Not your namby-pamby continental breakfast, beloved of Johnny European and those who consider themselves upwardly mobile, but the large plate of animal parts and fried accompaniments. To paraphrase the great Mel Brooks - 'A Full English Breakfast is like sex, even when it's bad, it's still good'

Is there anyone out there who doesn't know what constitutes a Full English? Well, if you now are, or ever have, resident in the UK, and you don't know, then I suggest you report to your nearest tall building and commence with the jumping out of the window and the uncontrollable screaming.

It's one of this sceptered isle's signature dishes, it's up there with Fish & Chips and Cottage Pie. (Note, it is not up there with Chicken Tikka Masala - Although I'm regularly informed that this is the most popular dish in the UK, and I enjoy it myself, that is Indian food, the clue's in the name.)

For those of you who are still with us, and have geographical reasons for having been excused defenestration, let me describe the standard ingredients:

Sausage: A tube of at least 80% minced meat, encased in a natural skin (OK, there's no way to say this nicely, intestines), bulked up with herbs and bread (Sometimes called rusk), vegetables or cheese. In Scotland this is sometimes replaced or accompanied by Lorne Sausage (or 'Slice') which is pretty much the same, but square.

Bacon: Now, for our American readers, what you term bacon, really isn't what I'm talking about. Over here, we call that 'Streaky' bacon and it's mostly used for cooking with, not eating on its own. I'm talking about what you might call 'Canadian bacon' and can be cooked anywhere between just opaque to 'you can hammer nails in with it', a good breakfast cook will always ask you how you like your bacon, if they do not, you are quite within your rights to roll your eyes, sigh, and find somewhere else to have your breakfast.

Eggs: You cannot have bacon in a breakfast without eggs, it's the law, whether they're fried, scrambled or poached (although, in fairness, if you ask for poached, there's a very good chance that the cook will spit in the water as they are a right faff to make properly.)

Beans: Not your normal everyday green fellahs - But, Baked Beans - Oddly, these are usually stewed, not baked, and packaged in tin, with a sweet, sweet, tomato sauce.

Tomato: There are two camps here, and it can provoke arguments of Blefuscuian proportions. One, quite rightly, says that the style of tomato that should be supplied is the skinned, tinned, plum tomato. Meanwhile, heretics and people of reduced mental faculty maintain that you should be given half a grilled tomato, which has the taste and consistency of a stale slug. Luckily these people are dying out due to the application of the laws of 'survival of the fittest' and food poisoning.

Now, you can sometimes be asked whether you would like beans OR tomato, the correct reply to this is to slap the person across the face and tell them not to be so bloody ridiculous.

Fried Bread: There should always be fried bread and plenty of it, it should be at least an inch thick and cooked in the fat rendered from the sausage and bacon (Which have been fried, not grilled, or griddled, or steamed or microwaved). Those amongst you who have ever been offered fried bread and have opted instead for its insipid cousin 'Toast'... well, I'm afraid you're dead to me now.

There are a number of optional extras that can be offered as part of the breakfast. These include, but are not limited to:

Field mushrooms, Sautéed potato, fried onions, Black pudding (or white pudding if you're squeamish about blood) Hash Browns (For those who have been to America, or shop at Iceland) and bread and butter.

It should also be served with a cup of tea (under no circumstances should you serve it with coffee, this is an offence punishable by flogging, and not the good, Public school, 'please sir may I have another?' kind).

Once you find somewhere that does the perfect breakfast, you should guard it jealously, never tell anyone but your closest, trusted cadre - When places get 'popular' the quality of food often suffers.

You may think that no-one needs to have the cooked breakfast explained to them, but let me leave you with this cautionary tale of a cooked breakfast gone horribly wrong.

I was sat in the breakfast room of the Croydon Hilton enjoying a buffet cooked breakfast which I would say probably ranked about 47 in my top 100 cooked breakfasts. There were many people staying at the hotel that week, including a couple of professional netball teams and a contingency of oriental types who, true to stereotypes, were very quiet and very polite.

My colleague and I were discussing what the day had to offer workwise when I noticed a small, fragile looking oriental girl, probably in her early twenties, approaching the buffet. She looked up and down the selection for a while, then took a large plate and put on some mixed fruits, peach slices, pears and mandarin segments - you know the type of stuff. She then bypassed the cereal, went to the cooked section and loaded up with bacon, eggs and baked beans. I have had meat and fruit before; it's traditional, very popular in fact in Tudor times. But her next addition was a bit of a deal breaker, she went to the... Well, I'm sure that there's a proper name for them, but they're effectively a bowser that holds the fruit juices and milk, and proceeded to pour the latter onto her breakfast.

She then took the plate to her table, sat down and ate the lot - she had a fairly disgusted expression on her face, and will probably never eat British food again - But you have to admire her tenacity.

So there you go. Quintessentially British food as it should be - Tasty, fattening, comforting and capable of flummoxing even the most inscrutable of foreigners.

50 - IT WAS A BRIGHT, COLD DAY IN APRIL, AND THE CLOCKS WERE STRIKING THIRTEEN.

This chapter is about the indignities suffered by your author at the hands of his Big Brother... Hence the title... It's the first line of George Orwell's 1984.

But then you knew that...

Right?

I'd like to think that this chapter has confused the many people who have Googled that line of that particular work and found this instead of something that would actually have helped them with their English Lit homework

-oOo-

So, this is a character assassination of my Brother, well no, it's not really... I love my Brother, if I had to make a list of the people who've helped me out most over the last forty years, he'd be at the top of it. But when we were little and everything, he was a monster. (At least, according to my Mother, who relayed these stories to me, although she did have a reputation for embellishment - So, whilst they are, to the best of my knowledge true, there's a possibility of artistic license in the details.)

Love you Man!

Let me do a little scene-setting. My Brother is ten years older than me, born in the fifties, grew up in the sixties, went to Uni in the seventies, got married in the eighties, rode the promotion rocket in the nineties, retired in the noughties and now lives in his hollow volcano, super-villain hideout in the Mediterranean eating Greek food and playing Star Wars: The Old Republic.

My earliest memory of my brother is, of course, one of torment and torture. (quelle suprise I hear regular readers gasp) When I was but a mewling, pewking, babe in arms, he was my babysitter whilst our parents desperately tried to have a social life. Remember this was the seventies, and parents having a social life was not yet frowned upon. As my Brother was a fairly normal pre-teen, his brand of babysitting often involved putting me where I would be least trouble and continuing with... Whatever it was he did... Watching TV, eating more walnut whips than was strictly good for him and suchlike.

His safe-place of choice on this particular occasion was a doorframe mounted baby-bouncer. If you haven't seen this kind of contraption, it comprises a clamp, attached to the top of the doorframe, then a long spring, some 'safety' straps and a seat, with holes for the feet, sort of like a plastic nappy. (One wonders if this is how fetishes start?) I was a needy child, which in fairness hasn't changed that much, and I enjoyed this contraption, but only if it was moving. Every once in a while my brother would wander over to me and give me a push, that would see me bouncing, or swinging, depending which way he pushed, into paroxysms of happy gurgling.

I guess on this one occasion, I had become particularly needy, and there was possibly some frustration on his part. But the next thing I knew, he'd taken hold of the 'gusset' of the bouncer, took a few steps back and let go. I went shooting into the other room, the spring stretched, then contracted, and sent me shooting back into the living room. I understand that I quite enjoyed this... Initially. Until he tried it again, and on this occasion took a few more steps back.

This time, I performed the same repeated trip between the two rooms, but at a higher speed, with my head snapping back and forth like an acid-fuelled Woody Woodpecker, and... Are you familiar with the Latin phrase ad nauseum? - Seemingly, I went slightly past that point. Well, let's say that I'm glad that I didn't have to pay for a new carpet.

The second incident is a Christmas story, one overflowing with comfort and joy. Our Father, at the time, worked at an electrical shop, and as such was the go-to guy for Christmas lights. We had everything it was possible to get; Flower-shaped ones, Snowflake-shaped ones, Cold-cathode ones that flickered like candles and, my personal favourite, a string of fairy lights where every bulb was a mini lava lamp - I poop you not! - All running on 240 volts, no transformers, no 'Ideal for outdoor use' labels, proper man's electricity, with all the danger and fire-risk that that suggests.

The setup for this story is the same as before, parents out, Brother babysitting, although I think I was a little older, maybe four or five. And I'm not sure how the subject came up, I think we were shining torches up each other's noses to make them glow red. And then 'someone' suggested that if I were to put a fairy light bulb in my mouth, my whole head would probably light up.

I think he panicked when he heard the crunch of broken glass, and ran to get a towel from the kitchen and 'encouraged' me to spit the razor-sharp shards into it. I can't remember that there was a lot of blood, which was definitely more by luck that judgement. It's not an experiment that either of us were in any great hurry to repeat - And I suggest you do not try it at home, or at B&Q or ASDA for that matter.

(And to clarify, the bulb had been removed from the light fitting, I mean, he wasn't mad or anything)

My final story for today is one of mayhem, death and destruction. It is the tale of a young child, sadly robbed of his innocence too soon, cruelly snatched from under his Mother's wing and thrust into the harsh, actinic glare of the real world with not a thought for his wellbeing, future trust issues, or length of his limbs.

The stairs at my parents' house were (and still are for that matter) very steep. My Dad would often arrange for Chris Bonington to come around to the house and give us tips on how to scale them safely. (Especially the difficult overhang on the West face) There was a family of goats on the third step from the top that you had to give a portion of your packed lunch to before they would let you pass.

Standing at the top, you got the same view that Hawaiian cliff divers get just before they take a deep breath and make like a Puffin, only the sea is made of deep-pile berber that the landlord got cheap after one of his other tenants 'tripped and fell'.

Steep, right?

Anywho, we used to play a mean game of cops and robbers, did my Brother and I. Well, I say cops and robbers, it was more sort of beat the poop out of me (in a brotherly and loving fashion), tie me up, stow me somewhere where I wouldn't be found too quickly, and then wander off and do something more exciting. On this occasion however, there was some 'Escalation' as I believe it's called in serial killer parlance. There was the standard light beating, as one had come to expect, possibly a Chinese burn or two, and then my hands were tied together with one of the many ties that my Father regularly got for Christmas but never wore.

Then the other end of the tie was loosely tied around the banister rail... As I am a kind and loving person, who never holds a grudge, I'll describe what happened next as me 'losing my footing'. Have you ever fallen downstairs? it used to be a weekly event for me when I lived at home. It involves a kind of rolling motion, designed to spread the trauma over your whole body. That can't happen when you're tied to a banister. So my ass took a real pounding.

No, there might be a better way to say that... Aw hell, you've read it now anyway.

He was very apologetic, once he'd stopped laughing and came downstairs and untied me.

So there you go, my Mother couldn't stop interfering in my life even after she died, my Father made free and easy with the Lords' little feathery creatures and my Brother was, well, one hesitates to use the words 'Fratricidal Maniac' doesn't one?.. So let's say, just a completely normal Big Brother - He even painted the number 101 on our shared bedroom door.

51 - JUST CALL ME 'SINESTRO'.

Good Afternoon...

My name's the Chimping Dandy, and I am one of the 10% of the population effected by one of the most under-reported and misunderstood syndromes in the history of Mankind.

I am left-handed.

Now I know that a lot of you will be sat there thinking 'So what? - I had a red tricycle when I was a kid, I really wanted a blue one, but I don't go crying about it on the Internet saying it's some kind of disease' And you'd be right, in the grand scheme of things I've not lost a leg or anything. But you normos (as Righties are often referred to by Lefties) don't appreciate the daily handism, which we have to suffer.

It's not a new thing, it's not one of the things that the modern age can claim to have invented. It started thousands of years ago probably. You all know the word 'Sinister', right? But do you know what it means? Let me save you the trouble of consulting a dictionary:

1. threatening or portending evil, harm, or trouble; ominous: a sinister remark.

2. bad, evil, base, or wicked; fell: his sinister purposes.

3. unfortunate; disastrous; unfavorable: a sinister accident.

4. of or on the left side; left.

Hang on a minute! Just wait one second! - 1.. Yeah, that's what it means, 2.. More of the same, 3.. OK, I get it, no need to ram it home, 4.. Sorry, what? It doesn't stop there, if you look further down the page you get this little gem:

1375–1425; late Middle English (from the) Latin: on the left hand or side, hence unfavorable, injurious

ON THE LEFT HAND - HENCE UNFAVOURABLE? - I should write to my MP! If I thought for a second that it would make a difference.

OK, so not only are all Lefties evil, base and wicked but we can't use scissors properly - Scissors made by the right-handed majority, for themselves, purely to subjugate us! We can't write with ink-pens because our left hands keep smudging it (Why is why, if you look, a lot of lefties will turn the paper through 90 degrees and write downwards), Corkscrews and screwdrivers are a bit of a faff, and don't get me started on tin openers!

I was going to search the Internet far and wide to secured some deep, meaningful scientific study of left-handedness, but because I'm threatening and ominous, I decided to just shout 'Buggrit' and check Wikipedia - Look what I found!

Other reported associations that may have decreased evolutionary fitness include shorter adult height, lower weight, puberty at a later age, possibly a shorter life expectancy, increased risk of accidents, increased risk of certain neurological and immunological disorders, and decreased number of children

INCREASED RISK OF ACCIDENTS? - What the actual Frak?

You can picture the scene, you're standing on the platform at the railway station, a Leftie walks up to you, you say 'Good Morning', he offers completely the wrong hand for you to shake, which makes things awkward to start with, then he trips and falls under the 07:53 to Chipping Norton, stopping at Penge, Romney, Hythe and Dymchurch (No refreshment car on this service)

Who knew? According to the fount of all knowledge I should be a tiny, skinny, under-developed in the trouser department, multiple trauma victim with a nervous tic, a runny nose and a single, ginger child called Phillip who wears National Health glasses and has abandonment issues.

Whereas friends and casual observers will know that I am a tall, fat bloke with fully descended testicles (thank you very much) who, despite being heavily scarred and susceptible to colds (due to losing the use of a lung to pneumonia) had to be spayed to avoid spontaneously impregnating people walking past the house!

Well I'll go to the foot of our stairs! as people used to say when the world was in black and white.

But it's not all bad...

Lefties are supposed to be more artistic - I'll give you that one

There are a higher proportion of Lefties in what we generally accept to be the more 'developed' cultures, than in the more 'primitive' ones. (Does that mean that Lefties are the next stage of evolution? - I think it might - Are you ready to open wine bottles for your Sinister Overlords?)

We were even prized historically for being the most effective first wave of foot-soldiers to be sent into a recently breached, enemy castle... Why? you ask, well, let me explain: Most spiral staircases in castles go clockwise upwards, giving the advantage to the (usually) right handed defenders, above and causing (usually) right handed attackers to flail about and not be able to give it the old hack, slash and stabby movements because their swords keep banging against the 'hub' of the stairwell - For Lefties, not a problem! - Much hacky-slashy goodness would ensue.

But the most bestest thing about being a Leftie is this little known fact... At birth, all left handed children are given a gift. A sacred present, that is non-transferrable, does not wear out, cannot be sold, traded or removed by force.

You might not believe this.

A lot of people don't

But all Lefties are impervious to Polar Bear attack

No, really, in all of recorded history there has not been one confirmed Polar Bear attack on a left handed person - Google it if you don't believe me (you might not want to Google it too closely in fairness)

This is because all polar bears, or at least those that have been studied, are Lefties and they can recognise this 'handedness' in others, by scent - They treat you as an honorary Polar Bear, which is why you might not want to visit the Arctic Circle in mating season unless you're VERY broadminded.

Anyway, to sum up, being a Leftie is a bit debilitating sometimes, but we're not disabled, we don't want your sympathy, we just want to be left alone to live our lives in peace, away from the finger-pointing and the chanting.

Until we become the majority of course, and we invade your cities on our Polar Bear mounts... And then you're all stuffed, sorry!

*Please note: The Author cannot be held responsible for any actual harm caused to a reader by a polar bear, or any other animal whether or not mentioned in this, or any other book at any time past, present or future.

52 - MAYBE THEY EXPLAINED IT BADLY?

One of my many jobs has been working in the IT Department for a large Aerospace company just around the corner from my house. It was great, I really enjoyed it and as with most of my tales, I will keep their identity secret. Suffice it to say their initials are neither Q.Q or S.S but something in-between.

And you know what I've never understood?

How aeroplanes fly.

I mean, I used to work for the UKs largest manufacturer of Aero engines, and I had it explained to me, in great detail, sometimes with diagrams, by engineering zealots all the time and at the end of it, I just looked at them like the Grumpy Cat meme that is so popular nowadays, shook my head, said 'Nope' and walked off.

I mean, let's examine the facts. Air, the things that aeroplanes swim through, the stuff that surrounds us, is light - it's the stuff that lightness is measured against, things are either 'Lighter than air' or 'heavier than air' (Although I guess, in fairness, things are also either 'Lighter than an elephant' or 'heavier than an elephant' - but that's not a very popular comparison, well, not in the UK at least, maybe they say it a lot on the Indian subcontinent... But in their local language, perhaps - I don't know.)

Aeroplanes, even what they laughingly call 'light aircraft' are pretty bloody heavy. You wouldn't want one landing on your head. They weigh anything up to five tonnes (Strangely, lighter than an elephant - who'd a thunk it?), and the big fellahs, the Jumbo jet for instance can weigh anything up to four HUNDRED tonnes on takeoff (about fifty-seven elephants if you wanted to willingly flog the analogy to death - Which is something I'd never do, especially not to an elephant).

So, you've got something the weight of a medium sized zoo, floating in something that weighs effectively nothing - Can't happen, sorry... Just doesn't make sense.

The textbooks say that it's all to do with the speed of the air going over the top of wings travelling faster than the air going underneath the wing, generating low pressure and effectively 'sucking' the plane into the air.

You're relying on, what Einstein called I believe 'The Weak Sucky Force' to keep a metal tube full of precious, precious human beings up in the air for hours at a time.

If you ask a proper physics type if that would actually work, they look all sort of uncomfortable, fidget in their chair, pick their nails, and then say 'Err... Well.. Kinda.. but no, not really' They'll tell you that it's actually all to do with something called 'Angle of attack', which you can experience yourself if you stick your hand out of a car window when it's travelling at speed. Hold your hand flat, parallel to the ground, and it will just feel a bit windy. If you imagine it's a plane taking off and angle it upwards a bit, the wind will hit your palm and it will lift your hand up, and depending on the speed, and whether there's a lorry coming in the opposite direction - It may well get torn off in a horrifically bloody fashion (If this happens, remember to tell the nice policeman/paramedic that I told you not to do it, but you went ahead and did it anyway).

So, the really scientific types say that the wind 'blows' planes into the air. Shyeeeah, riiiight! Next time you find yourself next to an aeroplane, do me a favour... Blow on it really hard, see if it leaps into the air, in fact, get some of your friends to help you - if you can get it into the air even a little bit, I will buy you all a Yorkie (and Kit-kats for the girls obviously).

Would you trust your life to something that even people who say they understand them can't decide whether they work by sucking or blowing? I know I wouldn't. Does that make me a Luddite? Probably - Does that bother me at all? Not in the slightest.

I would trust aeroplanes a lot more if their wings flapped like a bird's, at least that's a technology that's been perfected over millions of years - And it would look totally cool!

And here's a quick story from the annals of my Engine Manufacturing Company history - I must point out that this happened 'before my time' and is one of those stories that everyone gets told.

Our final assembly building was due to be visited by one of the Royals, and as happens before such an occasion, Special Branch, or whomsoever it was who looked after Royal security at the time, came to site and poked their noses into everything that could have an impact on the visit.

They walked around with one of the management team and had things explained to them, asked intelligent questions and gave instructions about how we should prepare for the visit.

At one point, allegedly, the rozzer walked around the room where almost completed engines were hanging in gantries above the ground, awaiting some small but very important parts being connected to them. He noticed that they were fixed to their frames by just four bolts, and commented that 'I'm glad that that's not how the fix them to the wings!'

The employee looked at the bolts, smiled, and said 'You're right, when they're on the plane they're only held on by three, and they're smaller and designed to snap easily.'

'What?' asked the Five-oh,

'Well, if the engine gets hit by something solid, it'll start to vibrate, the bolts will snap, the engine will fall away, and the plane keeps flying.'

'And if the bolts don't snap?'

'Well, once the engine starts to vibrate, the wing will start to vibrate, and then it will break apart, and they're full of jet-fuel...'

'Boom?' suggested the Poh-poh, making the expanding explosion handsignal with both hands.

'Aye... Boom!' Said the Engineer, doing the same.

He took a nonchalant step back, whistled nervously, and carried on with his inspection.

53 - LEVITICUS 19:28

It's easy to look down upon tattooed people isn't it? If you're a particular kind of person at least. Well, I say that, I look down on people with tattoos too, but then I think we've already established that I'm a bigot – And it does only tend to be people under 30 who have full sleeve tattoos, and they do tend to be making me a Venti Mocha with extra cream whilst I'm doing the looking down on them.

I'm a terrible person.

But tattoos, generally, they're great aren't they?

I realise that that might have sounded sarcastic, but no, I think they're great - I have tattoos, Mrs Dandy has tattoos, the Mini-Dandy wants tattoos. I've even designed the odd one (the very odd one in some cases)

Tattoos, tattoos, tattoos...

There are a few things that are still legal that are so divisive, there are two standpoints, you either love them or you hate them. No, hang on, that's Marmite... Marmite AND tattoos? Actually no, there are three standpoints, People either love, hate, or have no strong opinion on them at all.

Sorry, I came over a bit 'Monty Python's Spanish Inquisition' there didn't I?

Right, this chapter's going well so far isn't it? Do you get the feeling that I haven'y really thunk it through?

Do you know someone with a tattoo? I don't mean one jabbed into their skin with a pin melted into a toothbrush handle by someone called Fat Malcky in the exercise yard of your local Government internment Centre during Exercise Hour. I mean a work of art, often costing hundreds or even thousands of pounds, performed by a qualified, registered artist under sanitary conditions with some degree of skill.

Is that person a baby-eating psychopath? Chances are that they aren't, chances are that they're well-adjusted people who would not think twice about giving you their last carrot if you were short of one for your Sunday Lunch, or for use during a quiet night in on your own (Either way, they won't want it back).

So why the general vilification of the tattooed?

Well, I think it might be because the general populace, the huddled masses, Jane and Johnny Vanilla, can't tell the difference between tattooed people and people with tattoos.

What do you mean you don't know the difference either? C'mon people, work with me here!

Tattooed people are those who think about it first, ponder long and hard whether they should get some ink, think carefully about the content and placement, decide how it can be covered if that's a concern for them in their chosen sphere of employment, save up the money, listen to the artist's opinions and suggestions about subtle changes that can be made to improve the design, sit quietly and still, biting their lips as the job is done, then religiously following the aftercare instructions and ending up with a product that they're all too happy to show off.

People who have tattoos are those who, for instance, after Jeremy Kyle has finished, think 'I know, I'll have a duck tattooed on my eyelid'. Hunt down the back of the sofa, fail to find enough cash, raid their kids' piggy-banks for the fiver required to get it done by 'Our Sonia's boyfriend's brother' who does it in his bedroom at his Mum's house with a kit he bought from eBay, get the bus to some dismal Council Estate, wait for the shell-suited scrote to get back from scoring himself some weed, find out that he doesn't know what a duck looks like and then get convinced that what they really want is to have his thirteen year old, pregnant, girlfriend kiss your backside and then get it tattooed over, Manage to get the price down to three-fifty by showing him their cleanest Primark bra (But not doing what he wanted them to do to get it for free, because even they have standards), then going back to their council flat, letting it get infected and scratch at it until it looks like Nigel Lawson.

Easy mistake to make for the uninitiated I suppose...

As is becoming traditional, I leave you with a story told to me by a tattooist of my acquaintance.

One, quiet, sunny afternoon, a squaddie came into his shop and asked for his unit's insignia to be tattooed on or about his person. First of all, he didn't have a copy of what he wanted, so the artist Googled it and printed it out. He couldn't decide whether he wanted it black and white, or full colour, so the artist quickly did a black and white copy so that he could choose.

Then he couldn't decide where he wanted it, and after about three quarters of an hour, he decided to have it on his bicep. He took another half an hour to decide how big he wanted it.

After all of these questions, the artist thought that maybe a tattoo wasn't for this particular person and tried to convince him to go away and think about it, but try as he might, the squaddie was immovable, he wanted it done, and done now, so that it was healed for when he was sent back to... Erm... Afghanistan or wherever.

So an hour and a half later, the deed was done, the squaddie was happy, the artist was happy that the squaddie was happy, money changed hands and they went their separate ways.

All was well until the next day when the phone rang at the studio.

'Hello, Circling Dragon Tattoos, how can we make you more attractive?'

'Oh, Hi, I came in yesterday and you tattooed my unit's insignia on my arm?'

'Yes, I remember... Is there a problem?'

'No, no, it's great, really, there's just one thing...'

'OK, what's that?'

'Well I've tried on my fatigues shirt, and it won't roll up high enough to show it off, so I wondered if you could move it down onto my forearm?'

The tattooist was still laughing when he put the phone down, walked out of the shop, and threw himself under a bus.

54 - 'LEG GODT' AS THEY SAY IN DENMARK.

If you've read the story about my love of Charity Shops, you will have gathered that I'm a bit of a fan of LEGO.

It is, without doubt, the best thing that has ever been invented… No, seriously… It's amazing. You should go and get some right now. (Take this book with you so you don't forget what you went for – I do that all the time)

Please note that all trademarks used in this chapter are the Copyright and intellectual property of their respective owners and I have used them for illustration purposes only.

PleaseDon'tSueMePleaseDon'tSueMePleaseDon'tSueMe

I went up to the attic this morning, to push a fresh plate of fish-heads under my Son's bedroom door, when I saw a huge box of something that helped me decide what I was going to do this weekend.

If there's one word guaranteed to make any sane man weak at the knees, make his mind race and his mouth go dry...

It's LEGO!

Some of you may have read before about my almost slavish devotion to Ole Kirk Christiansen's building blocks. I can't remember a time when I wasn't surrounded by the colourful little beggars (and neither can I remember a time when at least one of my parents wasn't shouting 'Oooyah! Damn your eyes! I've just trod on some Lego! Pick it up before I wear your bladder as mittens -And yes, both of my parents were pirates of the South Seas before you ask!)

There's just something about the absolute mutability of it all. You can pick up a couple of decent handfuls of shiny plastic and make virtually anything with it. There's no guarantee that it will look anything like what it's supposed to be anywhere outside your imagination, but that doesn't matter.

You CAN make a scale model of the Titanic with four 'eighters', two flat 'sixers', a wheel and a Darth Maul lightsaber.

It's perfectly reasonable to expect someone to recognise that what they see as a pile of clear red and blue 'fours' are a steampunk version of the Mona Lisa wearing a pirate hat and cuddling a weasel - (If they can't, then they're imaginatively inept - You should shun them - Shuuuuuun Theeeeeemmmmm!).

My dear Son (Gawd bless him and all who sail in him) - In whose name 50% of the Lego is bought, likes to make guns. He doesn't constrain himself to just using Lego, he'll use sticks, cardboard, geese, cheese, anything really - But when we gets the Lego out, all bets are off. It's like there's an arms race between Rube Goldberg and Rowland Emett - His guns become fragile things with cogs and flags, they often also have windows and/or teeth. The one thing that most of them have in common is a removable magazine of some sort, A stack of blocks that can be connected under the breech (Oooohh, get me and my firearm vernacular!)

I asked him once, when he'd made a multi-coloured contraption that looked like a 3D model of the London Underground system mixed with an Avocet.

'So, where's the magazine?'

'You mean the clip?'

'Yeah, clip, of course, silly me,'

'Here,' He replied, removing what looked like a horse-headed duck.

'Gotcha, it's good that it has one of those.'

'Well, if it didn't, there wouldn't be any bullets,' He switched to the tone of voice that adults used to address the mentally challenged or new-born babies, shook his head and continued, 'And that wouldn't be a very good gun would it?'

And then the end fell off and smashed into a zillion pieces...

For every Cutty Sark we've made, there's been a three-legged centipede, for every Statue of Liberty, there's been a purple, one eyed, banana with rocket engines and an umbrella. Don't think it's just me and the boy though, Oh no! The Mini-Dandy gets involved too, but her constructions tend to be significantly more identifiable, houses, gardens, lakes and icebergs - that sort of thing. Mrs. Dandy occasionally takes a few minutes off from rocking backwards and forwards repeating 'Look at this mess, I'm not going to clear it up, it's not my mess.' to jam a few bricks together, from what I remember, she does a blinding small duck. (To clarify, not a small duck with a large spike coming out of the front of it - Although that would be perfectly possible, a small duck that is quite realistic - as far as one can be and still be made of Lego)

I could evangelise all day about Lego, I know for a fact that my Blog is read by at least two AFOLs (Adult Fans Of Lego) and one fully certifiable 'Brick Wizard' (He has a hat and a badge and everything, probably), and no, I don't mean certified.

But it comes down to this - Lego is the best toy that has ever been invented by man, It encourages thought, creativity, dentistry (as anyone who has ever tried to separate two flat blocks of the same size with their teeth will attest to), co-operation and parallel thinking. It prepares the little blighters for their adult roles, teaches problem solving and introduces them to the joys of the National Health Service and new words like 'Forceps' and 'Haemostat' when the nice doctor is trying to retrieve an orally, nasally or anally inserted mini-figure head.

I honestly believe, that if you have children that have gone past the 'put every gorram thing in their mouths or up their noses' stage and they are dextrous in any way, and you HAVEN'T bought them any Lego (or MegaBloks, or Kreo or whatevs, I'm not on the payroll - But Real Lego is bestest, obviously) Then you're a bad parent.

Baaaaaaaaaaad Parent!

We have a truly epic amount of Lego, most of it contained in a bedsheet, in a box that is about 24" x 18" x 18" - The horde of mini-figures and associated accessories that we have fill another, slightly smaller, box - Which contains the instructions for many things that we will probably never build again.

My one problem... The only rattlesnake in the yoghurt... Is how do I stop the idiot puppy from eating it all when it's spread all over the floor? The little faeces factory is constantly hungry but doesn't take the time to check that what he's about to ingest is actually edible - I think he's had a good half a dozen Lego tyres already.

55 - AH'M WITH YE JACKY-BOY.

I like Scotland me, it's a grand place, actually, I might go as far as to say that I love Scotland.

I've had many happy times there, the people are, for the most part, friendly, the food's different but not so different that you're not sure what you're eating, and if you get far enough away from the obviously touristy shortbread trail, up into the crinkly bits then it's truly amazing.

For myself and Mrs Dandy's Honeymoon, we went to a little place called Largiemore, near Otter Ferry on the banks of Loch Fyne - Very crinkly around there, almost corrugated you might say. We took the scenic route there 'o'er the tap' as it seems the locals call it, as in.

'Yah say ye came o'er tha tap?'

'Aye, seemed like the quickest way from Dunoon.'

'Quickest? Aye... Boot also the must dangerous, nea-yin goes o'er the tap if then dinnae have-tae'

It seemed that that was our 'in' with the locals, every time we went to the local pub, The Oystercatcher, the landlord would say to someone 'Hay, (Insert frightfully stereotypical Scottish name), they's the yin ah whuz tellin' y'aboot! Came o'er tha tap!'

Then there'd be backslapping and big grins all round, much clinking of glasses, and many, many opportunities to pretend we liked haggis.

But the funniest thing was, I got to practice my Scottish accent on the other tourists (Yes I realise that I said that where we were was off the tourist track, but some accidentally found their way there, it's not like there were coach parties or anything). Being on the West coast, about forty miles from Glasgow, you can (kinda) get away with thinking 'Now, how would Billy Connolly say that?' and then softening it a bit - I got a few tips from the locals, along the lines of'

'Nawwww... It's Awe Ayyyeeee', a chap looking exactly like John Laurie would say.

'Oh Eye?' I'd reply, sounding (I thought) exactly the same.

'Nawwww, nawww, naw... ye'd ownly say it lake thaat if'n ye didnea buleeve whut someyins sayin. Yea'd say, Oh Eye? an' raise an eyebrew.'

'OK, so, when would you say Awe Ayyyeeee?' (round of applause)

'Whun ye whuz tryin' to convince peepl' ye whuz Scots.'

I passed my exam in pretend Scottish one afternoon sat outside the pub. Mrs Dandy was talking to the wife of a family that had just arrived in the carpark, whose husband was labouriously emptying out the back of their car to try and find a football for the kids to play with on the beach. Now, Mrs Dandy, for those who haven't met her, was born in a Derbyshire village called Belper, but her Father thought that she would do better in life if she adopted a 'posh' accent, so her accent is an aggregation of Belper, Derby and received pronunciation and it's sometimes quite difficult to tell where she's from (Up until the point where alcohol takes over her vocal cords, then you can hear her accent quite clearly as she belts out the Metallica tunes).

'Have you been here before?' Asked Mrs Dandy,

'No, but we come to Scotland a lot, we love it up here. Is this your husband?'

'Aw-rayt,' I said, looking up from my book and touching the brim of my devastatingly stylish hat.

'Oh!' she exclaimed, 'Are you local?'

'Not... Exactly... ' Replied Mrs Dandy, 'We're from down the road a bit.'

'I love the Scottish accent, I wish my husband was Scottish!'

'Yeah, me too,' Whispered Mrs Dandy under her breath.

56 - THEN SMICK SAID THAT 'CHAP' WAS A BAD WORD.

All this Alba talk has got me thinking... We've not had a 'Me and SMick' story for a while have we?

OK, it's about time that you heard the story of my first trip to Dumfries (It's a lovely place, you should go there, it's got a river running through it and everything).

-oOo-

It was a sunny Saturday afternoon in the autumn of 1990, leaves were turning golden, squirrels were thinking about hibernating, and SMick and I were playing pool in the pub (The Station Inn on Midland Road in Derby, for those who are interested. Dave, the Landlord could easily be mistaken for a cantankerous Terry Wogan, and he serves half-decent Bass from the jug), sinking a few cheeky Newcastle Brown Ales.

'Ah feel like going home,' Said SMick, gazing wistfully out of the window.

'Oh, OK, we'll finish these and get off shall we... Bit early though innit?'

'Aye.'

So, about half an hour later, when I realised we were going in completely the wrong direction, I said,

'Dude, I thought we were going home?'

SMick turned, looked at me and said, 'I am...'

The trip North up the M6 / M74 was fairly without incident, we passed Gretna Green, Hadrian's Wall, lots of heather clad mountainsides and finally arrived at, SMick's mate, Doogie's house in Dumfries just as the sun was going down.

To be honest, I can't remember if I'd met Doogie before or not at this stage, but seeing as our first real conversation was about how many times we'd each seen Michaela Strachan's knickers, he was soon firmly filed under 'kindred spirits'. We had a couple of beers and then decided that it was time I experienced a real Sco'ish pub.

So we went to a place called The Joker on the Whitesands, this is where I nearly got killed the first time that day. As we got to the door, SMick stopped and put his hand on my chest.

'One thing, 'fore we go in.' He said, with a serious look on his face, 'You know how you're fond of using the word Chap?'

'Aye?' I said, wondering where this was going,

'Don't use it here, not a good word.'

'Ver' bad in fact,' Chipped in Doogie, 'S'a bit like calling someone a cu...'

'Aye, that's the one rule, don't call anyone Chap, goddit?'

SMick released his hand and brushed some imaginary dust off my T-Shirt, I looked down, he flicked me in the face, 'Ah, seeing as yer so gullible, you can buy the first round!'

We went into the pub, which was as busy as any town-centre pub on a Saturday night, the bar was two deep, SMick and Doogie got us a table by sitting down next to some Students and leering at them until they vacated their seats and I stood at the bar for ten minutes busily not being served. I heard a shout from behind me.

'Rab!'

Which I ignored, because they were obviously trying to attract someone called Rab's attention.

'Rab! turn roond yah big bast!' I looked around and Doogie was making the 'come over here you big bast' hand-signal.

'What?' I shouted over the jukebox, 'Difficult to get served innit?'

'Aye, y'ell haveta shoot, in Sco'ish or they won' serve yah,'

'In Scottish?'

'Aye, if they find oot yer Unglish, yer deed! Yah shoot "Three paints o' eighty" and then wait for the beyor.'

So I did shoot, I mean shout, and we did get the beer, Doogie did the same, then SMick, then it was my round again. I looked at the clock and noticed it was 10:45,

'I'll get us a couple each as it's getting late, OK?' I suggested,

SMick and Doogie looked at each other, shrugged, and said 'Aye!' with broad grins.

Six pints later, when it was my round again, I noticed that it was only about an hour later and both SMick and Doogie had four pints each lined up in front of them.

'When's last orders?' I asked, congratulating myself for being able to string those few words together.

'Mostly when people stop drinking,' Replied SMick, 'You might want to slow down a bit.'

I excused myself and went to open the floodgates, as my bladder pressure was rapidly approaching a valve busting level. After I had drilled a hole in the urinal by pure pressure of urine alone, I re-entered the bar and saw a chap... Sorry, bloke... putting a pound-note into a 'Fruitey' (A fruit machine or one-armed bandit) - Now, this totally threw me for two reasons. One being that I'd not seen a pound note for ages, since England started using pound coins some years before, and the other that I had never seen anyone use a note in a gaming machine. I stood and stared, open mouthed like a gasping haddock, for a few moments before overhearing the guy playing on the machine talking to his girlfriend about a TV program they'd been watching about Polar Bears.

Now, I'm a great believer in other people's education, especially when drunk, so I decided that I would impart some knowledge to them, that I had recently read (Which I later found out was completely untrue).

'Did you know?' I expounded, sounding very, very, English indeed, 'That your actual Polar Bear, isn't a bear at all, but a kind of giant weasel?'

'Whut?' replied the large, and getting larger all the time, Scotsman.

'Polar Bear, looks like a bear, with the claws and the Arrgghh!, right? Actually a big weasel!' (I think I might have actually made whiskery movements with my finger against my face).

'Y'tekkin the pish?' The guy continued to grow, which I thought was physically impossible.

'No, really, I thought you might find it interesting!'

'D'ya think ahm Styoopit?' He was about eight feet tall now, and showing no signs of stopping growing.

'Well, I don't know if... URK!' Luckily, my exclamation wasn't from him tearing off my arms like a bad tempered Wookie, it was from SMick and Doogie grabbing me by the shoulders and propelling me towards the door.

'Sorry! He's dronk!' Doogie yelled over his shoulder as they used my face to open the door.

'Are you actively trying to get yourself killed?' Asked Smick

'I didn't call him Chap, you said that that was the one rule!'

'OK, two rules, Don't call anyone Chap, don't try to educate anybody, right?'

'Fair enough... What're doing now.'

'We're going to go somewhere else and carry on drinking. You're going to sit quietly and give us money to buy drinks when it's your round.'

So, we went to a nightclub, whose name I can't remember, but I do remember it was up some stairs. And the bouncers were all huge, apart from one.

'NO TRAINERS!' Shouted one of the large bouncers from the top of the stairs.

'Whut?' Shouted Doogie,

'Him, wearing trainers, NO TRAINERS!'

I looked down and discovered that I was the 'Him'

'Don' s'ppose yah brought any boots with yah?' Asked Doogie,

'I didn't know we were coming, I didn't bring anything at all.'

We walked back to Doogie's house and he gave me a pair of his work-boots. Now, I am six feet tall, with size 10 feet, Doogie is, well, I mean, he's over five feet, definitely, with size 8 feet, on a good day. So, it was safe to say that my toes were in the main bit of the boots, but the rest of my feet were sort of where the laces were. I was walking like a drunken velociraptor.

Then I ripped my trousers, I honestly can't remember how, but it was a decent rip, from right knee, to groin and back down to left knee. Luckily, I hadn't yet adopted the 'All commando, all the time' fashion statement that I currently live by. I wish I could remember how I'd done it, it would probably have made a good story.

We walked back to the club, and I waddled up the stairs, which was being guarded by the smaller of the bouncers, who smelled like a trainee to me.

'Yer nay comin' in here dressed like that!' He shouted

'Sorry?' I replied, genuinely confused.

'Yer jeans, yah cannae com in here like that!'

'Look, pal, (I have since learned that 'pal' is something you shouldn't say either, it's not as bad as 'chap', but still a no-no) your mate said no trainers, so I went home and changed into these boots, now you're saying that I can't come in because I've got ripped jeans?'

'Aye, it's indecent!'

'I've got pants on!' I showed him my Spiderman y-fronts, 'Look, pants!'

'Naw, go haem, get some new jeans, then come back.'

'Look Chap!', SMick and Doogie both took a step back at this point, 'I've just driven two hundred miles because he said (I waved in SMick and Doogie's general direction) this was a good place to go for a beer. So I'm going in!)

'Naw, yah not!' The bouncer proceeded to roll up his sleeves and started down the stairs.

At this moment, another, more experienced bouncer came out of the doors at the top of the stairs and shouted, 'Whit's all tha bloody noise, Ah ken hear you lot over tha music!'

The situation was explained to him, he turned to SMick and said, 'Is he gonna be any trouble?'

'Nope, we've only brought him 'cos he buys the beer.'

'Aye, right, yah can come in, he sits in a quiet corner, doesnae cause any trouble, OK?'

And so we did, and that would have been the end of this particular tale, had we not bumped into some other old friends of SMick's, from the local Motorcycle Club (possibly The Fugitives, but I'm not 100% sure) and things got messy... Very... Very... Messy...

Maybe an hour later, I noticed a very pretty young lady standing at the bar, occasionally looking at me, I watched her for a while and thought it was odd that she was on her own. I stood up and SMick looked at me quizzically. This was the second time that I nearly got killed.

'I'm going to talk to the girlie at the bar.'

'Aye, one sec...' He turned to one of the guys from the Bike Club and said a few words, there was laughter and he said, 'OK, fine, off you go!'

I went over, bought her a drink and got talking, she commented that she liked my trousers and my pants and my accent, I told her that I thought that was strange as most of the locals seemed to hate the English. At this moment, the young bouncer came into the room, looked at me, went very, very, red and started towards us. I looked at him and raised a single eyebrow, he paled, turned around and walked back out.

'Alright!' I thought to myself, 'Result!' And carried on chatting up the pretty lady.

A few drinks later, the same thing happened again, only he got a little closer before I raised my eyebrow and she noticed him too.

'Aww... Shite...' She said,

'Everything OK?' I asked,

'Aye, that's my boyfriend.'

'Oh... Cock!' I held up my hands and backed away, found my seat and sat down, I probably mouthed the words 'Sorry' a few times too.

SMick, Doogie, and all the other lads were crying with laughter, literally crying.

'It's not funny!' I said, 'I could have gotten the crap beaten out of me then, you should have told me!'

'That's exactly why it was funny, plus the fact that when you thought that you were being all James Bond, all these guys stood up behind you and raised their eyebrows and wagged their fingers at her boyfriend too.'

A good start to a great weekend, which ended up with me losing my job, and nearly getting killed a couple more times. But I'll save that story for another day I think.

57 - A DISCUSSION OF PORNOGRAPHY, DO NOT READ.

This contents of this chapter have attracted a few readers to the Blog over the years, I think I may have found the Internet's level with this one.

But it's not really about porn.... Well, I mean it is, I know my titles can be a bit obtuse sometimes, but this one is... Oh, actually, just read it yourself and see what you think.

-oOo-

This might end up being a bit NSFW, if a page of text can be regarded as Not Safe For Work that is, I mean, I can understand someone sat at the desk next to you being offended by being suddenly confronted with a picture of an oiled, pneumatic, professional female model, wearing just a natural suntan and a length of knotted string appearing on your screen, but not a page of barely legible writing in a book.

Actually, hang on a second, thinking about that, I can't really understand. It might not be professional, it might not be what you're being paid to do, but the human body is a wonderful, beautiful thing... Well, I know mine is, I can't vouch for more than about fifteen other people's though.

I've worked in a lot of offices in my life and one thing I can say with surety is that I have seen many, many, more posters, calendars and desktop wallpapers that feature topless, oiled, zero body fat, elegantly coiffed, seductively posed, perfectly airbrushed, staring straight into the camera as if they are looking directly into your soul so that it makes you think they're in a relationship with you, MEN, than I ever have bikini clad WOMEN.

(OK, I've worked in a lot of factories and building sites where it was pretty much wall to wall boobage pictures, but that doesn't help my argument, so forget I said it, OK?)

I overheard a heated discussion between a pair of workmates once, in an office that we were upgrading. I think it was the guys birthday, and one of his mates had bought him an A2 sized poster of a Page 3 Girl, not a topless picture, she was dressed in swimwear, when a tweed clad harridan came storming across the office,

'Don't think you're putting that up in here!'

'Well, no, I was going t...'

'It's pornography, degrading to women, It's disgusting, it's against the code of conduct!'

The guy dutifully rolled up his poster and put it back in the tube, then looked at her and said, 'But what about the topless Fireman calendar you have next to your desk?'

'Obviously that's different, it's just a bit of fun, you're just jealous that you don't look like that!'

OK, so she was obviously a cow, and I know that all women aren't like that, not by a long way, because I wish to remain in possession of my external sexual characteristics. Women are great... Oh yes, definitely, I love me some women... Hoo yes... But, there seems to be a bit of a dichotomy where the old sexualisation is concerned, where the lines between erotica and pornography exactly are - Time for some definitions I think, via the OED:

Definition of pornography

noun

[mass noun]

printed or visual material containing the explicit description or display of sexual organs or activity, intended to stimulate sexual excitement.

Definition of erotica

noun

[mass noun]

erotic literature or art.

Hmm... That last one wasn't a great deal of help was it? Let's see what erotic actually means then:

Definition of erotic

adjective

relating to or tending to arouse sexual desire or excitement:

Now, it might just be me, but it doesn't sound like there's any real difference between the two terms. I guess you could argue (If you were a twunt) that Pornography is actually intended to provoke a physical, sexual response by explicit, graphic, depiction, where Erotica just 'arouses the desire' as it were. Although I think that that might just be splitting hairs.

I think that a more reasonable, and easy to understand, division for the vanilla masses would be, if it's targeted at Men, it's pornography. Because men are base animals who like looking at pictures of glistening ladyparts. However, if it's targeted at women then it's erotica, because women are beautiful, cerebral, floaty creatures full of imagination, romanticism and passion.

I don't like to bring up this example because it's lazy, but it's the elephant in the room as far as this subject is concerned. E.L. James' Recent Blockbuster, Fifty Shades of Grey. Described by Amazon as 'An Erotic Romance', Strangely not described as 'A BDSM porno primer for the Twilight generation' The book that did more for the average birthrate of the English speaking world than anything since Kim Basinger got herself covered in Trifle in 9 1/2 Weeks.

Shouldn't it really be regarded as porn? I mean, you can't tell me that all of its 65,000,000 copies have been purely read by people in stable relationships who have become heated whilst considering its adult themes and shown their love for each other physically after putting an interesting Guatamalan knitted bookmark carefully in the page and letting the cat out? Surely some have been read in ten minute sections by a young secretary in the disabled toilet cubicle at work with her Primark skirt up around her waist, some by students on the 08:34 from Ongar, where only one of their hands is visible above the table and the rhythmic to-ing and fro-ing of the train masks any other hand movement that's being made? And still more, curled up on the sofa, with a box of chocolates, a glass of crisp chardonnay and no underwear?

But still, whaddo I know? Maybe they've all been bought by fifty-something unfulfilled people who get a kick out of thinking how naughty they're being, who am I to judge? As long as it makes you happy, and you don't do it in the crisps and snacks aisle of Sainsbury's whilst there are kiddies about, more power to your elbow...

Actually, I suppose I could have put that better... Never mind

But if you really want to read some porn that's directed at women, get yourself some Anais Nin. It'll put hairs on your palms AND it's well written, that makes all the difference, trust me.

58 - YOU'LL DIE, AND IT WILL HURT ALL THE TIME YOU'RE DYING.

Health and Safety... There's a subject.

We've all been told stories by friends of friends (or in the red-tops) about bizarre rules that 'they' are trying to introduce that 'they' blame on Health and Safety.

The one where Butlins holiday parks banned the Dodgems, because people were using them as 'Bumper cars' (Did you know you were supposed to AVOID everyone else? I know I didn't), schools all over the country couldn't have sack races because kids might fall and bang their little nosey-woseys, or pensioners being forced to drag their old TVs down fifteen flights of stairs so that the burly council workers wouldn't hurt their backs.

Well, these are all well and good I suppose, but I've had a few health and safety talks in my life that actually made sense, gave you good advice, and helped to keep me sane, well adjusted, and more importantly, breathing.

I used to spend a lot of my time in computer rooms. You've all seen them on the TV, big football field sized rooms, filled with boxes of flashing lights, spinny-roundy tape machines and comfortable brown carpets. They have orange vacuum formed chairs and are entirely staffed by men from the 70's with huge moustaches, brown corduroy jackets and loafers, they're usually called Dave (The people, not the computer room... Who'd call a computer room Dave? That would be stupid). During my indoctrination for a company that will remain nameless, I was shown the fire suppression system for the computer room.

'This button releases the CO2 from those nozzles in the ceiling,' Said the HR guy who was giving me the tour, 'The last person leaving the room, when there's a fire, hits it on the way out.'

'What happens if there's anyone left in the room?' I asked, full of wonder and amazement.

'Well, the doors lock, then the CO2 pushes all of the air out of the room, the fire stops, we go in to recover the bodies of everyone you've accidentally killed, then you get the sack and charged with manslaughter.'

'So we check for people first then...'

'That would be the best plan by far, yes.'

Shortly afterwards, the CO2 extinguisher was replaced by Halon, a great gas that doesn't push all the air out of a room, right up until they found out that it gives you liver and kidney failure and does a great job of drilling a hole in the ozone layer. Now most companies just use a clone of Supernanny Jo Frost, who reasons with the fire until it realises what it's done and just goes out of its own accord.

Whilst working at the busiest airport in the UK, we (The new IT team) decided to go on a tour of the tunnels underneath the airport during a nightshift. The reason we gave the security guys was that we needed to trace a few cables and locate some comms cabinets. Actually, we were all bored to tears and thought it might make the nightshift go by faster.

The security guy who gave us the do's-and-don'ts was great, he showed us on a map where all the cool bits were, how to get into the hangers, where Concorde was (and more importantly which machines gave out the free coffee and what buttons you had to press to get it). He checked our 'Airside' passes, little cards that let you onto the parts of the airport where the planes live and said:

'If you hear the words [Deleted for National Security Reasons] come over the Tannoy, walk briskly back to the Terminal buildings, trying to look very innocent and British and non-explosive.'

'Why, what does it mean?'

'Well, we don't get a lot of military traffic, what with RAF Northolt being just down the road, but that's what they announce when we are getting some, it's only usually in an emergency.'

'Right, got it... What if we get stuck out on the far end of the runway? There is some kit out there isn't there?'

'Ah... Well that would be bad for two reasons.... One, the Military Security guys who come flooding out of the woodwork have no problems at all with shooting people, and Two, Military jets will quite happily land on bodies, dead or alive.'

And the last. And possibly most horrific one took place during a stint at a synthetic pharmaceuticals company - This was the only Health & Safety orientation I've had where there was a test afterwards. The H&S guy here was incredibly serious, he didn't take kindly to jokes or even to people who didn't take things as seriously as he did.

We had a tour of the factory, which is in a large City in the West Midlands (Mentioning no names, but it was a popular flight excursion location for members of the German Airforce in the early 1940's), and looks like a perfectly normal office building - However, a great majority of it is one huge room, with one way glass in the windows so that it doesn't scare anyone. Then we toured the laboratories... Well, we toured the corridors where the laboratories were. The H&S chap gave us a set of ground rules.

- You will never enter any of these rooms whilst procedures are in progress.
- You will never enter any of these rooms unless you have a legitimate reason for doing so.
- If you need to enter any of these rooms you will press THIS button and this button only and wait for someone to open the door, you will not bang on the glass.
- If the red light above the door is lit or flashing you will vacate the area and report to your normal work area and await further instructions.
- If the red light is flashing and an alarm is sounding, make your way to the nearest emergency exit.
- Do not ever open one of these doors, even if there is someone in the room that needs medical attention, professionals are on their way.
- If someone seems to require assistance but the red light is off, use the emergency telephone to summon assistance and then return to your work area and await further instructions.

He took a breath and I said, 'Why?'

'What?'

'Why can't we help people if they need help?'

'Are you trained to handle hazardous materials?'

'No... not as such,'

'Do you know the contents of the 1994 CHIP regulatory notices?'

'No, but if they...'

'Are you a trained Fire-fighter with hazardous substances training?'

'No...'

'Are you a Doctor? Do you own your own HazMat suit?'

'Well... No, not exactly, but..'

'Look, I know you mean well, but some of the chemicals that we regularly use here are incredibly dangerous, if someone who is trained in their use gets into trouble, what chance do you think you will have?'

'I don't know, but it...' I was starting to splutter by this point,

'I'll tell you, you'll have exactly no chance, if you're lucky, you'll only touch something that will make you violently allergic to all forms of plastic for the rest of your natural life, if you're unlucky you'll breathe something in that will instantly make you throw up your lungs whilst your intestines make a more southerly exit.'

'Right, so, let the professionals handle it?'

'Yes, touch nothing, ever. There's a good chance you'll die'

And you know what? - I didn't, luckily I didn't get a call to fix any kit in working labs. Although, I have fixed kit in operating theatres, which an operation was in progress.

Maybe I'll tell you about that one day.

59 - TO SLEEP PERCHANCE?

Did you know that these books that people who style themselves as a bit Fey tend to buy, called things like 'Find out what your dreams mean' and 'Force your opinions on your closest friends about what you think's troubling them' are all tosh? Well they are, the dreams you have and what they actually mean are specific to you.

If I dream about eating a hamburger, it might mean that I went to bed hungry, if you dream about eating a hamburger, it might mean that you're confused about your sexuality… I don't know, and neither does anyone else.

So the best thing to do is lie back, relax and watch the pretty pictures.

I was thinking about dreams this morning on the way to work, pondering the fact that I can't remember having dreamed for a long time. I appreciate that you often can't remember what your previous night's dreams had been about, but I actually can't remember having any at all recently.

Weird... Maybe I'm overtired, or I'm so good at working out my problems during the day that my brain doesn't need to thrash them out overnight using a tiger with Noel Edmond's face or a three eyed haddock called Raymond who can play the spoons... Pity really... It'd give me some easy bones to throw to you guys.

When I do dream, it tends to be fairly sedentary stuff, real world situations, no flying or turning into an ocelot or a trifle or what-have-you. Just me doing stuff that I would do if I had the time/money/social skills. The only major oddity I can think of is that I've never dreamed about a motorcycle, but I've had many dreams that feature me riding a motorcycle.

That's due a little explanation I suppose, I dream about the act of riding, but as far as I can remember, there's never been a bike. I sort of just float there, in the starfish position, with my hands on non-existent ape-hangers and my feet on completely fictitious forward controls. In fact, I remember having one dream where I tried to ride the (non) bike on several occasions and fell on my ass every time - It transpired that it had been stolen, but I hadn't realised - I actually went to a shop (in the dream) to buy another one, I remember wheeling it (and when I say it, I mean nothing) out of the showroom.

The only other real odd thing that happens to me, and I guess most other sentient life-forms in the Omniverse, is the prophetic or deja-vu dream. It's only snippets that I get, like I'll be dreaming about walking down the road, turning a corner and almost tripping over someone walking an amusing looking dog, and then a couple of weeks later, I'll be walking down the street, turn a corner and there's the dog, with the little wellies and a PVC sou'wester and the 'Please Gods kill me with a length of pipe' expression on its face, whilst the owner carries on about her business not realising what permanent emotional damage she's doing to the poor canine. Never had the lottery numbers though - not so far.

Now, scientists try to tell you that deja-vu is caused by impulses from the eyes being accidentally routed to the memory centres of your brain before being re-routed to the cognitive centres, so you see something, and think that you remember seeing it before and then do that double-take, puzzled look, point your finger whilst thinking 'Hang on a second', thing that they do in low-rent comedies that have a laughter track and say 'You have been watching' at the end.

I don't believe that for a second, I think that during sleepy-time, your brain is occasionally hit by a stray Tachyon (a theoretical particle that travels faster than light) and the minute explosion of Cherenkov radiation that's caused by it impacting a live electron in your brain causes you to remember things that haven't happened yet.

Plausible, I think you'll agree.

I also found out recently that according to current theories, all of the people that you see in your dreams are real - I mean, not real, they're dreams obviously, if they were real, physical people and you dreamed about a crowd, then your head wouldn't be big enough to hold them all and it'd like, go POP! or something and there'd be cerebrum all up the bedroom walls when you woke up.

Actually, thinking about it, your head wouldn't be big enough to hold even one physical person would it? Especially if they were wearing a big hat. Aaaaand, you probably wouldn't wake up either. Well, you might, but you might not like celery any more, or be able to smell purple and hear tartan.

But what they actually mean by that is that you haven't made any of these people up in your imagination, you've seen them all somewhere - On the bus or in a shop, you might have pointed at them in a police lineup or said 'Sorry' to them when you bumped into them whilst filming an amusing personal injury compensation lawyer advertisement.

Your brain stores their details for future reference, or for inclusion in dreams, or if they're particularly stereotypical, for thinking about when you're telling a joke that involves a little light racism.

People often dream about people they know, sometimes in unusual situations. Sometimes it's wish fulfilment, but sometimes you'll dream about things that would make Freud do some interpretive street-dance movements in his final resting place in Golders Green (OK, so he was cremated, but you know what I mean).

For instance, a friend of mine (who reads this Blog, whilst walking her dog - which doesn't as far as I know, wear wellies and a sou'wester) once had a dream about me. I know she won't mind me sharing it with you, as she posted it to her Facebook feed herself, and she requested that I write The Further Adventures of the crew of the Edward Teach.

I'll have to paraphrase what she wrote, as I can't find it on her timeline, but the gist of it was:

"I had a dream last night about an old friend of mine, called Dandy, some of you might know him. Anyway, I was the age I am now, and he was my Dad. I had done something wrong, I don't know what, but he took me to the park for my usual punishment.

This involved him kicking footballs at my head as hard as he could until I learned my lesson, I remember that he was a very good shot."

So, on that dreamscape I'll leave you.

Remember, dreams aren't real, they're fantasy, you shouldn't be embarrassed about them, and you certainly shouldn't make decisions based on their contents.

Till tomorrow... Sweet Dreams Children...

60 - WHY YOU LITTLE!...

Right then, our next topic is swearing...

Who here can honestly say that they don't feel better after a good old fashioned profanity session. I don't mean saying 'Cock' under your breath when you accidentally tread on a slug. I mean the lengthy stream of invective that you yell when you, for instance, hit yourself in the shin with a lump-hammer.

The type of thing that when you've finished yelling, you're breathing heavily and looking at the floor, your blood's pumping, your ears are ringing, and the Jehova's Witnesses that have wandered into your front room because the door was open have spontaneously combusted and turned into a small pile of ash on top of a very nice and shiny briefcase.

I like to start with the word 'You' and then try to, where possible, alternate between swearing and totally unrelated words, so it would go something like:

'You **** sucking, **** strangling, **** wiper... I will **** your **** juggling, **** eater of a **** guzzling, **** faced, **** Mother... After that, I will **** all over her **** flinging, **** and **** around your, **** kneading **** of a **** house that you only got in the ****ing first place because you are a **** who can **** the **** from a **** goat who **** the **** of the **** down the **** road, who **** his own **** of a sister!'

OK, that might be a bit strong... I'd save that for shouting at a book that had just given me a papercut or something... You should hear what I said to the dog after he knocked a mug of tea over me!

(This actually happened a couple of days ago, whilst I was watching 'Paul' on Sky Movies - causing me to have to watch the rest of the film naked and sticky - I tweeted @simonpegg and told him, but he was as strangely aloof and uninterested as you'd expect a big, Hollywood star to be... Maybe I should have tried @nickjfrost he seems a lot more down to Earth)

Actually, have you seen Paul? great film, lots of very creative swearing in there, mostly from Ruth Buggs (Played by the lovely Kristen Wiig - Did you know she was in Ice Age - Dawn of the Dinosaurs, playing a character called 'Pudgy Beaver Mom'? - There's something I never thought that I'd find myself typing in the daytime), Google it beeyatches - I ain't filthying up my book with any inappropriate language an' shizzle just to get more readers.

Although... Thinking about it... That might just work...

Anyway, sweariness... It really bugs me when people say "You only swear because you have a weak, limited, vocabulary!" So I usually either reply with something like... Oh, I don't know... 'Vos habent faciem et odorem mortuus porcus' or, more likely, I'll poke them in the eye and run off giggling whilst flipping them the bird with both hands. Although, oddly, I agree with them, at least about the people who are all:

'F'ing that, F'ing this, F'ing everything'

That shows no creativity, no sparkle, no wit, no grasp of the beauty of a well-constructed faecal epithet... Or as they used to say when I was a lad, 'It's not big, and it's not clever.' But it can be a wonderful way of dealing with stress if you do it properly. It can create shock and awe, it can establish you as one of those people who 'tells it like it is!'

But do it wrong, even once, to the wrong person or in an inappropriate place, like Church or during a boring PowerPoint presentation at a customer's office, and you'll be marked as an insufferable cock for the rest of your natural life, and will be shunned by the nice people that you were trying to impress with your knowledge of 8th Century Anglo-Saxon cursing.

So, go and bring sweariness to the world and don't look back, my little **** faced *** swiggers!

61 - SO HERE I AM ONCE MORE...

As well as LEGO, and motorcycles and stuff, I have also occasionally been known to listen to Rock music in all of its forms.

I therefore present you with an account, of a wonderful day in 1985, where I joined 79,999 other people to listen to almost exclusively hairy people spanking their planks.

-oOo-

I was feeling very musical this morning, which is odd, because I didn't actually listen to any music, or even stick a CD on in the car on my way to work. I did sing the Sheepy Magna song in my head, as I drove through Sheepy Magna though. It had different words this time, and I think it might be in danger of becoming a free-form sound poem, rather than your actual song. (Still, I sang it in a Scottish Accent though, if that helps)

Today I'd like to fast rewind to 1985 (That's twenty-eight years ago kids... Before some of you were born), when I had just turned seventeen and I was full of hormones and cider, and covered in long hair (well, my head was at least) - It was also the first 'Donington' (Not, you notice 'Monsters of Rock - It had been rebranded at 'Rockin the Castle' and was advertised as a ZZ Top gig with support) I'd been to with a real live girlfriend with her own long hair and breasts and spray-on jeans, rather than a selection of skinny boys with chests like xylophones, wearing inappropriate studded wristbands and huge white Hightop baseball boots that made them look like poundshop astronauts.

I (well, I should really say 'we' I suppose, but this Blog's about my recollections, and the time we spent together didn't end particularly amicably, so from now on I'm going to say 'I', OK?) arrived on site by bus, because that is without doubt, THE most Rock-n-Roll way to arrive at any Gig, Festival, Cattle Auction or Outbreak of Infectious Disease (All of which could be used to describe Donington) that there is.

Once I'd staked out a decent spot a few hundred yards from the stage, and complained about the heat a few times, Donington stalwart and professional bottle of urine avoider, DJ Tommy Vance came on to whip the crowd up into a state of mild annoyance. Now, a lot of people have had a go at Tommy (or Richard Anthony Crispian Francis Prew Hope-Weston as his Mother called him for some UnGodly reason), and broadcast, via the medium of chanting, far and wide of his imagined pleasure in solitary sexual pursuits. I remember personally commenting that there was no way that someone as old as him could know about what the 'Kids' wanted to listen to... I now appreciate that I am as old now as he was then - And I am a little embarrassed. But he did more to promote Rock and Metal music than pretty much any DJ or presenter at the time, I was an avid listener of his 'Friday Rock Show' on Radio 1, as was everyone I knew at the time, and he was really, very good at dodging bottles of urine and chunks of mud that were propelled at him all the time he was on stage. Rest in Peace Tommy, you W*nk*r!

OK, so... To the music. Magnum were first on - I'll be the first to admit that I wasn't their greatest fan, they always struck me as the kind of band whose name you'd see scribbled in ballpoint pen across the back of some spotty thirteen years old's denim jacket. But I have a vague memory of them not being all that bad, although the openers always had a reputation for just being there to soak up the first barage of plastic bottles, more than for their musical value.

Then there was a bit of a break, where I finished all the alcohol I'd brought with me, until Ratt came on. I've never being a fan of Hairspray rock, and I'm sad to say that I completely ignored their set and wandered around the ground trying to buy a t-shirt that didn't have the ZZ-Top Eliminator or a hand, clutching a dagger, coming out of a toilet on it (I failed) and getting a burger (I succeeded)

I got back just in time to see this bunch of hairy, denim-clad, long haired, Californian dudes who nobody had heard of, they were OK, a bit thrashy for me at the time - I quite liked one of their tracks though, it was called 'For Whom the Bell Tolls' - They were, of course, Metallica, with a twenty-two year old Clifford Lee Burton on bass (Who was to die in a terrible tour-bus crash the following year). They're another band that I wish I'd paid more attention to at the time, as Metallica get through Bass players like Spinal Tap get through Drummers.

Next up were Bon Jovi, who also weren't particularly famous at the time. Remembering that this was (just) before Slippery When Wet was released, so the only songs I recognised were In and Out of Love and

Runaway, and they were dressed like refugees from a Tom Baker era Doctor Who episode. Oddly, they headlined Monsters of Rock two years later, and played one of the greatest sets I'd ever seen there.

The sun was, whilst not exactly setting, but certainly heading for the trees when Marillion took to the stage. This band was the whole reason that I'd attended that year. I loved them, I bought all of their singles, albums, 12" EPs and would play their stuff constantly on whatever recording device was closest to hand. I knew every word to every version of every song that they ever released. They were the first band I ever saw that sounded exactly the same live as recorded.

Highlights of their set included Fish (The lead singer) asking the entire crowd of 80,000 people to 'Squash in a bit at the sides' so that he could take a photo for his Mum, as she still didnea believe that he was in a popular (prog) rock band. Fish sitting down and shouting 'Well you bloody sing it then' when the crowd started to sing Script for a Jesters Tear louder than he was, and the roar that went up, followed of course by a barrage of plastic bottles, when ZZ-Top's Eliminator car was flown over the crowd, slung under a Marlborough Cigarettes branded helicopter.

The headliners, of course, as has been mentioned on various occasions, were Texan Blues-Rockers, ZZ Top. Billy, Dusty and Frank were still riding high on the wave of their 1983 Quadruple (at the time) platinum album 'Eliminator', hence the flying car stunt. Their set was OK, I mean I liked their music and everything, but they just stood there and played... No pyro, no stunts, no nothing. Not what a seasoned Donington crowd were used to, or had come to expect. But they finished with 'Tush' my favourite song of theirs, so they redeemed themselves a little.

We all oooo-ed and Aaaaah-ed at the fireworks for a while and then found our way back to our respective car-parks... None of us aware that we had missed the best part of the entire gig, something we could have told our Grandchildren...

Secreted somewhere backstage was a fifteen year old Suzi Perry (off of the Gadget Show and F1 Coverage and stuff), and if you're a man, and the words, 'Suzi Perry' and 'Backstage' don't get your juices flowing, then you're already dead... (Note I said nothing about the whole fifteen years old thing... Not in the current climate... Hoooo no!)

62 - WELL, THAT'S NOT RIGHT, SURELY.

Here's a thing, despite what you might have gleaned from the past few pages, I like to consider myself a fairly honourable person. But there are occasions where that consideration drifts away like the smell of frying bacon on the wind.

But it's not just me…

Honour...

It's a very dated word for an idea that seems to have become equally dated. I can guarantee most of you had a picture of a knight in armour flash into your head when you read it (Unless of course you have experienced our justice system, where you might have thought of a judge)

Hold on tight kids, I'm going in for the definition:

Definition of honour

noun

[mass noun]

- high respect; great esteem: his portrait hangs in the place of honour [in singular]
- a person or thing that brings esteem: you are an honour to our profession (His, Your, etc. Honour) a title of respect or form of address given to a circuit judge, a US mayor, and (in Irish or rustic speech) any person of rank.
- the quality of knowing and doing what is morally right: I must as a matter of honour avoid any taint of dishonesty
- dated a woman's chastity or her reputation for being chaste: she died defending her honour

I'm mainly talking about the third one in the list, the quality of knowing and doing what is morally right. It's easy enough you'd think - You picture a situation that requires a choice, you decide (because it's usually obvious) what the 'right' thing to do is, and do it...

Simples! As an animatronic/CGI meerkat might say, before being replaced by a dry, scenery chewing, comedian whose character supposedly has a special set of angry clothing.

Not difficult is it? Really? You make the right choice, it gives you a warm feeling inside, you can be forgiven for having a bit of a smug little grin to yourself and the world keeps spinning round the sun like it has for the past however many billion years.

But now let's do some role-playing... Imagine for a second that you're a scrote.

(Some of you will find that easier than others obviously)

And we're gonna need a situation from someone in the audience... What's that sir? Waiting in the rain for a bus with a one-legged German and an Irishman? No, that doesn't really fit our purposes, Someone buying a live duck as a present for a Latvian single mother? - Seriously? What are you people on?

Forget it, I'll make something up. Howsabout, you're walking down the street behind a pensioner, she gets a real-live handkerchief out of her pocket, because they're the only people who still use them, and blows her nose. At the same time, she drops a fiver... No, no... She drops a twenty pound note... What do you do?

Well you steal it, obviously don't you, there's no-one watching (You did remember we were roleplaying being a scrote, right?) You make it so she has to fight the cat for its food for the next week until she gets her pittance of a pension so that you can buy another thirty cans of Dreadnought lager from Mr Patel in the corner shop, who you should really hate, 'cos he's an ethnic, but he's very chatty and always asks if your Mum's alright when you go in to buy Rizlas.

And the world STILL keeps spinning round the sun like it has for the past however many billion years.

Can you see where this is going? It seems to me that doing the right thing should the default setting, It's what my Dad taught me to do, it's what I teach my kids to do. But, being a dishonourable scrote is the way to make easy money; you can see why it's on the rise.

A case in point was the news story I heard on the radio on the way to work this morning. It seems a group of 'men' are wandering around the homes of the aged and infirm in the West Midlands claiming to be council appointed rat-catchers who need to check your house for... erm... well... rats. They gain entry, open their toolboxes, which contain previously killed rats (in a 'here's one I hit with a hammer earlier' stylee) and declare that you've got an infestation. Then they charge you for getting rid of it.

They charged one little old lady twenty-four thousand pounds...

I'll say that again on this new page so you can ponder the enormity of it...

TWENTY... FOUR... THOUSAND... POUNDS...

I mean, there must be some overheads, buying overalls and rat poison and so forth can't be cheap, but... That's obscene - Seemingly this has been going on for a while, but the 'going rate' for disposing of completely fictional, non-existent rats was about £400-£500 up until recently, and no-one particularly minded.

How much front does it actually take a pensioner's life savings? Would you have the brass neck to stand there whilst she thanks you for doing it?

No? Excellent! Well done - You are a well evolved human being and can commence telling people how brilliant you are - Go ahead, turn to the person next to you and tell them just how gecko-bleachingly wonderful you are.

But what if you answered yes? Well, I mean you wouldn't - No-one who reads this Blog could do that to another human being.

Could they?

You're all brilliant and kind and honourable. You do what's right because it's right, not for the reward, not because it's what people expect of you, but because it's what you expect of yourself, it's what makes you a valued member of society.

But you know... In the roleplay, it was only, like, £20... And I could do with a bit of a 'buffer' where the old petrol budget is concerned.

I mean, if I'd just found it lying in the street and there was nobody about, I wouldn't think twice would I?

Is there any difference? Should I really take it to the Police?

I probably should...

But I probably won't...

And I'd say that most of the rest of you wouldn't either...

Damn! We're all scrotes!

You know that person that you turned to a couple of minutes ago and told that you were great? - See what they think of you now...

I, personally, am very disappointed in us all.

63 - IF ONLY LOCK & CO MADE TINFOIL HATS.

A lot of the regulars out there will know that I'm pretty odd... Actually, who am I kidding, you've only got to read any of my posts that involve the words 'Haddock' or 'Spoon' or 'Transvestite Poundshop Christmas' to realise that I'm a purveyor of the rum and uncanny...

I actively enjoy the unusual. Normal, vanilla people and situations bore me senseless. I like it when OAPs tell me that they like hard-core Jungle music, or when quiet, unassuming office girls have one too many WKDs and say 'I make ferrets wear traditional Romanian gypsy dresses and film them dancing the polka'

That doesn't happen as much as I'd like, to be honest, but the opportunity's always there.

My favourite kind of people in all the world are conspiracy theorists... They're great, mad as badgers, every man-jack of them, but great. You usually find that they're very earnest people who strongly believe in something that they have no way of proving (trying desperately not to compare them with rabid fundamentalist Religionites here) Usually involving the Government, Aliens, Aliens in the Government, Government by Aliens or Aliens, in the Government, trying to keep the fact that we are being governed by Aliens, secret.

Every heard of Vril? Well, there are them that say that it's a type of energy, ('Them' in this instance being 'crazy people') described in a book written in the late 19th Century (as a novel originally, in fairness, but soon turned into cold, hard fact, a bit like the DaVinci Code I guess), that the Nazi's used to power their flying disk aircraft that they had all over the place between the two world wars... I know, right, I can't find a photo of the sky, taken between 1912 and 1944 that isn't choc full of Nazi flying saucers - They actually have to Photoshop them out of footage of battles you know. The Roswell Crash? that wasn't aliens, it was a Nazi flying saucer, powered by Vril.

In 1947-1948, a (strangely heavily armed) flotilla of US Navy ships, Commanded by one Admiral Richard E. Byrd were sent to the Antarctic on a 'routine survey mission' and were beaten back by a strong force of Nazi soldiers, backed up by flying disks. Huge cover up, tears before bedtime and everything.

Perhaps even more strange is the fact that the popular Beef Extract foodstuff Bovril (Made by giant chemical company Unilever) Gets its name from the words 'Bovine' and 'Vril' being cleverly portmanteau'd.

HAARP is a word you will have stumbled across if you've spent any time on the Internet at all. It stands for High (f)requency Active Auroral Research Project - Cleverly the 'F' of frequency has been omitted from the acronym as No-one could say HFAARP! without sniggering. HAARP does everything, it can trigger environmental disasters, down planes, burn the sky (or, at least make it look like the sky is burning, to possibly confuse our reptilian overlords), flip the North and South poles, and last, but by no means least... Control people's minds!

OK, so it does actually exist, there are vast arrays of strangely shaped antenna in Gakona, Alaska that shoot signals into the upper atmosphere to do strange and interesting experiments. There are certainly some odd things about it, it's run by the military and they freely admit that it can, sometimes heat the sky up a little bit... Can that be good? I don't know, I'm not a scientist - Google it, you'll have loads of fun trawling through all the 'HAARP ate my hamster' stuff.

Secret Societies are a VERY popular talking point too. Everything we see, do or feel is supposedly controlled by these trans-global mega think tanks. Be they Illuminati, Opus Dei, The Bilderberg Group, various Banking Clans such as The Rothschilds and, my personal favourite, The Freemasons. Whilst it would be stupid to say that the Hyper-rich can't also be the Hyper-powerful, some of the things attributed to these groups are - Is farfetched the right word? For instance,

The Illuminati - based on a group of German free-thinkers in the late 18th Century, have joined with the Communists to infiltrate Hollywood to pave the way for The New World Order (That's another one to Google on your own time - Ain't nobody got time for dat amount of explainin').

Opus Dei, a group within the Catholic Church, mostly comprised of lay-people, are said to have death squads throughout the world (again, an idea popularised in The DaVinci Code but now taken as 'fact')

The Bilderberg Group is an invitation only, annual meeting, of some of the most powerful men in North America and Western Europe who sit around and have a good old chat about the problems that the World is facing - They're definitely not deciding future global policy and the fact that there are no members from Asia, Eastern Europe, Africa or South America is only because those people are traditionally no very good at golf... Probably.

The Rothschilds have used their financial power to fix the outcomes of wars over the past few hundred years for their own financial gain.

The Freemasons... Ah, the lovely, lovely, Freemasons... I should probably admit that I know quite a few Masons, but I am not one myself. In my personal experience they're a great bunch of guys who really know how to party.

But to the pencils up the nose, pants on the head types, they've done everything from assisting the Illuminati and the Knights Templar in various plots to take over the world, worshiping their own personal God (called Jahbulon, for those who like to pigeonhole your deities), constructing the streets of Washington DC (and probably any other city that will stand still long enough) to strict numerological and Masonic algorithms and assassinating JFK.

Oh yeah, and according to David Icke, they're part of the reptilian alien conspiracy too - As if the rest of it wasn't mad enough.

Just to finish, I'd like to say that I bear no ill-will towards people who believe any of this stuff. Everyone has the right to believe whatever they want, who am I to judge? I just thought it might be a nice thing for people to trawl through the Internet for, maybe give people ideas for short stories? The worst thing that could possibly happen is that they all turn out to be right...

Sleep tight my friends - But watch out for the communist, kitten eating, Nazi, reptile, bank owner under your bed, slipping into your dreams and sucking out all of your positive energies.

And finally, for those of you who don't understand the title of this chapter, Lock & Co. are the oldest, and arguably best, Hatter in the country... Possibly the world. They are credited with the invention of the Bowler/Coke hat (or Derby, if you are of a Colonial persuasion) much favoured by our own resident brick-wizard and Flash-Fictioneer, James Josiah of The James Josiah Flash Project. (Google it, you'll be glad you did)

Their customer list contains the great, the good and the Royal and I have received word that popular comedian Al Murray has invested in one of their luxuriant head-coverings.

If you should ever find yourself in London, with the spare time and money, you should pop into their premises at 6. St. James' Street SW1 and make yourself a better person, well, certainly a better dressed person - which, for all intents and purposes is the same thing.

And if anyone from Lock's is reading this, and they feel like posting a new hat to Dandy Towers (for purely review purposes of course) Maybe something in a 'Stovepipe' or 'Fez', or even a linen cap as Summer is allegedly on its way, (or it was when this was originally written) well, that would just be spiffing!

64 - WHEN THE MAP WAS PINK.

So, tell me this... Where does being a proud member of your country end and being a racist Nazi begin?

(I've used the word, Nazi, quite a lot recently haven't I? Loads of times yesterday, about flying disks and suchlike... Great word, so many possible uses - Did you know it's a contraction of 'Nationalsozialismus' or the National Socialist Party? That sounds much more fluffy doesn't it, something you could really get behind?)

Anyway, back to the question in hand, I'm an anachronistic kind of guy, I like hats, I wear a beard and sideburns completely unironically, I wear silk waistcoats and regularly use a pocketwatch... You'd be quite within your rights to think that I live in the past.

In fact, you'd probably be right. Why do I do this? Well, it's obviously because the past was a better place. There was clean air and long summer days playing in the woods, you could make a bow and arrow and your Mum knew how to make jam. It wasn't all great obviously, there was slavery and quite a lot of syphilis, but that was a small price to pay for being able to go to exciting new countries and expect everyone you met once you got off the ship to be able to speak English.

Ah, there you go - You see the first warning sign right there, the expectation that we had (and still have to a large extent) that Johnny Foreigner will speeka-da-English. At the height of its 450 year history, the British Empire covered a quarter of the world and comprised a fifth of the total planetary population, the Sun quite literally, never set on it. We sailed to foreign parts, planted a flag, claimed the land for the King or Queen (delete as applicable) of the time, enslaved the natives (but we taught them English and Christianity, so technically they still owe us), spread a light smattering of syphilis and cholera, exported all their food, rinsed and repeated.

We invented stuff though, and built things. Everywhere you went there were huge copper and brass steam engines, pumping water and mining coal to keep massive copper and brass steam engines running so that they could pump water and mine coal, etcetera, etcetera, etcetera as Yul Brynner might say. There was cast iron and battleship chain and mass produced bone china - You might counter that with 'Yeah, but five year old children were being seriously maimed in woollen mills, and young boys were catching scrotum cancer from sweeping chimneys for fourteen hours a day.' And I'd look at you funny, because no-one likes to hear the words 'scrotum' and 'cancer' in the same sentence. But honestly, wouldn't you rather see children sweeping chimneys than hanging around on street-corners with their jeans around their knees, stabbing old ladies for an out of date tin of cat food? (And by children, I mean other people's children, obviously)

We had a Navy which ruled the waves (Which there's a song about, so it must be true) and an Army which kicked ass pretty much everywhere it went, especially when their cannons and muskets were turned on people armed with sticks and lengths of rope. We didn't have all the supply problems and the 'But I'm suing the Government because my Kevin had to buy his own body armour off of eBay and it came from China and it was made of papier mache' nonsense that we have today because we would take what we needed without a second thought... Without a first thought in some cases.

Sorry? What was that you said? Rape? Do you mean of the indigenous populace or the country? Both? Well, yes, I suppose there might have been a small amount of that sort of thing here and there, I mean you get a few bad apples in any expeditionary force don't you? It's not like we exterminated anybody is it? No native tribes ever got wiped out because they were a bit close to places where we could mine copper, or diamonds, or pitchblende... *cough*

The women of the Empire (which, even to me, sounds like badly written Star Wars fan-fic) were proper women, with the big hats and skirts and parasols. Demure and cosseted, they ate bon-bons from silver trays, brought to them at 3:00pm sharp by Philip, the nice dusky gentleman that they'd had brought in from Bechuanaland especially for this purpose. Most importantly, they knew their place, which was atop a pedestal, being showered with gifts and the only thing they had to do on a daily basis was to look pretty whilst their husbands got on with the very real and worthwhile job of being a good Captain of Industry and not getting gout... Or syphilis...

Wouldn't it be easier if things were how they used to be?

- The UK being the only real world power and thus guaranteeing no global war ever again?
- Children gainfully employed rather than roaming the streets like feral weasles?
- Women being sedate and wonderful and pretty and domesticated?
- Johnny Foreigner doing all the simple hard work in the hotter climates?
- Worthy but expendable lower-class people doing all the skilled hard work in Blighty?

You know it would, deep in your heart of hearts - A better time, a more rewarding existence for all... Well, all the important people like us at least. But it'd still be best to keep a few ampules of Doxycycline about your person just in case.

I'd like to finish with a few definitions, see if you can guess where they fit in:

anachronism (əˈnækrəˌnɪzəm) — n

1 the representation of an event, person, or thing in a historical context in which it could not have occurred or existed
2 a person or thing that belongs or seems to belong to another time: she regards the Church as an anachronism

satire (ˈsætaɪə) — n

1 a novel, play, entertainment, etc, in which topical issues, folly, or evil are held up to scorn by means of ridicule and irony
2 the genre constituted by such works
3 the use of ridicule, irony, etc, to create such an effect

65 - TAKE TWO AND CALL ME IN THE MORNING...

I mentioned, during my essay on why health and safety can sometimes be a bit of a lifesaver, about an incident I once attended in a hospital, here is that story (And another one for good measure).

-oOo-

Not to worry you or anything, but just to let you know, the vast majority of people who work in hospitals are normal human beings, not Super Heroes, not Angels, they don't have magic powers and they often get tired and grumpy, just like everyone else - This is important, try not to forget it. Be nice to them, it's in your interests in the long run.

I used to work at a couple of large Hospitals in the Midlands and I would do a lot of the 'Rapid response' stuff, you know, the sort of thing where people would have yelled 'Stat' at the end of every sentence if we'd been in America.

Once, there was a problem with an MRI scanner and of course, because it had cables connected to it, IT got called, and because it was medical equipment, I got the honour of trying to fix it. Once I'd found my way to the Medical Imaging department, I found a very red Sister and a flustered looking Nurse in the control room.

'Hey, I'm Dandy from IT, you've got a problem with the MRI?'

'Yes,' growled the Sister, 'It seemed that the PC got disconnected.'

'Disconnected?' I asked, not really liking where this was going, 'How did it get disconnected?'

'Do you really need to know?' Replied the Sister shooting a look at the cowering Nurse that would have boiled a stoat, 'or can you just (and she did the whole air-quotes thing here) Make It Work?'

'Well, I'm no expert, but I'll have a look at it for you... Can we not get the MRI people in?'

'They're expensive, but we can if we really have to.'

'Right...' It felt good to know that I was a valued member of the team, and not just the cheaper option.

The PC that displayed the MRI results was part of the desk, and to this day I've no idea of exactly what the nurse had done. but it looked like she'd maybe tried to move the whole desk and had panicked when everything went dark. I removed the panelling and went underneath... Have you ever seen the original Raiders of the Lost Ark? The bit where Indy lands in the pit and says 'Snakes! Why did it have to be snakes?' Well, that's pretty much what the space under the desk looked like, cables everywhere, big ones, small ones (but strangely, none as big as my head) - All sharing one commonality... They were disconnected.

'Are all these cables for this MRI?' I asked,

'Don't know, does it matter?'

So I spent a while, figuring out stuff, identifying other stuff, getting shocks from things until I figured out that maybe only three or four cables were actually for this bit of kit, and everything else had just been left there from previous equipment.

I crawled out, hit the main power, and everything sprang into life... No-one was more surprised than I was. The nurse, still looking quite embarrassed, did a few checks and confirmed that it was working.

'Can you hang around whilst we do the first patient? Just in case anything...'

'Sets on fire?' I suggested

The look she shot me let me know that perhaps I should keep my comedy to myself.

The patient was a little old lady, complete with 1940's tweed coat and a four-wheeled shopping buggy (which they convinced her that she'd have to leave outside the MRI chamber itself, as it had a metal frame, and they didn't want it flying around poltergeist style when the switched the multi-Tesla field on) and I went and got a coffee whilst they prepped the old lady.

I guess that might need some explaining, which will also make the rest of the story a little bit more understandable. MRI stands for Magnetic Resonance Imaging, Your body (not just yours, mine, the dog's, that girl whose backside you were staring at at the bus stop this morning) contains a lot of water, water contains Hydrogen molecules, the Hydrogen molecules contain little things called protons. Inside the donut of the MRI scanner is a bloody great electromagnet (about 750 times stronger than a fridge magnet) that they turn off and on really quickly and it makes these protons vibrate (or more correctly, resonate), then they take a picture. So you now understand why metal things behave oddly in a strong magnetic field. (Copyright - Explaining complicated things to people who really don't care - Chimping Dandy Books 2013)

By the time I'd got back, they were asking the spinster if she had any fillings or a false leg or anything to which she replied a resounding no.. Then they asked her if she was sure, which she was, and if she thought she might be pregnant. A question she treated with the contempt it deserved.

Finally they helped her onto the table and rolled her into the emitter. The nurse pressed some buttons, sighed, and rolled her back out again.

'Are you sure you aren't wearing any jewellery?'

'No dear.'

'Any piercings?'

'No.'

'Not... erm... anywhere?'

'NO!'

The nurse went into the store-cupboard and got out one of those 'wand' metal detectors that they use in court (or so I've been told *cough*) which she slowly moved around the old lady's body. When it got to her head, it beeped.

'You don't have a plate do you?'

'Pardon dear?'

'A plate, in your head, have you ever had surgery on your head?'

'Oh no, never,'

The nurse moved the wand again and it beeped by the lady's ear.

'What the?'

She looked closer and noticed a small bump on her ear, which she rubbed, and then gently scratched at, then she went to get some tweezers and some alcohol, and removed a small sleeper ear-ring... Which had been in her ear so long that the skin had grown over it, and the old lady had completely forgotten about it.

Ewwww... (The MRI scanner worked fine by the way, you don't need to worry)

We'd had a call about one of the PCs in one of the operating theatres being broken and needing to be fixed 'stat'. So I trudged halfway around the building, found the correct theatre, realised that it was 'in use', sighed, and pressed the buzzer.

An exasperated looking Nurse came to the door and said 'Yes?'
'I'm Dandy, from IT, come to look at the theatre PC, didn't realise that you were busy, shall I come back?'
'Don't know, wait there.' She turned around, closed the door, presumably scrubbed up again and re-joined her group.

About five minutes later, the door opened again, this time it was a Consultant, a not particularly happy looking one from what I remember, with a PC on a trolley. He pushed the trolley towards me and said,

'Fix it, we need it!' Then he turned around, closed the door, presumably scrubbed up again, and re-joined his group.

I looked at the PC, turned it on, did a few checks, connected to the network, made sure they could get onto the Internet, saw the homepage was set to Google (This single fact alone sent a chill down my spine) and stood there looking at it... I couldn't see a single thing wrong with it, so I pressed the buzzer.

A different exasperated nurse came to the door and said 'Yes?'
'Hi, erm... I'm supposed to be fixing this PC?'
'And...?'
'Well, I can't see what's wrong with it,'

She rolled her eyes and said, 'Wait here, I'll check.' Then she turned around, closed the door, presumably scrubbed up again, and re-joined her group. After a few minutes, the first nurse appeared again.

'There's no sound!'

'Pardon?' I replied in the style of Eric Morecambe – I needn't have bothered, she didn't find it funny.

'There's no sound... The sound, it does not work.'

'The sound?'

'Yes, sound,' You know that look you reserve for when you tread, with bare feet, in dog poop that has worms in it? Well, that was how she was looking at me, 'Mr. (insert Consultant's name here) doesn't work without music, no sound, no music, no surgery.'

I looked at her, she looked at me, I looked at the back of the PC, I looked at her, I held up the jack-plug coming from the back of the speakers, and plugged it into the back of the PC. There was a huge crackling noise, as it seemed the entire extent of their diagnostic process had been to turn the volume all the way up.

'Ta-dah!' I said, spreading my arms wide, 'That should work now.'

'Thank you,' whispered the nurse, begrudgingly, Then she turned around, closed the door, presumably scrubbed up again, and re-joined her group.

Remember where I said above that people who work in hospitals are normal human beings, not Super Heroes, not Angels, they don't have magic powers and they often get tired and grumpy, just like everyone else?

Well, a few of them are right arseholes too... just like everyone else.

66 - A SPACE HELMET FOR A COW?

Before you read this particular chapter, I'd like you to keep in mind that it was originally written before the BBC announced who the new incumbent of the role in question would be.

As you all know, I don't do 'Current Affairs' or 'Recent News' or 'Things that happened this century'. But there's an anniversary this year that definitely needs a bit of national celebration.

OK, so it's not really until the 23rd of November, but it's a biggie, so you'll probably be excused for getting overexcited, starting early, and making a mess in the corner.

Doctor Who is fifty years old this year!

There isn't a person out there (whose opinion counts for anything) that doesn't love Doctor Who. Most people have their own Doctors, often the Doctor who was in residence whilst they were growing up, I'm lucky enough to have two; Both Jon Pertwee and Tom Baker (Although I was a great fan of the occasional Patrick Troughton episode) are ingrained on my subconscious as the man in my particular funny blue box.

The on-going story of everyone's favourite 903 (approximately) year old adventurer from the planet Gallifrey, a binary star system in the constellation of Kasterborous have entertained all the members of the Dandy clan for the past 40 odd years. It has everything, adventure, pretty girls, rugged boys, humour, horror, suspense and in the later series (2005 onwards) an awful lot of running.

Don't get me wrong, it's not universally good, for me they could have quite happily left out the sixth Doctor, Colin Baker, completely as the job he did trying to channel William Hartnell was slapdash at best and at worst, jellyfish stampingly annoying and Sylvester McCoy did, in my opinion, more harm than good with his 60% Tom Baker, 30% Peter Davidson, 10% Charlie Chaplin portrayal. And whichever of the McGanns that it was that did the 'Americanised version'... Well, the less said about that the better (I understand he was quite brilliant in the Internet / Radio / Talking book versions though) But on the whole, the new mob are great, Matt Smith does do a particularly good Patrick Troughton, unfortunately sans the penny whistle.

It has generated a selection of words that have passed into the language, most notably 'Tardis' as used by estate agents to describe bijou one bedroom leasehold flats with staggeringly expensive service charges all over London that are the size of a biscuit tin on the outside and the size of a wardrobe on the inside.

'Sonic Screwdriver' has come to mean an item of equipment used to open containers that are proving 'difficult', it can apply to hammers, prybars, big screwdrivers or angle grinders, usually used thusly:

'Oi, Shadwell, chuck us the Sonic Screwdriver... No... Not that one, the big one.'

'Davros' can been applied to... Oh, I don't know... wheelchair bound people with a sense of humour, old people with dark tans who choose to wear fake leather jackets, or those unfortunates who have a single glowing blue eye in the centre of their wizened foreheads.

It's difficult not to use the word 'iconic' too much when you're talking about it, the enemies are all pretty iconic, Daleks, Cybermen, Silurians (both types) and their cousins the Sea Devils, Sontarans and The Master are all instantly recognisable... Well, I mean, the Master is kinda, at least in the Roger Delgado / Anthony Ainley years, but there've been almost as many Masters as there have been Doctors.

While we're on the subject, can you name all eighteen men and one woman who have played the Doctor in film or Television? (Not including body doubles or stand-ins you pedantophiles or people who might have been the Doctor) - Answer at the bottom of the next page. Don't worry if you didn't get them all, I had to look a couple from the late nineties up.

Hopefully, the adventures of the 'Raggedy Man' will continue for another fifty years so that the next generation of Dandies will be able to pick character traits to affect that will make them stand out, and I also hope that whoever takes over from Matt Smith next year will not urinate on the franchise from a great height.

Who would you want to be the next Doctor? There's not been a lot of talk about his successor as yet on t'Internet, but I'm sure everyone has an idea, maybe it's finally time for a female Doctor (although that presumably won't be the incarnation that marries Melody Pond... Although Alex Kingston has a history of playing 'open minded' characters), maybe we'll see the Ginger Doctor, or the one that doesn't have legs, Maybe the one that doesn't have legs is really Jim the Fish?

I don't know.

I know who my choice would be though...

He'd have to be suave and erudite, Well read, sarcastic, ironic, tough in a no second chances kind of way, in touch with his feminine side, able to quip, as disabling with a well turned phrase as with a stun-gun fashioned from a wind-up penguin and a bucket of butterscotch Angel Delight that smells faintly of sturgeon.

In a word...

Me!

For those who are interested, the people who've so far played the Doctor include:

William Hartnell, Peter Cushing (Played a human Doctor Who in the two 1960's films), Patrick Troughton, Jon Pertwee, Tom Baker, Peter Davidson, Richard Hurndall (Played William Hartnell's Doctor in The Five Doctors), Colin Baker, Sylvester McCoy, Paul McGann, Rowan Atkinson, Richard E Grant, Jim Broadbent, Hugh Grant, Joanna Lumley, (Comic Relief 1999) Mark Gatiss (Doctor Who night 1999 - Went on to write and star in several episodes), Christopher Eccleston, David Tennant and Matt Smith

Of course we now have to add John Hurt and Peter Capaldi to that august list – I'll bet they'll both do a great job, but they won't be as good as I would have been.

67 - I SEE A TALL, DARK STRANGER.

This chapter was originally posted at Easter 2013 – hence some of the references may point to, although it works pretty well during the rest of the year I think.

-oOo-

Better start writing I guess. I could go for the whole Easter story, what the Bible actually says about it, how it's another stolen holiday that the pagans celebrated ages before Christianity was brought to England, how commercialization has ruined it. How it's a travesty...

But in fairness, I really like chocolate, so it would be a bit two faced of me. So I sit here, on the verge of a four-day weekend pondering what to re-hash in a humourous fashion and entertain you guys with before you zoom off to Paris for the weekend (or whatever it is that you're telling your workmates you're going to do, we all know you're going to spend the days sat in a dimly lit room playing COD or FIFA, in your pants, whilst the snow falls outside like the cobwebbed cape of Thanatos himself.

So I thought long (lie) and hard (lie) about today's subject... Fortune telling.

There are many ways that people claim to be able to tell the future, there's palmistry (Reading of lines on the palms), hepatoscopy (Reading of entrails), scrying (crystal ball and water-bowl reading) and tasseography (Reading Tea Leaves - Which was a favourite of my paternal Grandmother), to name but a few.

I'm not saying it's all tosh, it could all be cockroach jugglingly true for all I know, but it's very open to abuse... And not in a good way. In the olden days, anyone who was a bit bald, and a bit mad, and fairly Greek, could set themselves up as an oracle, all it took was a bit of narcotic incense, and possibly getting someone from Handmaidens R Us to pop in on a Wednesday afternoon, wear the diaphanous robes and wiggle about a bit. while you talked about auspicious circumstances, stars rising in the East and the lion lying down with the lamb.

So I got to thinking, I'm a bit bald, and a bit mad, and I like Greek food...

Welcome to the Grotto of Dandyissimus, newest, wisest and most accurate of the new wave of oracular prophets. Cross my palm with coinage (but not the Euro, obviously, because that's worth less than a dog-fart in a crash helmet) and I will foretell your future with such accuracy as would blind a hamster.

You want a free trial?

Is that the marketing model that you're used to?

OK... Here goes - Some free glimpses into your future, but seeing as you buggers haven't paid me, I'm not going to tell you whose fortunes they are, or whenabouts they're going to happen. (These are in no way just things I have overheard, or have been told in confidence)

Your husband, who loves you very much, will start living a double life. Don't worry, he's not gay or having an affair or anything like that. He finds himself mixing jam, drinking chocolate powder and 'space dust' and spreading it over his body with your best spatula every time you go out. He will enjoy the feeling at first, but after a while it will become a compulsion, and his usage of it will get more and more extreme. Things will come to a head when you notice that your toothbrush is sticky and smells of strawberries and every time he breaks wind, it crackles slightly.

An entire group of people, who currently meet under social circumstances, will decide, after a celebratory night out, possibly after some kind of sporting event, to have commemorative tattoos. These will be done in ultra-violet ink and will look like random lines drawn all over their bodies. However, when they stand in a human pyramid, naked, at a local nightclub, the silhouette of Deliah Smith 'tasting a tangy sauce' personally prepared by Heston Blumenthal will be revealed.

Two separate people, in two wildly separate locations will start vociferously complaining about the quality of British cheese since we joined the EEC. MI5, intercepting their (completely separate) emails will assume that there is some kind of lactose intolerant terrorist uprising on the way and ban the sale of Stinking Bishop and Sage Derby to anyone without a Rolls-Royce. Questions will be asked in Parliament, which will lead to the leader of the opposition being 'outed' for running his own, black market trade in Dairylea Triangles.

Your wife will decide that her current position as your nearest and dearest, agree-er to your hair-brained schemes and backer-up of your obviously idiotic ideas is no longer enough. She will start her own business on eBay, buying up surplus fur coats, cutting them up and sewing them back together as suits for those bloody awful sphinx hairless cats. All will be rosy at first as all over the world people who have mistakenly bought these obscene creatures realise their mistake and buy a new coat for their hairless companions. Then there will be a short period where sales will fall off due to an expose in the press over allergy issues and then business will boom again as she branches out into fur coats for reptiles who wish to live in arctic areas. (P.S. she will also discover she is a lesbian and will take you for every penny you have – Although these two facts are un-related.)

The Government will decide that to bolster the economy, they will put a tax on ducks. Only privately held ducks are targeted and the bill (if you'll pardon the pun) flies through Parliament (if you'll pardon the pun) without notice by the general populace. The next morning you will be visited by agents of Her Majesty's Revenue and Customs, demanding £6,000,000 pounds tax on the 20,000 ducks that you purchased from a man that you didn't realise at the time was the Speaker of the House of Lords.

And finally.

One of you out there will realise that that thing that your Aunt left you in her will, that one on the mantelpiece that you hate, but can't bring yourself to throw away, the thing that makes you feel all tingly and nauseous in equal measure. The one with the purple stone that looks like it glows when you look at it out of the corner of your eye, is the key to the time machine that she had in her cellar. You'll realise this just after the developer you sold her house to, to make a quick buck, has bulldozed it and built a housing estate on top. You spend the rest of your life digging in peoples gardens in the darkness... You disappear one night, never to be seen again.

68 - LA-PISS LALOOZY IS HOW IT'S PRONOUNCED.

Well, herein is described an epiphany, where I describe that you can have all the fun of playing with LEGO, with none of the pesky clearing up afterwards.

I'm talking about Minecraft, obviously.

Well, I hope you all had a good Eoster, ate lots of chocolate eggs, prayed to Ishtar or clipped your local church in traditional style, whatever you heathens get up to in your time off.

I didn't do much myself, a quiet few days with the family, spent a few hours in casualty with Mrs Dandy on Sunday after she managed to blow the meniscus in her right knee after throwing some ill-advised, but still quite impressive, Old Skool breakdancing shapes at a party on Saturday night.

I tried to pace myself over the four days, tried not to peak too soon, watched all the episodes of Sons of Anarchy, Game of Thrones, Walking Dead, Bones and stuff that we'd Sky+'d. But mostly, I played Minecraft.

I don't know how many of you have experienced the joy that is Minecraft. For those of you that haven't, in its simplest form, it's Lego, you use 3' blocks of different materials like dirt or rock or iron to make 'stuff'. You can dig into the ground to find precious gems or to quarry more stone to build more things, you can make improbable looking buildings as the laws of physics only apply to yourself and certain other substances, like sand, water and gravel. I personally have many buildings that 'float' in midair, connected to their neighbours only by a three-foot square block of loose cobblestones, proudly sticking two fingers up at Sir Isaac Newton and reminding one and all that gravity is just a theory involving apples.

You can go on pretty indefinitely, I'm a noob and my current house, or base, or shelter, is made up of a seven storey tower, which gets significantly wider as it goes up. Completely unsupported bridges going from the third and fourth floors to the nearest village (populated by people who look like Gonzo from the Muppets wearing a dress), my stone quarry, my coal, iron, diamond and lapis lazuli (Which The Micro-Dandy insists on pronouncing La-piss Laloozy) mine and to my recently discovered island that is entirely populated by pigs and the nearby shallow seas are rich with oddly angular squid... I have named this 'Piggy-Squid Island' because I am so gorram original.

My outpost is surrounded by a 12' high 6' thick, medieval style crenelated stone wall 180' long on each side, I have also, in an effort to appease whichever Gods are passing by at the time, built a 36' high Meso-American / Egyptian carved sandstone pyramid (which started out as a spoil heap for all the dirt I found myself digging up, you can only conceal a certain amount in your trouser legs after all, even if you put drawstrings on the leg holes.) and a fully functioning Anglican Church, complete with bell tower and jaunty yellow and blue striped carpets. And I also have a potting shed, overlooking my carrot, potato and melon fields.

That makes it seem very straightforward... but there are a number of steps involved in doing everything, to make a blue carpet (I say carpet, it's actually a 'block' of blue wool) you have to shear a sheep to get the wool, and mine some La-piss Laloozy to colour it blue. But to be able to shear the sheep, you'll obviously need shears, which are made from iron, which you have to dig out and smelt. To dig out your first bit of iron ore, you need a stone pick, which you have to quarry stone to make, for which you need a wooden pick, which you will need to chop down a tree for which, luckily, you can do with your bare hands.

So, you make a wooden pick, quarry some stone, make a stone pick, mine some iron ore, make a furnace out of some of the stone you've quarried, smelt the iron into ingots (using some coal that you dug out of your mine whilst you were looking for iron ore), make the ingots into shears, find a sheep, shear it and then colour the wool blue... with the La-piss Laloozy that can only be found in the deepest, darkest corners of certain mines. Oh yes, and most of the tools you use are susceptible to 'wear', the more you use them, the more they'll break - So it's going to take you at least a good half-dozen iron picks to get enough blue dye for a whole carpet.

So why would you bother? I don't know, I really don't - It sort of just sucks you in. It's like World of Warcraft without the quests. You're presented with a random(ish) canvas and the game engine sort of just goes 'Off you go then chap, have a little play, I'll check up on you just before you die of dehydration'

But it never does, you can say 'I'll just put another layer of stone on this wall, to defend myself from the bad guys before I go to work,' Then you realise that you're too weak to move and it's the Thursday after next and they've given your job to a Romanian immigrant.

You see, I went and mentioned bad guys there didn't I? There are a number of 'mobs' in the game that do their level best to make you wake up injured and/or dead. There are zombies, skeletons with bows and creepers that explode to name but a few. They spawn in low light situations, so at night (They mostly come at night... Mostly) or in areas that you haven't lit with torches. There's nothing scarier, well, I mean, obviously, there are a plethora of scarier things, mostly involving rotating knives or finding a used condom at the bottom of a jar of Aldi mayonnaise, but it's pretty scary, being in a darkened mine, with no coal to make torches, and hearing a Creeper moving around behind you just before hearing him explode, and your family hearing the string of Anglo-Saxon invective as the contents of your inventory, along with your pixellated liver and other vital organs, are scattered to the four winds.

As I've said, I'm just a n00b at this game, there's a huge amount of stuff to discover, there're electrified railways, mob generating contraptions that you can use to 'farm' certain bad guys, traps, pistons, even an endgame where you have to travel to a different dimension and kill a Dragon Boss. I'm not even a bajillionth of the way through it yet, and it already eats all of my spare time, or at least it would if I let it.

I do have some self-control, contrary to popular belief.

69 - ANY WAY THE WIND BLOWS.

There was an American fellah, Joe Barton his name is. He's a bit of a big cheese in the U.S. Energy industry. He was Chairman of the House-Senate Energy conference committee when he said the following:

'Wind is a finite resource and harnessing it would slow the winds down which would cause the temperature to go up.'

Yes… Quite…

Anywho, I'd never heard of the chap until after I wrote this entry. I wish I had, I could have had an awful lot of fun at his expense.

-oOo-

Describe energy to me people... What is it? - Could you write an all-encompassing definition of what energy is that would satisfy a precocious eight year old?

No...

Me either...

If you look it up, all the definitions tend to be something like 'Well, it's like force innit?' and then you look up force and it says 'Well, force's a bit like vigour, Brah' and then you look up vigour and it says 'Why do you want to know an' t'ing?'

It's kind of an abstract concept, it's not a thing you can hold, you can't say 'Quick, hand me a bucket of Energy - Stat!' Although, you can pour all your energy into something...

You can't create it, or destroy it, you can only change its form - Take a second to drink that in... You can change the form of something that doesn't exist into a different type of something else that doesn't exist. Brain melted yet?

You can change kinetic or movement energy into heat energy for instance, by rubbing your hands together. (You also get sound energy too - Bonus!)

Or electrical energy into vibration energy (Loudspeaker) and the other way around (Microphone)

Then there's that wonderful thing called potential energy which is a type of something that doesn't exist that doesn't exist currently, but has the potential to not exist in a different way at some unspecified time in the future usually by the application of slightly more non-existent energy. (That stuff dripping down your neck is your cerebrum; do not be alarmed - That is quite normal.)

The reason this all came into my head in the first place was that I was thinking about wind turbines, you know, driving down the motorway, you occasionally see them don't you? Big white fellahs standing there giving it the old 'Pray to us bitches, we are the future.' attitude thing - I keep expecting to see a ring of rabbits and stoats around them offering gifts of acorns and daisies, gently waving backwards and forwards until they get hypnotized by a mixture of the slow rotation of the blades, the whomp-whomp-whomp noise and some slightly fermented potato juice that Steve the Badger forced them to drink down at the back of Farmer Jim's Hay Barn last Thursday week.

What I wondered was, all that wind energy that they're capturing and converting into electrical energy... What should it be doing? what was it going to do if the turbine hadn't stolen it away? Wind's been with us for, quite literally, ages. Probably since the very world began - So at least fifty thousand years... *cough*... And it does some pretty cool things, it used to blow sailing ships to far flung places, it lifts aeroplanes up into the air (possibly) - It's great stuff generally - windmills, both flour grinding and the pretty toy ones, wouldn't work without it. OK, I mean occasionally it can spin around a bit sharpish and wipe things off the face of the planet leaving just some tinder and a single dolls head for poignancy, but still!

All wind must have a purpose, Gaia or Nature or the Gods or our rubbery overlords from Zeta Reticulii don't put things on the planet just for the crack, except Duck Billed Platipii and possibly Pangolins. So, the wind that we're capturing and converting should be doing something else - But what? Does it have a function that we're not aware of? Does it somehow trigger 'Spring' perhaps? - All evidence would point towards the fact that maybe it does.

Or could we be facing an altogether more armageddonal problem? Could the light winds that the turbines capture regulate the planet's temperature? Could Wind Turbines be causing climate change? Will the heat radiating from the molten core of our planet slowly build, without this breeze to cool it, until the mantle of the earth liquefies and the fragile crust tears to pieces like a soggy sheet of Plenty kitchen towel (Other brands are available) and we all have just enough time to yell 'Damn you Charles F. Brush!' and wave our skinny fists towards the heavens defiantly before turning into a greasy speck in the burgeoning magma?

It's a possibility.

So, the next time some hippy says 'Tear down this coal fired power station and put in a wind-farm, Man!' You have my permission to nail him to something solid so he can't do any further harm.

70 - NO, NO, NO, NO, NO, NO, YES!

A few of you may know that in my spare time, as well as the writing, and the drawing, and the motorcycling, I am a live sound engineer. I practice this particular type of witchcraft at my local Church, the one where we hold the free bacon-sandwich-a-thons that I'm always banging on about (Do not be confused – There's no point in me banging on about them here, they're live events).

Now, even if you're not a Religionite, you'll know that Easter is a pretty important time in the Christian calendar, lots of flowers about the place, talking about hairy fellows coming back from the dead and rolling stones away from sepulchres and what have you.

Not so many rabbits or chocolate eggs to be fair, which I think is a bit of a missed trick on their part, I think they'd get a lot more bums on seats if they gave away creme eggs and planted a bloody great plywood Easter Bunny in the graveyard, He could maybe carry a basket of eggs and one of them could be a hole, where you put your head through and had your picture taken... OK, so there's the chance that it could also look like he was carrying a truckle of severed heads, but I think most people'd get the gist.

Anyway, staying on track for a second, Yesterday was Quasimodo Sunday (No, really, that's what it's called) which, although it isn't as 'sexy' as Easter Sunday, still holds a certain reverence, what with the whole St. Thomas thing and the sticking of fingers into holes in wrists made by nails (I am so waiting for the movie version of the Bible stories directed by Dario Argento - It would rock like a hurricane, as Klaus Meine might say). The Church wasn't particularly full, probably because it was the middle weekend of the local schools Easter holidays and lots of people with kids were away.

Unfortunately, on Sunday, this also included the Vicar and 95% of the music group. So really, there wasn't a great deal for me to mix - Easy gig, I thought... But it turned out not to be quite like that.

The mixing desk itself is great, it does all kinds of cool things, and with all my knobs, faders and flangers I can make Gods-awful crap sound a little less Gods-awful. What it can't do is make the proverbial silk purse magically appear from a female porcine's aural cavity. I knew I was going to have to get a bit creative, when the young lady who was to deliver the sermon came up to me and said,

'We're going to have some songs, but from a CD'

'OK,' I replied, waiting for the other boot to drop.

'But I've been told that our main CD player is a bit... erm... temperamental?'

And she was right, the CD player that had come with the desk was actually a DVD recorder, with no screen attached, so you've got no way of knowing what track is currently playing, this important piece of information is the only thing that the little LED display doesn't show. And it keeps things very exciting.

'So, how would you like to do it?' I asked, genuinely interested.

'Well, I thought we could play it on a portable CD player, and put one of the music-group's microphones close to the speaker.'

'Do you have someone to select the track and press play and things?'

'Yes, that's all taken care of.'

'Great, should be a piece of cake.'

To assist in making everyone feel like one, big, Anglican family there's a laptop with a projector that puts the words to whatever song is currently being played, so you can sing along, on a 10' square screen at the front of the Church... So far, so believable, right?

Now, let's add a few more levels of oddity shall we? The young chap who was operating the CD player was wearing a camo-pattern onesie.

Yes, you read that right...

A onesie...

Camo pattern...

Completely unironically...

And the couple who were operating the laptop, with the words, for the songs, that everyone was going to sing, on a PowerPoint presentation, kept displaying random pages of lyrics from other songs that the parishioners would be singing throughout the service, as opposed to the strictly next... next... next... procedure that was required of them. Don't get me wrong, they're lovely people, she writes poetry, but they were just a touch technically inept on the day.

The person giving the sermon was helping them out, and at one point there seemed to be a bit of a scuffle for control of the remote, which ended in a lot of scowling and finger-pointing.

Then the chap in the onesie faded the song out halfway through (Which is something he continued to do throughout the service). But with true Dunkirk spirit, we soldiered on. Someone delivered a reading, cleverly ignoring all the radio mics that had been setup for that very use and relied solely on her own voice projection ability, so she had the air of a codfish on a sandy beach, you could see the panic in her eyes and her mouth opening and closing, but no sound came out. This went on for a minute or so until the person giving the sermon pointed her lapel mic at her and audio was restored.

This was followed by a slightly longer reading about some cannibals, which I didn't really see the point of, followed by another song, this one had everything, the combat onesie, the muffled audio, the complete lack of cogent lyrics, but we actually added two new levels of frisson... The person delivering the reading didn't turn off her mic whilst she sang, and the CD player started skipping.

Now, if I'd been any kind of real sound engineer, I would have run to the front, taken the CD out, cleaned it and started it off again before anyone noticed...

Instead I chose to hide behind the mixing desk, alternating between laughing uncontrollably and trying to slash my wrists with a stiff piece of A4 paper.

71 – STEVE THE HEDGE

Kids are great, aren't they though? I like kids so much that I went and got some of my own. I decided to get one of each, you know, so I could experience both sides of the coin as it were.

I know that a few of you out there in the Blogosphere have children. I mean, I've accidentally read... Oh, I don't know... Literally tens of Blogs that say things like:

'And this is little Clinton taking his first steps, we bought a new deep-pile carpet for the whole house in case he falls over.'

'Jocasta looks absolutely scrummy in this Anne Geddes original Bumblebee costume that I bought from Fortnum & Mason (in the sale, Tarquin tells me that he's not made of money, hahahaha!)'

'We took the BMW so that Phillipe and Hermione could have enough room for all of their imaginary friends'

And I suppose I can sympathise to a degree, net-savvy Yummy-Mummies spending their time between glasses of Veuve Clicquot filling the empty void left in their lives after they gave up their full time job as a Business Analyst or Advertising Executive to be a real woman, just like their own Mothers', by telling their equally vacuous friends how their offspring regularly exceeds the targets that some book or other has set for them, whilst they're trying to re-invent the previously non-existent neon coloured school satchel market in their spare time.

But for every one of those, I have five, or maybe ten people who I follow via Twitter or Facebook that regularly say things like:

'Oh for God's sake, my idiot offspring has crapped in the bath... AGAIN! And he's NINE!'

'Well, I'd told her not to lick her fingers and put them in the socket, then there was the bang, but I knew she was OK because she was crying.'

'So, I got a call from the school and this very nice lady told me that HellChild had said "That's not a willy... THIS is a willy!" which it seems is frowned upon in a mixed ability PSHE lesson nowadays.'

See if you can guess which of the people I count amongst my friends? I'll give you two guesses, but the first one doesn't count.

Anywho, back to my own little bundles of joy... As I said, there are two of them. The Mini-Dandy is a teenager, who writes a Blog (very) occasionally, that some of you even follow. She's the thinly veiled heroine of the Edward Teach stories and is quite odd, in an individualistic, original way. She gets her sense of humour, irony, fair play and indignation from me. Her mood swings, irrational behaviour, clothes sense and general female-ality are all from her dear Mother.

My Son, who despises being referred to as The Micro-Dandy, so I won't, except just then, which he won't see so it doesn't matter. Is a completely different tray of spiced giraffe tongues. He's also odd, don't get me wrong, sometimes supremely odd. I mean, you'll often wake up after having a bit of a snooze on the couch and he'll be standing there, staring at you, just about breaking a smile, then turn around and walk out of the room. He's got a mind like a steel trap, and can find a hole in any argument faster than a Teflon stoat in a greasy Swiss cheese factory.

He's logical, calculating and almost autistically anal about things. Which is great if you need him to remember something, I mean, he can quite honestly quote chapter and verse things that he finds interesting that have happened over the past five years. But ask him what he had for lunch of course and he looks at you as if you're an idiot and says 'Can't remember.' He's also the basis for the Ice-Demon killing, Pig Exploding hero, Mal Ak'hai the Hunter

But he's not one for whimsy, which can be a bit of a handicap in the Dandy household... Or at least he wasn't, until last night... He came into the living room and said,

'Dad, I've written a story, do you want to hear it?'

Being a kind and loving parent, I ignored the obvious, intuitive answer and replied;

'Yes, I'd love to hear your story.' And you know, I'm glad that I did - It's a gem. I present it below, I have taken the liberty of correcting his spelling and punctuation, for clarity's sake.

Steve The Hedge.

Steve the hedge lives in fire hydrant land.
Steve is always watered, because of the fire hydrants.
But if you dig a trench, from the lake to Steve, it would make Steve very happy.

It's a thing of beauty, I'm sure you'll all agree. It's got everything, whimsy, abstraction, nonsense, descriptiveness, at the end - fatalism bordering on the Dadaist. I loved it. I've had it framed and I keep it on my desk.

I was slightly worried about him, in a John Wyndham, Midwich Cuckoos kinda way, but now I'm not. He's one of the Firm now, definitely 100% on target to be a gen-u-wine, solid gold, stone cold, thousand yard staring, klaxon blaring, Dandy of the old skool...

Maybe of the new school...

Maybe that's even better...

But more likely, very much worse! –

MuahahahahahaahahahahahahHAHAHAAHAHhahah!

I think we should all beware, just in case, start stocking up on tins, and maybe dig a fallout shelter. Because if either of the smaller Dandies ever makes a bid for global domination, the chances are that it's going to be him.

Yet another reason I'm sinking all of my spare cash into the space program.

72 - THEY CAME OUT OF THE SUN, ALL DAKKA!-DAKKA!-DAKKA!

Last year, we had a note from the Micro-Dandy's school, saying that they were doing a project about what Britain was like after the Second World War... Rationing, National Service, stuff like that. His first thought was to talk to his Grandfather about his experiences, what with him being alive at the time and everything - But because he is almost clinically lazy, the task of listening to his Grandfather's stories fell to me.

So one night, I trudged around to his house, notepad in hand, and asked; 'Dad, what did you do in (the years just after) the War? - The stories he told had to be quite heavily edited for their intended young audience, but I'll tell you pretty much what he told me.

(Note: Yes, this is my pigeon exploding Father, just so as you know what to expect.)

Our story starts in 1947 when he was conscripted into National Service (Which we should definitely still have in my opinion), and sent for eight weeks training at RAF Innsworth in Gloucester.

It was here that he learned to shoot;

'We were all on the range one afternoon, taking pot shots at these targets with Browning 9mils, bloody horrible things they were, used to grab the skin between your thumb and first finger when the hammer came down, really heavy trigger too... Rubbish... Anyway, there was this clot who comes onto the range with a Sten Gun, waving it about, coming the big I Am. Fired a couple of shots down the range and it jammed, no lubrication you see, you had to keep 'em clean, and he obviously hadn't been. So he took the magazine out, banged it against his boot, stuck it back in and pulled the slide back, which is something you don't normally have to do, I think this might have confused him. He fired a couple more rounds holding the barrel, not the magazine like they tell you to and, it got hot, so he moved his hand back and his fingers got caught in the ejector mechanism - took the ends of his fingers clean off, started running about the place screaming and crying and p*ssing blood everywhere. We couldn't stop laughing long enough to help him.'

He learned to throw grenades;

'Grenadier training was a waste of bloody time, we spent days throwing de-activated Mills bombs into pits then covering our heads and counting to seven, just to make sure we could throw 'em forty feet so as not to blow ourselves up. I wouldn't have trusted half the blokes there to throw a teabag in the bin, never mind chuck something that could blow their bloody heads off!'

How to use a parachute;

'I didn't get to jump off any of those fancy towers that you see in the documentaries. My parachute training consisted of sitting on a bench in the back of an open truck with fifteen other blokes, driving at forty miles an hour across a bumpy field with a great bloody ape of a Sergeant kicking us all off the back at ten yard intervals. You learned how to land properly pretty bloody quickly!'

And hand-to-hand combat;

'We shared the base with a load of bloody Rock Apes (Note: this is a derogatory term for members of the Royal Air Force Regiment, although this term wasn't in use at the time, my father never misses an opportunity to be offensive to people he considers inferior as new insults become available.) who did the guarding duties, general rule was, if you wanted to join the RAF they asked you three questions - Can you breathe through your nose? Can you spell your own name? Do you know who your Father was? - If you answered yes, you got into the RAF, if you said no, you got put in The Regiment. I said this to one on the main gate one night as we were coming back to barracks, he didn't take kindly to it, I got some lumps that night...'

After this training was complete, he got transferred to Flensburg in Northern Germany, promoted to Sergeant, and joined Transport Command as a Radio Operator. He spent the next few years flying all over the world. Cyprus, Hong Kong, Iraq, Libya, Malta and Malaysia were all popular destinations for him and his crew.

He also did a number of 36 hour shifts during the Berlin Airlift (Of which there is ample information on t'Internet, so I'm not going to go into the whys and wherefores of it here.) And tells many similar stories about flying cargos of coal and food and mail into Berlin, refuelling then turning around and flying back to base, but these two stick in my mind.

'We were coming in to land behind this Dakota (an American transport aircraft), we were packed in about 200 yards behind him and still about 500 feet up. We'd just cleared the fence at Tempelhof airport when he lost control and dropped onto the deck, We'd already committed to landing and the pilot was just about to grab a handful of throttle and yank the stick back when a couple of bulldozers appeared from the side of the runway and pushed the wreckage out of the way, we just cleared it - I needed to requisition a new pair of trousers when we got back to base that afternoon.'

And;

'We'd just landed and taxied over to the hard-standing where the ground-crew were going to unload us when this Penguin (an officer with no flying experience) waddles over with a clipboard and says "Right lads, need you to stay on board while they juice you, you're taking fragile cargo back so try not to shake it about too much." Then this truck backs up right to the cargo doors, some sheets go up and we feel the plane shaking about. We get the all clear and take off back home. When we landed, all these ambulances turned up and all these kids got out of the back of the plane and were whisked away. Turns out we were transporting German evacuees.'

And as you can imagine, he had a fair old repertoire of things going wrong.

'We had a heavy landing with this York at RAF Uetersen, so heavy in fact that one of the tyres blew and we swerved off the runway and into the weeds, never had an entire aircrew simultaneously s*it themselves before, it smelled like the Elsan (Chemical toilet) had exploded!'

'There was this CO at one of the airbases we were visiting who was keeping his hours up (If you wanted to still call yourself aircrew, you had to do a certain amount of flying time every year.) when we needed to get something signed, he was just doing laps of the airfield, about 200 feet up in an Oxford, or maybe an Anson. So we got a cuppa and went and sat outside NAAFI to wait for him to finish. He was coming in to land when he got hit with a crosswind, our pilot had commented on it as we came in the previous day, but it caught his plane and flipped it on its side. The tip of one of his wings just clipped the ground and he cartwheeled across the runway and burst into flames, poor bugger never stood a chance...'

But his favourite story, about his favourite plane, which he never tired of telling, and never tired of embellishing as old soldiers often do, was this one.

'Towards the end of my time, the RAF had done a deal with the Post Office. The P.O. were taking surplus Mosquito fighter-bombers, painting them red, and using them to carry mail. Our crew got the job of flying loads of them from Germany back to the UK, then cadging a lift back and doing it all over again. All this flying over The Channel got very boring after a while, and to make it more exciting the pilot would see how low he could fly, or how fast, or see how long he could fly on a knife edge (with the plane tipped at 90 degrees to the surface of the water) or any combination of the three. There was this one time when the navigator spotted a fishing boat on the horizon right in front of us, so the pilot dropped us down to the deck and throttled up to about 300Mph, at the last moment, we popped up, flipped onto a knife edge and flew in between the derricks on the deck. Then we buggered off sharpish, hoping they were too busy s*itting themselves to make a note of our squadron markings.'

□

□

73 - HE SAID BABY, BABY, BABY, WHO?

Now, I'm not one for your actual fishing, I mean, I can see the appeal of sitting by the side of a picturesque lake, in the sunshine, with a bucket full of cold cans and a bacon sandwich, but the whole stabbing worms and having a mouthful of maggots has never appealed to me, jus' nah ma t'ing Brah!

Anywho...

I read a news report this morning about a certain Mr Justin Bieber, who, on a recent visit to the Anne Frank museum in Amsterdam left a message in the guestbook stating:

"Truly inspiring to be able to come here. Anne was a great girl. Hopefully she would have been a Belieber."

OK, so it was ill advised, probably a spur of the moment thing. Who amongst us can say that the nineteen year old versions of ourselves have never done anything stupid? I know I can't... I really, really can't.

Effectively, if I was feeling charitable, I'd imagine he was saying, 'I hope she'd have liked my music, or my personality.'

Uncharitably, I'd be thinking, in the back of my mind, that he meant 'Hey grrrl, the whole dying in Belsen thing musta been real whack, and I don't really know your story, but you musta been fly as they gave you your own museum. You'da liked me, I'm da shizznit'

What I think might be MY personal problem with him hoping that she'd have been a Belieber is that there are a vocal hardcore who viciously dive on anything anti-Bieber and tear it apart with their rabid, pre-pubescent fangs. There's an even smaller, even harder-core sect of Belieberdom that does the same to people who have stood next to, kissed, looked at, or even breathed the same air as La Bieber - How would the world have been changed if Anne Frank, generally seen as the very personification of persecuted youth, had joined those hallowed ranks?

Now, I know it's against the laws of the Internet to invoke the name of a certain Austro-Hungarian born fellah with a toothbrush moustache and side-parting, but I am quite fond of using the word Nazi as you may have noticed in previous chapters. One of the first traits that people think of when you say the word 'Nazi' is fanaticism. (Along with the whole 'Aren't those Hugo Boss designed SS uniforms darkly fashionable' thing.) And fanaticism is something that Bieber's fans are keen to show in spades. You only have to look at the replies that Drake Bell, popular Nickelodeon actor, guitarist and Belieber troll got when he suggested that Mr Bieber might not write all of his own material, or possibly could benefit from guitar lessons.

Not only were aspersions cast on his sexuality, musical talent, sanity and relationship status, but there were honest to goodness, actual death threats. With one young lady going to the lengths of tweeting 'live' threat updates as she got her Dad to drive her to the airport where Mr Bell had 'challenged' the irate Superfans to meet him and air their grievances in public.

Seemingly, when it came down to it, there was little 'carrying through' of threats, but some generally good natured banter ensued.

You have to worry if stuff like that is just advertising hype though, designed to raise their profiles. I hope it's not, I currently quite like this Bell chap, (my Daughter was a great fan of 'Drake & Josh'), and would hate to have my regard for his integrity dented by the foul mistress that is the Hollywood fame machine.

So, I thought I'd conduct a completely non-scientific media experiment.

This morning, I tweeted the following message:

So, #Bieber thinks Anne Frank would be a #Belieber, strange, when she spent her life hiding from death threats, not issuing them.

Complete with hashtags designed to ensure that the most bottom-feederish, hardcore, Belieberettes would rise from the murky depths like fame-addled sturgeon hunting for frozen peas. Just to see if they turn their spindly hate-antennae towards me, or just concentrate on the famous Hollywood types.

So far I've been re-tweeted by someone called Justin Bieber - I'm going to go ahead and assume that it's not the real songstrel himself, or even a real person, as the Twitter ID of this person is @JustinBCookie, but they do have 3,462 followers, which is a start.

But we'll see what happens when the USA starts to wake up in a few hours - I'll keep you in the loop.

Wish me luck fellow citizens of the Blogosphere, but the chances are I won't need it.

AND NOW as they say in American multi-part dramas, what happened the next day!

Well, if you tuned in yesterday, you'll know that I conducted an ill thought out experiment to see if I could bait a Belieber into threatening me with bodily harm.

I admit I didn't try very hard, I just commented on the whole Anne Frank/Justin Bieber news story (There's a link to the story on the BBC website in yesterday's Blog) and said something to effect that Beliebers are more likely to make death threats than they are to be effected by them.

You'll be pleased to know that I've not been threatened, or had my sexuality or the very reason for my existence questioned, unlike some people I could mention.

There have been no DMs from 14 year old girls from Oregon telling me to leave their future husband alone or face the consequences. Neither have I had clouds of youngsters with nary a pubic hair between them camped on my front lawn burning effigies of whichever member of One Direction is popular at the moment which they've quickly drawn a moustache and titanic sideburns on to make it look more like me. My cat has not been nailed to the front door and my goldfish has not been blown up with my own pair of antique, Victorian fire bellows.

So, this lack of affirmative action leads us to a number of possible conclusions.

1. I am not important enough to bother with.

Now, this is my favoured explanation, I assume that the people who issue the threats are only interested in clashing swords with the great and the good. A sort of Munchhausen by famous proxy deal. By abusing a famous person, they belie(b/v)e that they become famous themselves, or at least they interact with people that they see on their 50" plasma screen balanced precariously between the sink and the toilet of their aloominum skinned single-wide trailer.

2. I wasn't obvious enough

I like to think I'm fairly subtle. I mean, I enjoy knob jokes as much as the next man... As much as the next few men all rolled together if truth be told, but you know - I do tend to dress things up in 'purty talk' more befitting my inferred Dandy status. Instead of comparing the antics of his more psychotic fans to things that may have gone on in the latter days of the Wiemar Republic - I should just have said something like 'Beebur iz gay an Sucks Donkey D*ck' and let them have at me. (Please note: I have no insider knowledge of the 'artist' in question's sexuality, or his propensity for performing fellatio on farm animals, I include this section purely for dramatic effect, as an example of the language that his fan-base would be familiar with, no offense is inferred, implied, intended or suggested - Just in case there are any multi-armed cybernetic lawyer machines watching).

3. It's all a big con, engineered by his management to keep media attention on the pint-sized popinjay.

Contrived? Well, if your manager is a real life Van Wilder from the nation that can turn the honest and honourable sport of all-in wrestling into a mass market soap opera, then why shouldn't you take the angst and hormone fuelled attention of love-starved teens with unformed emotional compasses into a huge (but supremely moist) cog in the media machine. After all, you've turned a nineteen year old from a prosperous suburb of London (Ontario) who started out posting videos of himself singing on YouTube, into what I understand is termed a 'Wigger' and a polished, preened and soul-less cash cow. What's one more offence against youth helping to weigh your soul down into the fiery pit?

Whilst we're on the subject of his management, I wonder if Mr Braun has had a quiet word with him about the whole Anne Frank debacle, what with his own grandparents having only narrowly escaped the holocaust themselves?

One would hope so... Wouldn't one?

Anyway, the only thing that happened to me was that I had my original tweet immediately picked up and forwarded by what I presume to be a Bot... And the number of hits on the Blog was slightly higher that I would have expected (23 hits in the first few minutes, rather than the normal 10-15)

On the whole, a bit of a damp squib, which by a strange quirk of fate, is, I beliebe (LOL), the name of Mr Bieber's next album.

As an aside, during the rigorous research procedure before the publishing of this chapter (the customary flick through Wikipedia to check names and dates) I noticed a couple of (semi) interesting facts.

London, Ontario (The City of Mr Bieber's birth) is in the county of Middlesex. Which goes to show that if you don't nail things down, people will steal them, geography included.

There's a river running through it called the... See if you can guess... That's right, The Thames!

There's a Blackfriars Bridge, a Victoria Park, an Oxford Street, and the township of Westminster (which includes the village of Lambeth)

However, the most unintentionally funny thing that I read is that there was a fire in 1845 which destroyed a fifth of the (then) town... That's not the funny part though; the funny part was that one of the first 'casualties' of the fire was the only fire engine that the town had.

I know that Americans don't understand irony, I wonder if the Canadians do?

74 - I NEED YOUR CLOTHES, YOUR BOOTS AND YOUR MOTORCYCLE.

I like a good party, me. I'm a great fan of the alcohol and the moving of parts of the body in a rhythmic style to phat, dench, beats and so forth. But more and more, recently, I've found myself being invited to parties hosted by people I don't know hugely well.

I mean, I know these people, don't get me wrong... I don't just wander up to any building that sounds like it contains people 'Getting their groove on', knock on the door, hold up a four-pack of Carling and say 'Dave invited me' ('cos there's always a Dave around somewhere isn't there?). But I've probably only seen them a couple of times a month, over a few years. I guess I'm maybe what they used to call in the olden days 'a face'. Someone you see around the place and nod at who you think might be more important/mysterious than they actually are.

They usually follow the same sort of timeline:

- We (because it's invariably a 'family' invite.) arrive about 15-20 minutes after the posted start time, because you don't want to seem too keen.
- We look suspiciously at all of the other 100+ people in the room, few of whom we know. We get scowled at quizzically in return.
- Eventually, someone we know quite well turns up and we annexe a couple of chairs/tables and set up court, where we can be visited by other party-goers (including our original inviter or the person for whom the party has been thrown) at their leisure.
- We have a few beers
- Dancing ensues
- The decision is taken whether to leave the car at the venue and get a taxi home is discussed and summarily rejected.
- I drink more Coke / Lemonade than is strictly good for me
- I comment pointedly on the tightness of / lack of clothing on some of the female guests to any of my male compatriots within earshot.
- I further research the above subject until I'm noticed doing so by the wife.
- We go home, in the car, in a generally frosty atmosphere.

But we got invited to an 18th Birthday last year which went a little bit differently. First of all, the invitation contained those two words specifically designed to stab fear into the heart of every right-thinking Englishman. (No, not that, Bring Your Own Bottle is four words)

'FANCY DRESS' - But at least there was a theme, 'Heroes and Villains'

So we all went and had a bit of a think... The Micro-Dandy was fine, he had a Darth Vader costume already, The Mini-Dandy wanted to be a Jedi (we have the Force-FX lightsabers and everything, so it was just a case of making her a costume - Good job I can sew innit?). Mrs. Dandy has a fine selection of Goth stuff, so 'Generic Vampire' was her choice. So it was left to me, I really wanted to go as Iron Man, but there wasn't enough time, or money, or talent available to make a decent costume in time (which I wasted a significant proportion of sulking about it) So I had to go with something I already had. Now my normal, day-to-day wardrobe contains all the items required for a decent Neo or Morpheus, Connor Macleod of the Clan Macleod or H.P. Lovecraft, but I fancied something different.

I decided to go as 'The Terminator', which I had the clothing for but not the prosthetics, because of course, I wanted to be a battle damaged T800 (and who doesn't deep down?) - So I searched the web and saw many, many videos of Americans with too much time on their hands sticking LEDs and theatrical PVC appliances to themselves and thought 'bugger that I'll just paint it on'.

So, if you'll picture the scene, I had my selection of acrylic paints that I once used for painting toy soldiers, in the upstairs bathroom, with one of those shaving mirrors screwed to the wall, you know, the ones with the comedy extending boxing glove type fitment. painting my face, right-handed (I'm left handed) without my glasses on (I'd tried just painting over my glasses, but it didn't look very effective).

So we got our accessories together and took some pictures, the smaller Dandies grabbed their lightsabers, Mrs. Dandy grabbed our new puppy (that I had made a pair of bat-wings for) and I picked up my shades, the freshly painted, over and under Nerf shotgun and my .50AE Desert Eagle... For how does one terminate properly without devastatingly powerful projectile weaponry?

We then started on the party timeline as described above. We got as far as the 'Someone we knew turned up' stage when suddenly there was a massive influx of Darth Vaders and Jedi. Now, my son took umbrage at this because he'd had the idea of coming as Darth Vader first and he did no more than to storm across the room to set about these poor people with his lightsaber. I don't know if anyone here's ever been twatted by a seven year old, full of righteous indignation, overarm, with a solid blade lightsaber - But it bloody hurts. And I admit I felt sorry for these poor teenagers trying to defend themselves with the little plastic extendy-blade lightsabers, or in one case, the cardboard core of (I think) a roller blind with the end painted red.

Not sorry enough to stop laughing and do anything about it of course, but sorry all the same.

Then things went downhill, the guns got borrowed and they danced around the room for a good hour or so and spent their time being discharged into the faces of villains by heroes, or slightly more often, vice-versa. As did the puppy, who, even if I say so myself, was incredibly cute dressed as a vampire fruit bat. And I seem to remember at one point having a lightsaber duel, with the Mini-Dandy, between songs, in the middle of an empty dance floor.

The night wore on, more coke was drunk and the number of people in PVC hot-pants dancing to 'Gangnam Style' seemed to multiply every time I looked up.

I took a few minutes out to write something on the 'guestbook', well, I say write something.. What I actually did is stand there for ten minutes with my mouth open, thinking of some edifying advice for someone who'd just entered adulthood, then gave up and drew a dragon wearing a cowboy hat, which I then mislabelled as a dinosaur wearing a cowboy hat and wandered back to our little group of tables.

Can you think what had happened in my absence? Have a guess...

Nope, wasn't that.

Not that either.

It certainly wasn't that, but only because I don't think that there's that much oil-based lubricant in the East Midlands area.

What had happened was that a number of our friends had turned up a little more than fashionably late and had, as a group, dressed up as 'The Scooby Gang', complete with improbably attired, lizard based villain.

Oh yes, and my seven year old son had field stripped the Desert Eagle into its component parts and spread it out on one of the tables, he'd had an encouraging audience and everything.

I tapped him on the shoulder and said:

'Dude, you gonna put that back together?'
'Nope.'
'And why not?'
'I don't know how...'

So after the slowest sliding facepalm in the world, I sat down and set about re-assembling the gun, it took longer than I'd expected, as the breech cover had fell off the table and rolled away, and it was dark, and I had the same drunken audience.

On the whole, a great party, I need to go to more like it. And so do you guys, you owe it to yourselves.

And if you do, don't forget to send me an invite. Oh yeah, you need to mingle, the mingle's the thing(le)

75 - IF I HADN'T SEEN IT I WOULDN'T HAVE BELIEVED IT.

I know you guys like to hear about how much the real-life world of IT is like the one depicted in 'The IT Crowd', so I thought I'd recount some of the fun and exciting things that happened to me during what I consider to be my first 'Real' job.

The year was 1985, the wreck of the Titanic had just been discovered, Axel F by Harold Faltermeyer hadn't been totally buggered by that frog thing and Mick Jagger and David Bowie were at the top of the charts with 'Dancing in the Streets' (Whilst not looking at all gay in the slightest)

I was seventeen and worked for a small (and now sadly defunct) marketing company, based in a renovated stable, in the small Derbyshire village of Brailsford. It was run by a couple, let's call them J and M (Because they were the first letters of their names) who had, if I was being charitable, delusions of grandeur. They'd drive around in his slightly scabby Alfa-Sud, him in a sharp three-piece suit and her in tight-fitting business-wear where the blouses were low-cut and the skirts were short, as was the fashion in the 80's if you wanted to do business.

Their core business was printing promotional items, little metal signs, t-shirts, that sort of thing, but they'd just bought into a PC network reselling scheme and they were doing their best to tout it around local businesses. They weren't technical, and at the time, I wasn't particularly either, which was recipe for hilarity if ever I heard one.

A normal work day would be: Get the bus to work and then wait outside in the rain and the wind for the bosses to turn up. Put the kettle on and go to the newsagents for the Daily Express. Make coffee and fire up the camping stove. Listen to J reading out the headlines whilst M tutted and I cooked bacon for sandwiches. Drink strong coffee and eat the sandwiches. Do the Express crossword. Print a few t-shirts. Go to the Pub. Offer to exchange printing services for beer. Stay at pub for two hours. Stagger back to the office. Drink Coffee. Wait for J & M to fall asleep. Get bus home.

Very little I.T. related stuff there, I think you'll agree. But that all suddenly changed after I'd been there about three months. Then we got a couple of PCs delivered from the resellers and I started demo-ing them to prospective customers. Business really took off... Kinda...

We arranged a demo for Charing Cross hospital in London and I arranged to meet J at the railway station so we could travel down together and discuss 'Strategy'. He didn't turn up (Bearing in mind this was before mobile phones so I couldn't chase him), luckily we'd had the kit sent to directly to site, so I arrived and set it up in this chap's office. The demo went as well as could be expected seeing as I was not a salesman, merely a scrawny, long haired, metalhead. The demo was finished by lunchtime and the customer turned to me and said.

'Shall we get some lunch?'
'Yes... That'd be great, thanks.' I replied.
'You do have an expense account, right?' He asked.
'Ah, no, not really,' I looked in my pocket and found the grand total of £3.45
'OK,' He said, 'I'll pay, but I'm going to send your company a bill for it.'

Which in fairness was exactly what he did, we sat in the pub for a couple of hours talking about how awful my company was and how he didn't blame me, then I caught the train home. We never recovered the kit. J's excuse was that he'd had a skinfull the night before and had forgotten all about it.

Another time, we had the chance of demo-ing the system to Shell UK. I knew this wasn't going to go well, but I had my suit dry-cleaned anyway. The demo took place at, what was then, Shell House on The Strand (again in London) and this time we all drove down there in the Main Distributor's Jag, with the kit in the boot. The demo was due to take place in the mid-afternoon and we arrived there at about eleven-ish. We unloaded the PCs and took them up to the conference room, where I was left to unbox and set them up whilst everyone else went to the pub. five minutes or so before the demo was due, my bosses, the distributor and the Shell guy who'd arranged the meeting all rolled through the door, giggling and doing that 'Shush' thing to each other and the other ten Shell senior managers in the room, that you do when you're drunk and people are scowling at you.

Again, the demo went OK, we had to stop a few times when J forgot what he was saying, or had to ask me about how the system actually worked, or had to go to the toilet. Luckily not a great number of people were actually paying attention, as M was perched, bleary eyed, on a chair in the corner with her skirt ridden up so far that not only could you see she was wearing stockings, but also a thong (She allegedly had a friend who worked with Janet Reger, and we would often be treated to an impromptu fashion show when she had acquired a new item).

At the end of the demo, the distributor asked if there were any questions, accused the chap who asked the first one of storing half of his breakfast on his tie and then promptly took a step back and fell over his chair.

Upon our exit, J did a stage wink at the Shell chap who'd taken them for lunch and said:

'Cheers Brian, the cheque's in the post'

We didn't get the business, and the most surprising thing was that J was surprised.

As business started to slump, they gave me a key to the office and they started to come in less and less. This suited me just fine, and would have suited me even better if the Internet had been freely available. I'd come in at about 10-ish, wait for M to ring to check I was there, go to the pub, back to the office for an hour and then go home. During this time, I became friends with the landlord of the local pub, The Rose & Crown. I would often trade printing services to the landlord for beer and food. In fact, during my time there, I completely refreshed all of his signage and designed him new menus. I also became addicted to Salmon & Salad cream sandwiches.

One lunchtime he came over and said:

'Can you use a hammer?'

'Yes, of course.' I lied, nodding like a loon - In fairness, at this stage I wasn't particularly sure which end you held and which end you hit yourself with.

'Come with me...'

We went into the somewhat dilapidated beer garden and he showed me a long strip of concrete that he'd had laid.

'Very nice,' I said, not really sure what it was I was looking at.

'It's my new skittle alley, if you give me a hand putting a roof over it, I'll pay you in beer and sandwiches.'

So, I spent the summer of 1986 building a skittle alley (which may or may not still be there), a huge chicken coop for his 'fancy hens', and learning some very interesting things from a barmaid some seven years older than myself.

One Friday morning, I was sat in the office, spinning around on the chair, waiting for my check-in call from M. The phone rang, I answered it, it was M. But this time the call was a little different.

'Dandy, what are you doing on Monday?'
'I don't know, whatever you tell me to I suppose.'
'Right, we're going on holiday for the month, and I need you to feed the cats.'
'OK.'
'I'll come and pick you up and show you what needs doing.'

So I sat and waited, and then waited, and then waited a bit more and eventually the popping and banging from the exhaust of the Alfa announced her arrival. I locked up and went out to meet her.

'Sorry I'm late,' She said, 'Pippa and Debbie turned up, so we all had a bit of a drinkie.'

We drove to her place, which was an apartment in an old manor house down the road and she showed me where everything was, how much the cats ate and where the tea and coffee was. It turned out that they wanted to me close the office and come and stay all day in their apartment whilst they were away.

Everything was sorted, and she was just about to drive me to the nearest bus stop when I had a call of nature. M directed me to the correct area and I went into what was a very well appointed Victorian style bathroom.

Which just happened to have a life-size naked, photograph of her over the bath. It answered a couple of questions for me, the first one being that her blonde hair hadn't, as I'd first though, come out of a bottle, and the second was that certain parts of her anatomy, that I'd thought had been surgically enhanced, probably weren't.

When I left the bathroom, some twenty minutes later, she looked at me and said,

'Perhaps I should have warned you about that... I used to model when I was younger'

I just nodded, as I didn't really want her to hear how out of breath I was. The drive to the bus stop was a little bit weird in fairness, but I'd just about pulled myself together enough to go to the pub that night and tell everyone I knew, and a lot of people that I didn't.

On Monday I went to her flat, and her next-door neighbour let me in. I fed the cats and made a coffee. She had some bayonets hanging on the wall, so I had a bit of a fiddle with those, wandered around the gardens and had a general sniff around.

I found some modelling photos, and then more modelling photos, and then some photos that weren't exactly of her modelling, I mean she wasn't looking at the camera in most of them, neither was the other person in them, and they were probably taken by a third person. If I was her, I would have probably have hidden these away from prying eyes, rather than leave them on display, in the back of her underwear drawer, under what amounted to a tightly fitted false bottom.

The next four weeks virtually flew past. And when she called me on the Monday to make sure I was back in the office she sounded quite upset, I asked her what was wrong and she said:

'Those people! The neighbours we left the key with! They've been through my stuff, even my underwear drawer! I'll never speak to them again!'

I expressed my shock at their despicable behaviour... And left it at that.

It just goes to show that you never really know anyone until you've seen them naked.

ABOUT THE AUTHOR

Rob Grimes has been working in IT for various companies around the UK for the past thirty years. He enjoys drawing, writing, Piña Coladas and making it home just before the rain starts. He's often up at midnight, but usually slumped in front of a hot laptop, not in the dunes of the Cape.

He would very much like to give up IT and start writing full-time if you can help to make that happen, please and thank you.

He lives in Derby and is married with two wonderful children who will be lucky to make it to their next birthday if they don't stop squabbling over nothing.

The second volume of The Collected Chimping Dandy (The Pangolin Yodels) will hopefully, if anyone buys the first volume, be released in June 2014 – Closely followed by a collection of short stories (Forever Girl and other stories) with the first volume of the Edward Teach stories (which has yet to be named) to follow in 2015

If you've enjoyed this book, please take the time to 'Like' us on Facebook

www.facebook.com/TheChimpingDandy

Or follow us on Twitter

@Chimping_Dandy

Or drop us an email to:

TheChimpingDandy@hotmail.co.uk

Printed in Great Britain
by Amazon

54150445R00176